AF553360

ROLE AND PERFORMANCE OF DIETs

ROLE AND PERFORMANCE OF DIETs

By

Dr. D.V.Subba Raju

M.Sc., (Botany) MA (Eng.)

M.Ed., M.Phil (Edn.) Ph.D. (Edn.)

Principal

Nagarjuna College of Education, Nidadavole,

West Godawari district

Andhra Pradesh

&

Prof. K.P.Subba Rao

M.A., (Pub. Adm.) M.A.

(Edn.) B.L., Ph.D. (Edn.)

Dean Faculty of Education

Andhra University, Visakhapatnam

Andhra Pradesh

DISCOVERY PUBLISHING HOUSE PVT. LTD.

NEW DELHI-110 002

First Published-2010

ISBN 978-81-8356-620-6

Published by:

DISCOVERY PUBLISHING HOUSE PVT. LTD.

4831/24, Ansari Road, Prahlad Street
Darya Ganj, New Delhi-110002 (India)
Phone: 23279245, 43764432 • Fax: 91-11-23253475
E-mail: parul.wasan@gmail.com
info@discoverypublishinggroup.com
Website: www.discoverypublishinggroup.com

Printed at:

Sachin Printers
Delhi

Dedicated to
my beloved
parents

Foreword

Efficiency and effectiveness of new knowledge, generated through research, depends a great deal upon its extensive and effective dissemination among the potential users. Where as the citations of the output of knowledge embodied in books or research works, may reflect their contemporary relevance, quality and standard, citations themselves depend upon the accessibility of users to this new knowledge. Publication of new knowledge resulting from research is an effective means of its dissemination, and making it accessible to readers. Greater the relevance and higher the quality, larger is likely to be the number of users of the knowledge disseminated through publications.

I am very much happy that the book titled "Role and Performance of DIETs in Andhra Pradesh State" published by Discovery Publishing House is a very useful contribution to the existing literature on the subject. It is comprehensive in its coverage. More importantly, every aspect covered has been dealt with very competently. The treatment of theory simultaneously with the empirical exercises in the study is another distinguished feature.

The teachers are the builders of the nation and the training institutes produce these teachers. So, we must imagine how much importance should be given to the quality of education imparted in the training institutes. DIETs train primary school teachers and they give primary inputs in the training period, which is the basis of education and the whole edifice of education stands upon this foundation.

The book consists of five chapters. In chapter one the author(s) emphasized the importance of training and its historical background with recommendations of various committees and commissions. They also incorporated a detailed information on the functionaries of DIETs, role and performance of DIETs, facilities, support for conduct of inservice Training Programmes, conduct of action research etc. The book is very useful as a reference material to the DIET teacher trainees, faculty and the Heads of the institutes.

This book covering five chapters, with an analytical rigour, richness of contents, varied and enhansive range of methodology, abundance of empirical evidence to support the functionaries of DIET.

This study is illuminating an innovative approach and intuitive insights. Students, teachers, researches, planners and policy-makers will find relevant, interesting and useful as a work of reference for research and helpful in teaching and training.

Dr. M.S.R. Sarma
Senior Faculty
DIET, Bheemunipatnam
Visakhapatnam District
Andhra Pradesh

Preface

Knowledge is power. Knowledge is acquired through books or by observation by making use of our sense organs. Knowledge can also be acquired through precepter .The concept of teaching is an age-old tradition. In the early days of human history, knowledge was transferred from generation to generation orally through guru to his sishya on one to one basis. As such the role of the teacher became much crucial to the alround development of the human race. Knowledge received through teacher is more concrete and it sustains for ever. The human society at present has been gaining knowledge in all fields mostly through the teachers. Gradually the teaching has been institutionalized and hence the schools and colleges have evolved, so also for the training and preparing of teachers.

The teachers were prepared through basic training schools, teacher training institutions (TTLs) in the earlier period, in which only, pre-service, primary teacher-training was being conducted. According to NPE-1986, the then existed one of the prominent TTIs in each district in India was upgraded as district institute of education and training (DIET) to impart not only

pre-service teacher training but also adult and non-formal instructors training, academic supervision of upper primary, primary and adult and non-formal schools in the district and other academic support for the district educational administration.

The main aim of the establishment of the DIETs is to enhance the quality of primary education. Evenafter a lapse of 15 years after the establishment of DIETs there was not witnessed the expected quality in the field of primary education in Andhra Pradesh.

The present piece of research aims at enquiring the present status of DIETs and its role and performance in the wake of NPE-86. There are two reasons to embark on the present work. One is that there is dearth of studies in the area of DIETs role and performance. And the second one is though the DIETs are existing in allover India, there are considerable differences and deficiencies regarding quality training. These are due to various reasons particularly the region in which the DIET is established; the DIETs are scattered in various locales, these imbalances are bound to appear.

It is an in-depth analysis of the working conditions of the DIETs in Andhra Pradesh state, comes certainly in handy for personnel in the DIETs of Andhra Pradesh in particular and India in general.

Author(s)

Acknowledgements

A good work of research can be successful with the whole hearted cooperation and involvement of many a good persons. I feel I am only successful in my endeavour, if I could pay my due regards to all those persons who have encouraged and inspired me to undertake this task.

I strongly feel that I do not find the most suitable words to express my deep heart felt gratitudes to my Research Director Prof. K.P. Subba Rao, Professor and Dean Faculty of Education, Andhra University, for his truthful and amicable guidance, cooperation and help extended by him all the way in completing, this study at every stage.

I express my sincere thanks to Prof. L. Venugopala Reddy, hon'ble Vice-Chancellor of Andhra University for giving me the opportunity for doing research in this university.

I express my thanks to Prof. J.V. Prabhakar Rao, Principal, Colleges of Arts and Commerce for his cooperation in completion of my work.

I am equally thankful to Prof. Nimma Venkata Rao, Head of the Department of Education for his kind help in the completion of my work.

I am grateful to Prof. V. Krishna Murty, Prof. Y.F.W. Prasada Rao, Prof. R.S.B. Ratna Raju, Prof. O.R. Reddy, Prof. G. Latchanna and Dr. S. Paul Douglas, Assistant Professor for their heartful cooperation for completion of my work.

I am thankful to all the Faculty members of Education, Adult and Continuing Education, Special Education and IASE, Andhra University for their cooperation extended for my work.

I am really indebted to all the Principals and Faculty members of 23 DIETs of Andhra Pradesh for their cooperation in providing data for research work.

I am sincerely thankful to Sri M. Suryanarayana our Principal, L. Vaikunta Rao, Senior Lecturer, Dr. M.S.R.Sarma, Senior Lecturer and all my colleagues in DIET Bheemunipatnam for their cooperation and encouragement.

I am really indebted to my life partner and family members for extending me all cooperation for the successful completion of my work.

Last but not least, I am specially thankful to Mr. R. Vijay Kumar, Mrs. M. Radha, Mrs. P. Subba Lakshmi of Vijay Software Solutions for neat typing and computing my work.

D. V. SUBBA RAJU

Contents

Foreword

Preface

Abbreviations

1. Introduction 1
2. Review of Related Literature 35
3. Methodology 65
4. Analysis and Interpretation of the Data 79
5. Summary and Conclusions 220

Bibliography 254

Abbreviations

APPEP	Andhra Pradesh Primary Education Project
AE	Adult Education
AIE	Alternative and Innovative Education
APIIC	Andhra Pradesh Industrial and Infrastructural Development Corporation
BC	Backward Class
B.Sc.	Batchelor of Science
B.A.	Batchelor of Arts
CEO	Chief Executive Officer
CLIP	Children Language Improvement Programme
CTE	College of Teacher Education
CIE	Central Institute of Education
CMDE	Curriculum Material Development and Evaluation
D.Ed	Diploma in Education
DBE	District Board of Education
DIET	District Institute of Education and Training
DPEP	District Primary Education Programme
DRU	District Resource Unit
DRDA	District Rural Development Agency
DSERT	Directorate of State Educational Research and Training
DE	District Educator
ET	Educational Technology

EE	Elementary Education
GOI	Government of India
HRD	Human Resource Development
IASE	Institute of Advanced Studies in Education
IFIC	In-service Field Interaction Innovation and Co-ordination
IIE	Indian Institute of Education
MDO	Mandal Development Officer
MHRD	Ministry of Human Resource Development
NGO	Non-Governmental Organisation
NCTE	National Council for Teacher Education
NFE	Non-formal Education
NLM	National Literacy Mission
OBC	Other Backward Classes
OC	Open Category
OHP	Over Head Projector
PAC	Programme Advisory Committee
PE	Primary Education
POA	Programme of Action
PSTE	Pre-service Teacher Education
P & M	Planning and Management
QIP	Quality Improvement Programme
RJDSE	Regional Joint Director of School Education
RCE	Regional College of Education
SC	Scheduled Castes
STEI	Secondary Teacher Education Instution
SCERT	State Council of Educational Research and Training
SIET	State Institute of Educational Technology
SLM	Self Learning Material
SRC	State Resource Centre

SEC	School Education Committee
SSA	Sarva Siksha Abhiyan
ST	Scheduled Tribes
STE	Secondary Teacher Education
SIERT	State Institute of Educational Research and Training
STC	School Teacher Certificate
SSC	Secondary School Leaving Certificate
SE	Secondary Education
SIE	State Institute of Education
SVU	Sri Venkateswara University
SOPT	Special Orientation Programme for Primary School Teachers
TLM	Teaching Learning Material
TTI	Teacher Training Institute
TTC	Teacher Training Certificate
TE	Teacher Education
UT	Union Territory
UNICEF	United Nations International Childrens' Education Fund
UGC	University Grants Commission
UEE	Universalization of Elementary Education
VEC	Village Education Committee
VCP	Video Casette Player
WE	Work Experience

1

Introduction

Education was regarded as the most important tool for self-realization. Education is an act of training. Education aims at the modification of the behaviour of the child and man. Education is the back bone of a progressing nation and teacher is the pivot in any system of education, since the teacher has a key role in the educational process. It thus enhances the need for better programme of preparation of more and more good teachers.

It is aptly said that a true teacher never ceases to learn, and each school year, whether the first or the fortieth, should be viewed as a challenging experience. The first of these teaching experiences is usually student teaching. Learning will have strong impact as the art and culture of a country.

HISTORY OF TRAINING

Training is a process of preparing a person for a sport or job or profession. It is a means to bring a person to a desired standard of efficiency, behaviour etc. by instruction and practice. Human resource can be developed by subjecting personnel to certain renovating/refreshing/rejuvenating programmes like short term/long term/pre-service/in-service input activity. This is required for inputing the changed or modified, revised strategies so as to achieve desired results. Hence training is necessary in the field of education.

In Education Department the college teachers (lecturers and professors) also need training. But in Indian situation only pre-primary, primary and secondary teachers only are being trained initially for one or two years.

HISTORICAL BACKGROUND OF TEACHER EDUCATION

Ancient Period

The status of the teacher reflects the sauce-cultural ethos of a society. It is said that "No People can rise above the level of its teachers." (National Policy on Education, 1986).

A special feature of the teacher in the ancient period was that he took a personal interest towards each pupil. Sometimes so many students came to the teacher that he could not fulfil his responsibilities towards them. Hence, he used to seek the assistance of meritorious students of higher classes. They were called 'pattacharya'. They assisted their teacher *(guru)* in teaching, used to be his pupils. If the teacher sometimes went away, the teacher used to entrust the whole work of teaching and the school to such students.

This system was in fact the monitorial system in which some prominent students of the same class and some students of the higher classes assisted the teacher in the performance of teaching and other allied works. The students who were entrusted with this work, used to become efficient teachers and school organizers in the course of time. After having been thus trained, they used to devote themselves to teaching work in future.

Medieval Period

The chief aim of a Muslim ruler in medieval India was to propagate their religion and to convert Hindus into Muslims. Consequently, excepting a few rulers, they did not pay much attention to Muslim education. In such a condition, it was very difficult for them to have any idea of teacher education.

Modern Period

In fact teacher education in the systematic form was introduced in the modern times only. The following were the mile-stones in teacher education during the Modern Period. Early efforts, in the modern period, were the Educational Boards of Bombay, Madras and Calcutta for the first time felt the need of teacher education and they established a few training centers but only the teachers of primary schools were imparted training in these schools. The Native Education Society of Bombay, trained 25 teachers and sent them to different parts of the province, so that the standard of teaching in the primary schools might be raised. In 1812. Calcutta School Society was established at Calcutta. This society made the provision for the training of the teachers on the basis of monitorial system. In order to encourage the work of the society, the East India Company started giving Rs. 500 per month, since the year 1825. In accordance with the suggestions of Munro, a training school was established by the then Governor of Madras for the training of the teachers at Madras in the year 1826.

Wood's Despatch (1854)

Wood's Despatch mentioned that: "We desire to see the establishment, with as little delay as possible, of training schools and classes for masters in each Presidency in India". The wish that was expressed by the Directors of the company in Wood's Despatch with regard to teacher education could not be fulfilled.

Lord Stanley Despatch: 1859-1882

Lord Stanley has mentioned in his Despatch that a special attention should be paid to the training of the teachers. After transfer of the 'power it was not possible for the British administrators posted in India to ignore or disregard the orders of the Secretary for State of India. Consequently, they worked with enthusiasm for the establishment of training schools for the teachers of primary schools, and as a result of their effort, many training schools were established in each province by the year 1892. In 1892 there were existed seven and two training schools for men and women respectively. The number of students studying in those schools was 553.

In 1862 normal school system was started in Bengal. According to this system the teachers of the native schools or their relations were sent to normal schools. In 1874 Campbell, the Governor of the province, prepared a new scheme for the training of the teachers, and consequently 46 normal schools were established.

In Madras there were 32 training schools and nearly 927 students were receiving training in those schools. Likewise, provision of training of the teachers of primary schools was made in other provinces also. In 1902, there were 106 normal schools in the whole India and about 3,886 men and women were trained in those schools.

Indian Education Commission (1882)

The regular system of teacher education was started in accordance with the recommendations of the Indian Education Commission, 1882. Consequently by the end of 19th century, there were six training colleges at Madras, Lahore, Allahabad, Kursan, Rajahmundry and Jabalpur, and 50 training schools in the whole country.

Education Policy, 1904

Lord Curzon paid sufficient attention towards education and training of the teachers. The Government resolution of education policy of 1904, after considering all the aspects of the teacher education, made the following recommendations :

1. Provision should be made for higher training of able and experienced teachers for the Indian Educational Service.
2. The importance of the establishment of the training colleges is almost equal as that of general colleges.
3. The training period for the graduates should be only one year and there after they should be granted degree by the university. The knowledge of teaching methods and practical training should also be included in the curriculum. The training period for the non-graduates should be two years.
4. Theoretical training and practical training should be mutually connected with each other and there should be a practicing school connected with each training college.

5. Training college should be connected with ordinary schools so that the teachers may apply the methods learnt in the training colleges.

Calcutta University Commission (1916-1917)

This commission devoted special attention towards teacher education and made the following recommendations:

1. The number of trained teachers should be increased.
2. Research work in education should be encouraged.
3. A demonstration school should be attached with each training college so that practical work may be done in it.
4. The subject of education should be included in the curriculum of Bachelor of Arts and intermediate classes.
5. Education Department should be established in Calcutta and Dhaka Universities.

Hartog Committee (1929)

The Hartog Committee emphasised the training of the teachers of primary schools and recommended the following:

1. Education standard of the teachers should be raised.
2. Training period should be extended.
3. Able teachers should be appointed in training institutions and their number should be increased.
4. provision of refresher courses should be made from time to time for the teachers of primary schools.
5. In order to attract able persons to the teaching profession the conditions of teachers should be improved and made attractive

TEACHER EDUCATION IN PRE-INDEPENDENCE PERIOD

In 1947 there were three types of institutions existed in India :

(*a*) *Normal schools* – Teachers of primary schools were given training in those schools.

(*b*) *Secondary training schools* – These schools imparted training to the teachers of middle schools only. Those students who passed matriculation were admitted in these schools.

(*c*) *Training Colleges* – The teachers of high schools were given training in these colleges. Only graduates and post graduates were entitled to get admission in these colleges.

TEACHER EDUCATION IN POST-INDEPENDENCE ERA

Praiseworthy steps have been taken in the field, by expanding the facilities of teacher training in the post-independent period. Suggestions given by the University Education Commission (1949). Secondary Education Commission (1952-53) and Kothari Commission (1964-66) were being implemented by the Government, among which those of Kothari gained popularity.

DEVELOPMENT OF TEACHER TRAINING IN INDIA

Indians were following their own pattern of education in the patashalas, the *Madrassahs*, the Persian schools called *'Maktabas'* and other schools teaching through modern indian languages education in temples, and domestic education too in *gurukulas* formed the basis of what the British termed the indigenous education almost till the end of 18th century. The missionaries became active in the eighteenth century.

Teaching is praised as the noblest of all professions. Kothari Commission (1964-66) earmarked that "The destiny of a nation is shaped in its class-rooms". Hence, the person commanding the classroom, the teacher, has a great role to play in shaping a nation. Thus, the teacher has to be given training on ideal and sound lines. Moreover the quality of our school education is lower than that in some of the African countries. The improperly trained teacher transacts his unhealthy attitudes unauthentic knowledge and false notions to the impressionable young. These students after educated join the teacher training institutions

(TTIs) and still further bring down the educational standards. According to the findings of earlier researches, most of the teachers are just being drafted into the profession. The cream of the college students prefer to go to jobs other than teaching profession. We attract the average and below average students and also who are selected out for other jobs. Thus the dull part of the student population were being entered teaching profession. This ultimately resulted in the fall of the quality education.

But presently the younger generations are greatly motivated and are attracted to the Education Department due to attractive salaries offered in the department. Hence, there is rush of first class students seeking admissions into the teacher training institutions.

Teaching in an art. One cannot teach in the way another teaches. It is a technique of communicating the ideas to the pupils in a more meaningful way. The teacher training institutions have been instructing a number of methods for the purpose of teaching, but the teacher has not been following any of these methods purely but adopts a hybrid of methods by combining knowingly or unknowingly a few of these methods with his own method, in an ill-equipped and overcrowded classroom. The relevancy of the presentation of the lesson-plan is also doubtful. There is also difference in the lesson-plan practiced in the training institution and that actually being demanded by the inspectorate. This suggests that the teaching practice in the training institutions is not so relevant to the classroom teaching.

Coming to the content, which is also necessary because theoretical knowledge, including that borrowed from other disciplines is getting modified and enriched at such a great speed that the content in the syllabus soon becomes old, and in certain cases, even obsolete and out dated. Developments are being added to the corpus of knowledge everyday, which makes continuous restructuring of the curriculum neither imperative to help it nor become upto date and contemporarious. In this age of communication, a number of tangible innovations and experiments in the field of education are being conducted and their results deserve to be disseminated for wide replication. Since many of them are useful for improving the present practices, their inclusion in the curriculum would equip the teachers to perform their professional roles meaningfully. The change in the curricular competencies, constantly required at training level in order to cope-up with the fast changing world knowledge which is to be imparted to the younger generations. The fund of world knowledge is being constantly renovating hour-by-hour which in-turn changing the tone of the curriculum. But the curriculum of teacher education is not so positively being changed proportionately. Much care is not being taken up in revising the curriculum of teacher education.

While viewing the taught, the knowledge of most of the students is much discouraging as they get automatically promoted into higher classes not basing on their achievement rather than on their attendance. In Andhra Pradesh since 1968 the result is the sample, the trance, gets into the teaching practice, is the uninterested and reluctant lot. Thus the need to orient the trainee in the proper direction, so as to face such pupils and come out successfully. The 'teacher' is the mind, 'teaching' the spirit and the 'taught' is the body-factors which form the combined force of education. Teacher is the link between the activity 'teaching' and respondent, (i.e.) the taught. This link should be strengthened and tried on the altar of practical pre-service experience.

The foremost task before the educationists at present, is to bring drastic change in the attitudes of teachers inherited. Thus they should be ready to rethink and change the criteria and basic situation of the teaching profession, in which the job of educating and stimulating students is steadily superceding that of simply giving instruction. It is a general opinion that parents are to be educated before attempting to educate the child. Parents are the first teachers to their children, and they are to be given training to see that the school expectations are realized from the child, so also the teachers are to be trained in such a way to realize the educational objectives. But the present scenario reveals that the teacher education is at cross-roads.

RECOMMENDATIONS OF KOTHARI COMMISSION (1964-66)

1. *Removing the isolation of teacher training:* In order to make the professional preparation, effective, teacher education must be brought into the main stream of the academic life and educational developments on the other.

2 *a.* *To remove the existing isolation of teacher education from university life;* education, as distinguished from pedagogy, should be recognized as an independent academic discipline and be introduced as an elective subject in courses for the first and second degrees, and schools of education should be established in selected universities to develop programmes in teacher education and studies and research in education, in collaboration with other university disciplines.

b. *To remove the existing isolation of teacher education from schools:* extension should be regarded as an essential function of teacher training institution (TTI) and an extension service department should be established in each institution-pre primary, primary and secondary-as an integral part of it.

- Effective alumni associations should be established to bring old students and old faculty together to discuss and plan, programmes and curricula.
- Practice teaching for teachers under training should be organized in active collaboration with selected schools which should receive recognition from the Education Department as co-operating schools and special grant should be given for equipment and supervision, and
- Periodic exchange of the staff of the co-operating schools and of the teacher training institutions should be arranged.

c. An intensive effort should be made to remove the existing separation among the institutions preparing teachers for different stages of education or for special fields such as Craft or Art or Physical Education by:

- Implementing a phased programme of upgrading all training institutions to the collegiate standard with the ultimate objective of bringing all teacher educators under the universities.
- Establishing comprehensive colleges of educators in each state on a planned basis.
- Establishing a state board of teacher education (SBTE) in each state to be responsible for all functions related to teacher education at all levels and in all fields.

3. Improving professional education: The essence of a programme of teacher education is "quality" and in its absence, teacher education becomes not only a financial waste but also a source of overall deterioration in educational standards. It is a programme of highest importance, therefore, it has to improve the quality of teacher education.

4. *Duration of training courses:* The duration of the professional course should be two years for primary teachers who have completed the secondary school course. It should be one year for the graduate students but the number of working days in a year should be increased to 230.

5. *The State Board of Teacher Education* should conduct a survey of teacher education programmes and curricula and initiate the necessary revision.

6. *New professional courses* must be developed to orient Headmasters and teacher educators to their special field of works.

7. *Quality improvement:* Early steps should be taken to improve training institutions for teachers for the improvement of quality in the teacher education.

NATIONAL POLICY ON EDUCATION (NPE) (1986)

National Policy on Education (NPE) (1986) emphasized the following aspects on teacher education:

1. *In-service and pre-service components:* Teacher education is a continuous process and its pre-service and in-service components are inseparable. As a first step, the system of teacher education will be overhauled.
2. *Continuing education:* The new programmes of teacher education will emphasise continuing education and the need for teachers to meet the thrusts envisaged in this policy.
3. *Establishment of DIETs:* District institute of education and training will be established with capability to organize pre-service and in-service courses for elementary school teachers and for the personal working in non-formal and adult education.

PROGRAMME OF ACTION (POA) (1986)

Programme of action, which is a follow-up programme of national policy on education (NPE) (1986) gives the following details about the upliftment of teacher education. Professional training of teachers to be employed in elementary and secondary schools, is a pre-requisite in all parts of the country. The facilities of the training institutes should be improved and the curricula should be revised.

Keeping in view the central place of teacher education, NPE (1986) calls for its overhaul as the first step towards educational reorganization. Giving particular importance to the training of elementary school teachers, it is envisaged that selected existing teacher training institutions would be developed as district institute of education and training (DIET) both for pre-service and in-service courses of elementary school teachers and for continuing education of the personnel working in non formal and adult education programmes. Reorganization of secondary teacher education system is also implied in the policy.

DISTRICT INSTITUTE OF EDUCATION AND TRAINING

Types of Training Programmes Being Given in DIETs

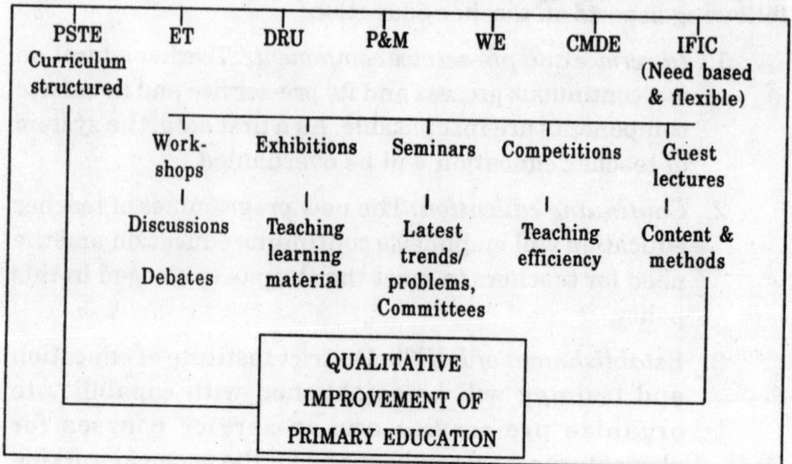

The following are the ten examination papers constituting the syllabus for the two year D.Ed. course.

1. Education in Emerging India
2. Educational Psychology for Elementary Teacher Education.
3. Elementary Education, Planning, Management, Teacher Functions
4. Perspectives in Pre-primary, Primary Education.
5. A) Computer Education and Capacity Building.

   B) Health and Physical Education.

   C) Art Education.

   D) Work Experience.
6. (a) Methods of Teaching Mother Tongue (Telugu) (or)

   (b) Methods of Teaching Urdu (in selected DIETs)
7. Methods of Teaching English.
8. Methods of Teaching Mathematics.

9. Methods of Teaching Sciences.
10. Methods of Teaching Social Studies.

IMPORTANCE OF PRE-SERVICE TRAINING

Those who intend to enter teaching as a profession, must undergo a sufficiently long period of good training before they join in to the service. No one should be appointed without proper training, both academic as well as professional. In other words, teachers are required to know what to teach, how to teach and why to teach. The knowledge of content, method and purpose of teaching is the three-fold pre-requisite for the professional teacher. The pre-service training should include the courses in the subject of specialization, courses in educational methodology and courses in Philosophical and Sociological Foundations.

IN-SERVICE EDUCATION

For implementing the In-service education for teachers through Agencies, it is necessary to have full support of state, in terms of policy, programme and finance. Unless the Government is concerned about developing the quality of education and improving the teaching profession in the country, no effort of professional organization or academic institutions is going to bear fruit. In India, Government is looked upon as the authority that can inspire and initiate new schemes and can sustain them for good. Whatever the Government ignores, the people tend to neglect.

Unless the Government takes a positive stand and works as an active partner in the professional development of teachers, all schemes of educational improvement will fall flat and result in wastage in money. It has to play a new role in free India and adopt effective measures for promoting the standards of the teaching profession. Some of the measures suggested are outlined here:

- Formulation of a national policy and programme on teacher development in view of the needs of the country.
- Moral, material and legal support to the professional organization of teachers in the country.

- Active collaboration with the educational institutions and the professional groups in organizing programmes of training, research and extension for teacher improvement.

In-service Training

It is the education, a teacher receives after he has entered the teaching profession, and after he had his education in a teachers' college. It includes all the programmes educational, social or others, in which the teacher takes a vital part, all the extra education which he receives at different institutions by way of refresher and other professional courses, and all he travels and visits which he undertakes. The advantages of the in-service teacher training are listed below.

Professional Growth

In-service training is most essential for the professional growth of the teacher. He needs to renovate his experiences, refresh his knowledge, develop a wider out look, benefit by the experiences of others, acquire new information and hence reorient himself.

Upto Date Knowledge

The Kothari Commission suggested that every teacher must receive two or three months of in-service education in every five years of service, because education is dynamic i.e., ever changing. Theories which were considered true 20 years ago, are no longer hold good today. Obviously a teacher who received his training 20 years back, must receive new training today. He must remain in touch with latest trends in education. He must have the up-to-date knowledge of new problems, new methods, and new techniques in education.

Critical Awareness

In-service education develops the power of critical awareness. The teacher enriches his personal experiences, holds self examination., compares him with other in the field, avails of the experience of others, conveys to others his own good or bad experiences and finds opportunities to trash out common problems on professional platform, shares his knowledge and experiences, learns from others experiences, gets competitive spirit, knows his position in the teaching community, corrects himself, becomes communicative, makes himself to the changing class room situations.

Sense of Security

When the teachers meet in seminars or workshops, they develop a sense of security, a like-mindedness, a team spirit and a feeling of belongingness and tries to find himself updated.

Training in Democratic Way of Knowledge and Living

While participating in discussions and conferences, the teachers get a training in democratic way of living. By deliberating in seminary they arrive at mutual decisions after healthy discussions, respecting others opinions, inviting criticism for members of the group, sharing ideas etc.

PROGRAMMES OF IN-SERVICE TEACHER TRAINING

1. Refresher courses
2. Workshops
3. Study groups
4. Conferences
5. Experimentation
6. Seminars
7. Extension lectures
8. Content enrichment training
9. Methodology orientation
10. Induction training courses
11. Action research training
12. Adolescence awareness training

13. Quality Improvement training
14. Language improvement training
15. Awareness training courses.

INCENTIVES FOR IN-SERVICE TEACHER EDUCATION

Incentives are essential for the promotion of in-service education. The following incentives are suggested :

1. Promotion to higher salary scales and greater administrative positions on the basis of in-service education.
2. Attendance of refresher and short-term professional courses should be credited towards preparation for degrees.
3. Leave or absence with lower pay should be granted to those who wish to go for further study, for specialization in teaching or for educational tours.
4. Grants should be given for educational tours.
5. Pay should be according to the qualifications and not according to posts held.
6. Increment should be refused to those who do nothing to improve their professional qualifications for several years.

Views of Programme of Action (POA) (1986) on In-service Education:

RESPONSIBILITIES OF SCERTS

A great responsibility would be given to SCERTs. They would have the major role of planning, sponsoring, monitoring and evaluating the in-service education programmes of all levels of teachers, instructors and other educational personnel.

SCERTs would also prepare suitable material for in-service education of teachers, undertake orientation for key resource persons, monitor and evaluate the programmes. Similar steps for training of teachers in vocational stream should also be taken by SCERTs.

RESPONSIBILITIES OF DIETS

The district institutes of education and training for the primary level would be the major agency to conduct the programmes of in-service education for primary teachers. Assistance would be sought from school complexes in the district. In case of secondary school teachers, the programme should be extended through teacher training institutions and the centres for continuing education. The district level education officer will help in effective conduct of the programmes.

ORGANISATION OF IN-SERVICE PROGRAMMES

All in-service education programmes cannot be organized in face-to-face modality, especially in view of the numbers involved. Distance in-service education programme will be prepared and extended with the help of broadcasting Agencies. SCERTs would be equipped with necessary resources for the production of learning material other than print. Minimum essential equippment to record audio and video programmes would be provided to each SCERT. The comprehensive colleges of education as well as DIETs would also be provided production facilities in a phased manner. The production facilities at DIETs and the colleges may not be of professional quality but which would produce material which can be used in its own training programmes and can also be shared by other sister organizations. Experiences especially those of voluntary organizations should be drawn upon in designing courses, development of material and strategies for in-service education.

DISTRICT INSTITUTES OF EDUCATION AND (DIETs)

After the adoption of the national policy on education 1986, a centrally sponsored scheme for re-structuring and re-organising teacher education was being implemented since October 1987. One of its components are establishment of district institutes of education and training [DIETs].

By the time of adoption of NPE 1986, elementary and adult education system were already too vast to be adequately supported by national and state level agencies alone. The NPE-86 implied their further expansion and also considerable qualitative improvement. Provision of support to them in a de-centralised manner had therefore become imperative. The NPE and POA accordingly envisaged an addition of a third, district level tier, to the support system in the shape of district institute of education and training. With this, expectation would be of wider quantitative coverage as well as equilaterally better support as these institutes would be closer to the field and therefore more alive to its problems and needs.

PROGRAMME OF ACTION (POA) (1986) ELEMENTARY TEACHER EDUCATION AND DIETS:

Chapter XXIII ['teachers and their training'] of the programme of action (POA) prepared to implement the NPE has this to say:

> "Keeping in view the central place of teacher education, NPE calls for its overhaul as the first step towards educational reorganization. Giving particular importance to the training of elementary school teachers, it is envisaged that selected teacher training institutions (TTIs) would be developed as district institutions of education and training (DIET) both for pre-service and in-service courses of elementary school teachers and for continuing education of the personnel working in non-formal and adult education programmes".

FUNCTIONS OF DIETS

Paras 18 and 20 of the chapter say that "functions of a DIET" would include:

- Pre-service and in-service education of teachers for the formal school system.
- Induction level and continuing education of non-formal and adult education Instructors and Supervisors.
- Training and orientation of heads of institutions in institutional planning and management and micro-level planning.

- Orientation of community leaders, functionaries of voluntary organizations and other influencing school level education.
- Academic support to school complexes and district boards of education (DBEs).
- Action research and experimentation work.
- Serving as evaluation center for primary and upper primary schools as well as non-formal and adult education programme.
- Provision of services of a resource and learning center for teachers and instructors.
- Consultancy and advice, for example to DBE's.

THE FIRST LOT OF DIETs

They were sanctioned in February-March 1988. During 1987-88 and 1988-89, the first installment of central assistance for non recurring items were sanctioned for 101 and 114 DIETs respectively. Thus up to September 1989 central assistance had been sanctioned under the teacher education scheme for setting up a total of 215 DIETs in the country.

RESTRUCTURING AND RE-ORGANISATION OF TEACHER EDUCATION IN SEVENTY PLAN

It has been taken up during the Seventy Plan Period with the following five components.

1. Mass orientation of about five lakh school teachers annually to make them aware of their role in the context of the new policy thrusts and improve their professional competencies.
2. Setting up of about 400 DIETs.
3. Strengthening of about 250 secondary school teacher education institutes (STEIs), about 50 of them as Instutions of advanced study in education (IASEs), and the remaining 200 as colleges of teacher education (CTEs).
4. Strengthening of SCERTs.

5. Establishment of university departments of education through the U.G.C.

MISSION AND ROLES OF DIETS

The DIETs were established, to provide academic and resource support to the field of elementary education, adult education and non-formal education at grass root level.

Through DIETs the following objectives were expected to be fulfilled, namely.

(a) Universalisation of primary/elementary education

(b) NLM targets in regard to functional literacy in the 15 to 35 Age group.

The DIETs have to work in accordance with the needs of individuals of state and districts as specific role.

PACE-SETTING ROLE OF DIETS

In pursuit of excellence the DIETs have to perform two interrelated aspects, namely.

(a) Excellence in the institutes own work

(b) Helping the elementary and adult education system in the districst in achieving excellence.

To achieve and promote excellence the DIETs have to be equipped with all necessary resources and man power.

In this context DIETs will also have a very important pace setting role to play. They will be expected to become models for other educational institutions in the district in terms of meticulous, efficient and effective planning and execution of functions. Harmonious and creative organizational climate, maintenance of a clean and attractive campus.

DIETs cannot therefore afford to view themselves in isolation and must faithfully discharge their role of supplementing and complimenting other parallel initiatives.

THE MAJOR FUNCTIONS OF DIETS

A DIET will have to perform three main functions viz.,

(1) Training: Both of induction level as well as continuing training.

(2) Resource support: extension, guidance, development of materials aids, evaluation tools etc.

(3) Action research:

BASIC TRANSACTIONAL APPROACH FOR THE DIETS

The transactional approach for the DIETs is child centred approach as envisaged by the NPE and POA 1986. The most important aspect of the reform will be to make education a joyful, innovative and satisfying learning activities rather than a system of rote, cheerless and authoritarian instruction. In case of adult education programmes the approach should be participative and learner active mode. This approach facilitates teachers, instructors to tackle the problems of high pupil-teacher ratio, multi-grade teaching, inadequate physical facilities and so on, but not mere transmitting the ready-made knowledge to the learners, so that the teacher should act as a designer, facilitator of learning experience, a manager of Institution and learning resources and an active contributor to the all round development of the learners. In all the programmes of pre-service and in-service teacher education and training of AE/NFE personnel, the DIETs have to adopt the same approach. This basic approach would improve the transaction of all programmes in a DIET. Some of the implications would be as follows:-

1. Programmes will be need-based.
2. Trainees will be enabled to experiment, discover, learn, practise and innovate for themselves. Learning activities will be suitably organized in individual and group modes.
3. Maximum possible use will be made of the local environment in the learning process. Curricula and learning activities will be suitably related to it.
4. Good work will be duly recognized, encouraged, displayed, and published.
5. The DIET will itself adopt to the attitude to the life long learner rather to that of an oracle or know all. It will receive as much from the field as it would endeavour to give to it.

The district will serve as the school for its learning experiences while it may carve out one or two special areas as its lab-areas.

TARGET GROUPS

As per the emphasis of NPE on universalisation of elementary education (UEE), special attention is being given to the following target groups as identified as disadvantages.

(a) Girls and women

(b) Scheduled castes and scheduled tribes

(c) Minorities

(d) The physically challenged

(e) Other educationally disadvantaged groups, eg. working children, slum dwellers, inhabitants of hilly, desert and other inaccessible areas etc.

GUIDING PRINCIPLES, AUTONOMY AND ACCOUNTABILITY

In view of the structural and functional aspects described above, DIETs would need to be given adequate functional autonomy-academic, administrative and financial and would at the same time be accountable *vis-à-vis* clearly laid down objectives and norms. They would be institutions of the state Government or Union Territory administration and will therefore be ultimately answerable to them. The state Government / Union Territory administration may exercise its supervisory functions through the SCERT and SRC.

The DBEs are set or state Government may designate SCERT/SRC or some other suitable educational authority to perform the DBEs functions vis-a- vis DIETs.

DIETS AS NON-VACATION, RESIDENTIAL INSTITUTES

The DIET activities like, in-service and programmes for AE/ NFE personnel would go on throughout the year, but peak during summer vacations because when the institutes resources would be free from the work-load of pre-service training, and also because that would cause minimum dislocation in schools.

STRUCTURE OF A DIET

Looking at the above functions, a DIET would need to have staff strength in the following areas:

(1) Foundations of education and pedagogy.

(2) The subjects taught at the elementary stages – namely

   (i) Languages taught at the elementary level in the district (these may be two, three or even four, depending on the number of languages which are introduced in a state at the elementary stage, and factors like bilingual character of a district).

   (ii) Mathematics

   (iii) Environmental Studies-Social Sciences.

   (iv) Environmental Studies-Sciences

   (v) Work Experience

   (vi) Art Education

   (vii) Health and Physical Education

(3) Non-formal education

(4) Adult education

(5) Curriculum, Material Development and Evaluation

(6) In-service Programmes, Field Interaction and Innovation Co-ordination

(7) Planning and Management

(8) Educational Technology.

THE STRUCTURE

In the study the structure was used to refer to physical, financial and human resources available as per the norms stipulated by MHRD Guidelines (1989).

Organizational Structure of a DIET

Principal

Academic staff	**Office staff**	**Model school staff**
1. P.S.T.E Sr. Lecture r - 1 Lecturers - 7	2. Superintendent-1 3. Accountant-1 4. Senior assistant-1	1. School assistant-1 2. Secondary grade
2. I.F.I.C Sr. Lecturer - 1 Lecturer - 1	5. Junior assistants-5 6. At tenders-7 7. Sweeper-1	
3. E.T. Sr. Lecturer - 1 Lecturer - 1 Technician- 1		
4. D.R.U Sr. Lecturer - 1 Lecturers - 3		
5. C.M.D.E. Sr. Lecturer - 1 Lecturer - 1		
6. W.E Sr. Lecturer - 1 Lecturer - 1 Instructor - 1		
7. P & M Sr. Lecturer - 1 Lecturer - 1 Statistician- 1		

ACADEMIC BRANCHES OF A DIET

1. PSTE - Pre – service Teacher Education including Health and Physical Education.
2. DRU - District Resource Unit
3. IFIC - In-service Programmes, Field Interaction and Innovation, Co-ordination.

4. WE	-	Work Experience
5. ET	-	Educational Technology
6. C M D E	-	Curriculum, Material Development and Evaluation.
7. P & M	-	Planning & Management.
8. H.R.D.	-	Human Resource Development

(HRD branch was existed for Andhra Pradesh Primary Education Programme (APPEP) during the year 1989-1996 in Andhra Pradesh state only)

THE LIBRARY

(1) A DIET library should be run on open access system i.e., its members should have free access to the book-stacks so that they can consult or browse through any book of their choice at any time during library hours.

(2) The library should remain open longer than the normal Institute hours so that trainees can use it even beyond regular hours. It would be desirable if it could also remain open on Sundays and public holidays.

(3) To facilitate (2) above, some special allowance may be engaged to man the library beyond Institute hours , on payment basis. For this purpose a panel of interested and needy students could be prepared and they could be given basic training in library management.

(4) Certain guidelines regarding selection and procurement of books and journals for the DIET library as given in the Guidelines manual to be followed.

(5) For smooth and efficient functioning of the Institute library, after its initial setting up at the project stage, a library advisory committee may be set up with the following composition:

(1) Principal	Chairman
(2) Vice-Principal and all Sr. Lecturers	Members
(3) Two Lecturers to be nominated by the Principal	Members

(4) Two pre-service trainees to be nominated by the Principal — Members

(5) Two experts in the area of Library Science/Book Promotion/ elementary teacher education/ AE/NFE — Members

(6) Librarian — Secretary

The Comittee may take decisions regarding all important matters concerning the library, including procedure for selection and purchase of new books, selection of journals for subscription, optimal utilization of the library budget and resources, etc.

THE HOSTEL

(1) As already stated, every DIET will have separate hostels for men and women. The capacities of these hostels will be decided mainly keeping in view the ratio of men and women among various groups of trainees who would be coming to the Institute.

(2) The Principal may appoint either a common warden for both hostels or separate wardens – as may be found locally suitable – from among the faculty members. In case of separate wardens, the one for women's hostel may as far as possible be a lady.

(3) While servicing, the residential part of the hostel will be the responsibility of the institute staff, all recurring expense in connection with the mess (including remuneration to cook, etc.) will be borne by trainees. In case of pre-service trainees, they will bear it themselves, while payment for other trainees will come from the funds provided for the conduct of the relevant programmes. The institute will only provide furniture and utensils for use in the mess.

(4) The hostel mess may be run either by the students as a co-operative, or through a contractor, as may be found locally convenient.

PHYSICAL FACILITIES

A DIET with the kind of functions and structure spelt out above would also need to have adequate facilities like:

(a) 10 acres of Institute campus.

(b) Buildings – Administration, Classrooms, Hostels, Staff quarters.

(c) Other facilities.

(i) Library and reading room.

(ii) Laboratories for Physical Sciences and Life – Sciences.

(iii) Equipment for Psychology experiments, Social Studies and Language teaching.

(iv) A work – shed/garden for W.E. activities.

(v) Equipment for Education in Visual & Performing Arts.

(vi) Equipment and playground for Physical Education & Sports.

(vii) Audio – visual aids.

(viii) Computer room.

(ix) Equipment for education of the physically challenged.

(x) Special materials and equipment relevant for AE/ NFE.

A DIET is an expensive Institution to create and maintain in non-recurring as well as recurring terms. It has therefore, to be ensured that it has enough clientele to justify the investments it requires. It is accordingly recommended that :

(a) Relating the DIET structure to the characteristics of the district.

(b) Relating DIET structure to the elementary teacher population of the district.

(c) Co-ordinating the various branches in DIET.

PROGRAMMES AND ACTIVITIES ORGANIZED IN DIETS

The following are the main programmes and activities organized in DIETs.

(1) Pre-service teacher education programme.

(2) In-service programmes of elementary teachers, Headmasters, Heads of school complexes, and officers of Education Department up to block level.

(3) Field Interaction. (visiting elementary schools and guiding teachers in the implementation of the innovative ideas.)

(4) Training programmes for personnel of adult and non-formal education.

(5) Workshops for the development of curricular, teaching learning material, testing, tools and techniques of evaluation, low cost teaching aids etc.

(6) Orientation programmes for members of DBE school education committees (SECs), community leaders, youth organizations and other educational activities.

(7) Field studies, action research and experimentation.

PROGRAMME ADVISORY COMMITTEE (PAC)

Every DIET will have a programme advisory committee which will advise and guide the Institute in the planning and conduct of its entire range of programmes and activities. The committee may have the following composition :

(1) Pncipal, DIET : Convenor

(2) One representative each from all agencies with which the DIET would have linkage e.g.

- (i) District Board of Education (representative to be chosen from among the board's non-official members)
- (ii) SCERT, SIET and SRC
- (iii) Nearest university department of education,

(iv) Nearest CTE or IASE, and in the absence of these, any other good secondary teacher education institution located nearby.

(v) District Educational Officer.

(vi) District level officers in-charge of AE, NFE and women and child development.

(vii) Chief Executive Officer of district rural development agency (CEO, DRDA).

(viii) Station Director of the local radio station (wherever applicable).

(ix) District Information and Publicity Officer.

(x) In case a DRU is wholly or partly outside the DIET, the Head of such DRU.

(xi) Co-ordinator of Nehru Yuwak Kendra.

(xii) NGOs in the district working in the area of elementary/adult education.

(3) Representatives of client group and staff

1. Two students of the pre-service teacher education course.
2. One elementary teacher, one Headmaster and one instructor or Supervisor each of AE and NFE who may have undergone in-service training in the Institution during the last one year.
3. Three representatives of the faculty of the institution of whom one would be Vice-Principal/Senior Lecturer In-charge of DRU, one other Senior Lecturer and one Lecturer.
4. Others

   (i) Two eminent educationists/teacher educators/ teachers, with a substantial record of service, who may be interested in associating themselves with, and contributing to the activities of the DIET.

   (ii) Two other eminent citizens of the district, whose association with the DIET may be of benefit to the institution.

FUNCTIONS OF THE PAC

Preparation of five year and annual institutional plans of the DIET have been indicated.

Meetings of the PAC may be held at least twice a year. It may set up sub-committees to go into various categories of programmes conducted by the DIET e.g. teacher education (TE), AE, NFE, field interaction, action research, etc. The sub-committees may co-opt in their work experts and other concerned persons who may not necessarily be members of the PAC.

CO-CURRICULAR ACTIVITIES

While DIETs organize a large number of formally structured, curriculum-related training and other programmes, they would also be expected to organize a wide range of Co-curricular Activities in which faculty members and trainees (especially pre-service trainees) would participate on voluntary basis, depending on their individual interests. Though these activities would be outside regular curricular programmes, they would play an important role in enriching life on the campus.

Pre-service trainees would be the main beneficiaries of these activities, since they are the ones who would be at the Institute for long duration, but participants of the in-service programmes would also find many of these activities interesting and useful.

Co-curricular Activities will be expected to be organized chiefly through clubs and societies formed ;for the purpose. Each such club/society would have one or two staff associates/advisers, and trainees would enroll as members of such clubs/societies depending on their interest. The office bearers of each club/society would be chosen from among such trainee members in accordance with rules which the Institute may frame for the purpose. The following are some of the areas for which clubs/societies could be constituted.

(1) Debates and elocutions.

(2) Literary activities.

(3) Trecking and mountaineering.

(4) History and Archaeology.
(5) Current affairs.
(6) Fine arts.
(7) Music, Dance and Drama.
(8) Environment.
(9) Science.
(10) Hobbies.
(11) Athletics/Gymnastics/Aquatics.
(12) Various games and other sports.
(13) Yoga/Judo/Karate.
(14) Social Service.
(15) Scouting and Guiding.

DISTRICT INSTITUTES OF EDUCATION AND TRAINING (DIETS) IN ANDHRA PRADESH

Under national policy on education (1986) Government of India has formulated a central scheme for restructuring and reorganizing of teacher education. Under this scheme, Government of India has sanctioned 23 DIETs, one each for every district in a phased manner with cent percent central assistance.

The objective of DIETs is to improve the facilities for pre-service and in-service teacher training for elementary education (EE) including non-formal and adult education. Also, it aims at improving the quality of teacher training programmes for these sectors of education.

Government of Andhra Pradesh state has upgraded 23 then existing Government teacher trainining institutions in the state into DIETs in a phased manner i.e. nine DIETs during 1988-89, eight DIETs during 1989-90 and the remaining six DIETs during1990-91.

Under this scheme, Government of India has sanctioned 38 additional posts, both teaching and non-teaching for strengthening each DIET with seven departments and one more department exclusively in Andhra Pradesh for Andhra Pradesh Primary Education Project (APPEP) as department of human resource development up to February 1996.

All the 23 DIETs were provided pucca buildings for smooth and quick completion of civil works, the construction work, has been entrusted to Chief Engineers of roads and buildings (R&B) Panchayat Raj and Andhra Pradesh Industrial and Infrastructural development corporation (A.P.I.I.C.). All the 23 DIETs buildings were completed.

THE PRESENT STUDY

In the context of the importance of DIETs as institutes of elementary teacher education, the present study has been undertaken to examine the role and performance of DIETs In the state of Andhra Pradesh. In the present scenario the improvement of quality in elementary education is being practised by using various interventions of DPEP and SSA through DIETs.

The importance of this study is that the success of U.E.E. is on the shoulders of the teachers. Hence, the teacher education at elementary level is very important. The teacher education will be imparted by the DIET at district level as envisaged by the NPE (1986) and its P.O.A.

DIETs are also expected to improve the perspectives and philosophy as well as approaches where the programmes are designed depending on the needs and are presented through child centered activities which require better infrastructure facilities, better qualified faculty and more wide range of programmes compared to the erstwhile teacher training institution (T.T.I.) pattern.

TITLE OF THE PRESENT STUDY

The title of the present study is stated as:

"A Study on the Role and Performance of District Institutes of Education and Training of Andhra Pradesh State" with special reference to Guidelines of MHRD, Government of India.

NEED FOR THE PRESENT INVESTIGATION

Various commissions and committees were being appointed by the Government from time to time and their recommendations were being reviewed' and policy statements were being issued to effect needed changes in the present system of education. Any change in the society can be brought only through education. The aspirations of the people are frequently changing due to the advancement of science and technology . Accordingly the changes in the system of education also need to be brought in from time to time. In any society, a sound system of education which enables the people of that country to keep their five fingers in their mouth is needed. Kothari Commission has emphasized the need for vocationalization, universalisation of our education and Science Education especially at secondary level. Accordingly, Rajeev Gandhi, the former Prime Minister of India has felt the need for utilization of human resources in the nation's spirit . Hence national education policy was introduced to revamp the primary education, secondary education, vocational education, adult education, women education and teacher education. If teachers are well, all is well. The deterioration in the quality of secondary education may be because of ill-trained and ill equipped teachers in schools. The national policy of education 1986 and the statutory body of NCTE have given top most importance for maintaining quality of education in teacher training institutions in the country. Since independence the efforts made by the Government to improve the quality of education at any level have faced a failure and the students after leaving the school or college are facing a gloomy future, which leads to students unrest. Our society is unable to utilize fully the human resources, though they are abundantly available. The teachers are the architects of the nation. If they are properly trained in developing the capacities in among children, the challenges of the 21st century can be easily met by our country. Accordingly huge funds were being spent for upgrading teacher training institutes as DIETs.

Some suitable programmes and interventions are being planned and implemented through DIETs from time to time to achieving desired quality and universalization of elementary education (UEE). Even after 17 years of DIETs establishment there is not much improvement in the quality of elementary education.

Hence, the investigator felt that whether there is any serious deficiency in the DIETs in Andhra Pradesh in promoting the quality in elementary education? Whether there is any significant deviation in the provision of resources of DIETs in Andhra Pradesh from the MHRD Guidelines? Whether there is any inappropriateness in the role performance of DIETs for bringing the desired quality? It is in the study of DIETs in Andhra Pradesh is to be conducted in terms of their role and performance and the intervention of SSA. Hence there is the need for the present investigation.

2

Review of the Related Literature

The researcher has reviewed several Indian as well as foreign studies which are related to the present study.

Mehta, R.D., (1985), *An Investigation into the Change in the Attitudes and Values of Teacher Trainee with Respect to Some of Their Personality Variables,* Delhi University.

The objectives of the inquiry were: (i) to study the relationship of extroversion (E), psychoticism (P), neuroticism (N) with (a) change in attitude towards teaching as a profession (ATP), (b) change in attitude towards child control (ACC), (c) change in attitude towards classroom discipline (ACD), (d) change in attitude towards classroom instruction (ACI), (e) change in attitude towards teacher-pupil relations (ATPR), (f) change in theoretical value (TH), (g) change in economic value (EC), (h) change in aesthetic values (AS), (i) change in social values (SO), (j) change in political value(PO), (k) change in religious value(Re), and (ii) to study the main effect along with interaction of extroversion (E), psychoticism (P), and neuroticism (N) on ATP, ACC, ACD, ACI, ATPR, Th, EC, AS, SO, PO, and Re.

The findings of the study were: (1) The impact of the teacher training programme in the CIE (Department of Education) was such that a significant positive change in attitudes towards teaching took place in all the subgroups of subjects, and the maximum positive change took palace in the sub-group of high extroversion, with low psychoticism and low neurotism. (2) The interaction effect of extroversion, psychoticism and neurotism was non-significant in producing any significant change in the said attitudes, namely attitude towards child control, attitude towards classroom discipline, attitude towards classroom instruction and attitude towards teacher-pupil relations. (3) The impact of the teacher-training programme was such that theoretical, aesthetic and political values changed negatively as a result of the effect of extroversion, psychoticism and neurotism.

Maria Emenon, (2002). *Perception of Future and Current Teacher in the Organization of Elementary Schools : A Dissonance Approach to the Investigation of Job Satisfaction.*

The study compares the satisfaction ratings of future and current elementary teachers with respect to the main aspects of school organization and administration. Data were collected from 66 in-service teachers and 79 PSTE trainees in Cyprus. The application of factor analysis on the data resulted in the identification of the following main dimensions of the school organization.

Major findings of the study were: First the ratings of the two groups differred significantly for the first four factors. Secondly, future teachers reported lower satisfaction ratings than their in service counter parts in the Headmasters role, school organization and school climate factors and higher ratings in the teacher incentives work conditions factor.

SIERT, (1966), *Teacher Education at Primary Level in Rajasthan.*

The main objective of this survey was to have a global picture of the primary teacher training institutions in the State.

The study revealed: (1) The average intake was about 130. The qualifications prescribed of admission to the STC course was the high/higher secondary examination. (2) About two-thirds of the trainees belonged to Rural area. (3) The minimum age prescribed for refreshers was 18 years whereas the ages of the trainees ranged for 18 to 45 years. (4) In the teaching staff, there were Headmasters, subject teachers, and Craft, Agriculture Physical Education and Drawing Instructors.

Shukla, A.G.B., (1975) *A Critical Study of Curriculum Development at the Stage of Elementary Education in the State of Gujarat; 1940-1970,* Ph. D. Education, Gujarat Vidyapeeth.

The major objectivities of the investigation were : (i) to review the changes introduced in the curriculum of primary education during the years 1940-1970.

The major finding of the study were: The major defects of the primary school curriculum were lack of practical knowledge inadequate arithmetic in the lower classes, emphasis on information rather than understanding a heavy load of subject matter, absence of moral education, low level of instruction in History region and Geography, the local trade industry etc.

Arora, K., (1976) *Difference between Effective and Ineffective Teachers.*

The major objective of the study was to find out the characteristics differentiating effective and ineffective teachers.

The findings of the study were : (1) The age and the length of service were non-differentiating characteristics. (2) A greater number of ineffective teachers passed examination while in service.

Bhatt, M.H., (1966) *Kapasan Scheme of Improvement in Teacher Training,* SIERT, Rajasthan.

The study was taken up on the assumption that qualitative improvement in education was possible by preparing better teachers in training schools. A scheme based on this assumption was developed and tried out at the Government Basic Training School, Kapasan.

The study revealed : (1) As a result of the training, there was improvement in lesson planning and standard of teaching. (2) On the basis of pre-and post-tests trainees' knowledge of the content was found to be much improved.3. Teachers were encouraged to teach in a planned manner.

Chander, R. (1976) *Studied on Relationship of Attainments in Theory Subjects in B.Ed course with Attitude as a Teacher and Teaching Efficiency.*

The study attempted to investigate the relationship between the attainments in a training course with the teaching efficiency in the classroom and attitude as a teacher.

The major findings of the study were : (1) Factor analysis indicated three different factors-namely factor A-theory subjects, Factor B-principles of education, and Factor C teaching efficiency. (2) Attitude and teaching efficiency had loadings on Factor A alone and only two other variables, techniques of education and Educational Psychology had appreciable loadings on it. Factor A had only small correlations with factor B and Factor C; then for the variables of attitude and teaching efficiency had little to do with the existing theory courses other than those in educational techniques and Psychology.

Thakur, T., (1976) *Who is a Good Teacher? (A Study Based on the Opinion of Senior Pupils),* SIE, Assam.

The main purpose of the study was to analyse the characteristics of a good teacher as perceived by his pupils.

The major findings were: (1) Most of the pupils were from economically deprived homes. (2) The outstanding positive traits of the teacher as viewed by the pupils were good teaching, kind and pleasing manners, good advice and guidance to pupils, regular and punctual attendance and equal treatment to all. The pupils were in favor of strict discipline and strict administration. The pupils loved to get regular assignments and wanted that the teachers correct pupils was loved by all. A teacher who did not let down pupils was loved by all. A teacher who could identify himself with his pupils found his class teaching easy.

Mohini, B.K., (1977), *and Others,, A Study of the Development of Teacher Effectiveness through Teaching Practice.* SNDT College of Education for Women. Pune.

The objectives of the investigation were : (1) to find out at which lesson or lessons in the teaching practice period, the teachers effectiveness in general reached the maximum. (2) to assertain if this point experienced development was the same or different for experienced trainees and freshers and whether this point differed with different school subjects.

The major findings were: (1) The coefficients of correlation obtained between the overall grade and the grade computed on the basis of assessment of components were quite significant in respect of both the experienced and the fresh teachers. The relationship was higher in the case of subjects in which subject experts observed higher percentages of lessons (2) In the case of experienced teachers effectiveness in general reached a limit on sixth, seventh or eighth lesson in all subjects except Science.

Sharma, N.D., (1978) *An Experimental Study of Teaching Natural Sciences at the Primary Level in Central Schools,* Patna. University.

The study was undertaken : (i) to ascertain the existing position of teaching Natural Sciences at the primary level in the central schools, and (ii) to compare the effectiveness of different methods of teaching Science at the primary school level.

The results of the study were : (i) Most of the teachers used traditional methods for teaching Natural Sciences. Some tended to make Natural Sciences teaching at this level activity-oriented. (ii) The teachers were not well equipped for teaching Science at this level. (iii) It was admitted by most of the teachers that activity should be the basis of teaching Natural Sciences at the primary level. (iv) Guided activity was more effective than self-activity in respect of concept formation, development of scientific attitude and acquisition of scientific knowledge, training in scientific skill.

Das, R.C., (1979) *Effectiveness of Teacher-Training in Reducing Educational Wastage,* SIE, Assam.

The main aim of the study was to find out the impact of teacher training on educational wastage and stagnation in primary schools.

The major findings were: (1) The training of teachers at the primary level had no significant contribution towards reduction of wastage and stagnation in schools with multiple-class teaching. Training of teachers had no significant impact on the system of education at primary stage. (2) In the case of multiple-teacher schools when a majority of teachers were trained, the impact of training did contribute effectively towards checking wastage.

Bhatnagar, T.N.S., (1980) *Studies and Literature on Student Teaching and Other Practical Work in the B.Ed. Programme in India - A Review,* Department of teacher education Project, NCERT.

The main objective of the study was : to analyze the contents of studies and literature on student teaching and other practical work in the B.Ed. programme and to suggest the future perspective of studies in these areas.

The major Findings were : (1) A few studies revealed that student teaching was the weakest link in the teacher – education programme a. primary as well as secondary level. (2) Most of the literature of this period spoke highly about micro teaching training approach.

Malik, S., (1978) *Personality Correlates of Real and Ideal Self-concept of Teacher Trainees,* Agra University.

The objectives were: (i) to find out the relationship between real and ideal self-concepts of teacher trainers, (ii) to find out the relationship of the real and ideal self-concept with some selected dimensions of personality of teacher-trainees, (iii) to find out the relationship between the teacher-trainees' attitude towards the teaching profession and their real and ideal self-concept.

The findings were: (1) Teacher trainees' self-concept consisted of conservatism of temperament, adaptability, confidence and relax were the personality variables that were found associate with the real self of the teacher-trainees, whereas bright emotional stability, conscientious, venturesome, shrewd, self-controlled, socially group-dependent, adaptable, confident and relaxed were the personality characteristics that were found associated with their ideal self.

Ekambaram, B., *(1980) A Study of an Experiment in Creating an Effective School Climate.*

The major objectives of the investigation were: (1) to change the teachers verbal behaviour by proper training and regular feedback programme. (2) to study the effectiveness of the inputs in bringing about changes in respect of organizational climate, leadership behaviour and teachers morale.

The major findings of the investigation were: (1) As a result of teacher behaviour training and regular feedback, the teachers changed behaviour in the experimental group. (2) There was increase in the use of categories, 8 and 9 which lead to increase in pupils talk in the experimental group. According to Flanders ten category system the pupil talk involves the two categories, namely Category 8, Pupil talk response

This category is used when the teacher has initiated the contact or has solicited pupil statements, when the pupil answers the question asked by the teacher or when he responds verbally to a direction, the teacher has given anything that the pupil says that in clearly in response to initiation by the teacher.

In general if the pupil raised his hand to make a statement or to ask a question when he was not prompted to do so by the teacher – Sharma R.A. (1993) page 568, "Advanced Educational Technology".

Mohan, K., (1980) *Has Studied on Effectiveness of Teacher Training Programmes.*

The investigation was designed to find out the effectiveness of the teacher training programmes in the colleges affiliated to Avadh University, Faizabad.

The findings of the study were : (1) The teacher training departments did not have adequate buildings or equipment (2) None of them had hostels for girl students, the hostel facilities for boys were not satisfactory (3) quite a few teacher educators were not adequately qualified to supervise teaching practice in the subjects in which they were supervising the lessons.

Rajput, J.S., Saxena, A.B., Jadhao, V.G., (1980) *A Research Study in Environmental Approach of Teaching at Primary Level, Regional College of Education,* NCERT, Bhopal.

The objectives of the project were : (i) to study the existing awareness towards the scientific and social environment in children, and (ii) to identify the available community resources, which can be gainfully utilized for teaching.

The study revealed; (i) Only one of the four groups (2 schools × 2 classes) was significantly different on environmental awareness at present stage, whereas at the post test stage two experimental groups were significantly better than the control group. (ii) The difference between the experimental group and the control group on a traditional achievement test was not significant.

Sinha. U., (1980), *The Impact of Teacher Education Programme on the Professional Efficiency of the Teachers.*

The main aim of the study was to find out the impact of teacher education programme on (1) The effectiveness in classroom teaching (2) Teachers competence to perform non teaching roles, such as maintaining good interpersonal relationships with students, colleagues, and Principals, doing office work, giving guidance to students, participating in the activities of associating, comittees and community life, and participation in curricular activities.

The main findings of the study were : (1) In the sphere of professional efficiency the trained teachers were better than the untrained teachers about the aims of the lesson, its appropriateness, its organization, the use of teaching devices, presentation, questioning, answering, students questions, the use of blackboard and other teaching aids, eliciting students cooperation and participation and effective closure.

Yadav, D.D., (1980) *A Critical Study of Teacher Education in the State Haryana and Its Comparison with That of CIE, Delhi and the RCE,* Ajmer, Raj. University.

The objectives of the study were: (1) To critically evaluate the trends and issues of secondary teacher education in the state of Haryana, (2) To compare the teacher education programmes of the Central Institute of Education (CIE), Delhi, and Regional College of Education (RCE), Ajmer.

The findings of the study were: (1) The growth of the colleges of education was not need-based in the state of Haryana. (2) Though there was only one Government college of education in Haryana, yet the Government was encouraging other colleges of education by giving grants-in-aid to these institutions without fulfilling the conditions laid down by the universities.

Balachandran, (1981) *Teaching Effectiveness and Student Evaluation of Teaching.*

The main objectives of the study were : (1) to evaluate teaching effectiveness of college teachers by their students and (2) to find out the feedback effect of student evaluation on teachers in terms of their teaching effectiveness.

The major finding of the study was: student rating and self rating of teaching effectiveness were positively and significantly related, but the self rating was significantly higher than the student rating.

Dash, S. C., (1981) *Introduction of Work Education in Primary Schools- a Pilot Study, SCERT, Orissa.*

The major aim of the study was to develop models of curriculum in work education for primary classes (standards). The specific objectives were; (i) to identify the situations related to Work Education, (ii) to develop necessary instructional materials, and (iii) to develop tools to evaluate outcomes of activities related to Work Education.

The major outcomes of the pilot study were: (i) The curriculum of Work Education could be conveniently divided into three groups as for standard I, and II standards (classes) III, IV and V, and standards (classes) VI and VII. (ii) Curriculum for Work Education should be based on local resources and work situations available.

Gupta, U., (1981) *has Studied on Job Involvement and Need Pattern of Primary School Teachers in Relation to Teaching Effectiveness.*

The major objectives of the study were : (1) to find out the inter relationship between job involvement and personal factors, psychological needs and detaching effectiveness (2) to find out the effectiveness between male and female primary school teachers with respect to personal factors, psychological needs, Job involvement and teaching effectiveness.

The major findings of the study were : (1) In the case of rural males and females, job involvement was not significantly correlated with personal factors, while in the case of rural females and urban males age and experience were significantly and positively correlated with job involvement but, income was not significantly correlated with job involvement. (2) In the case of rural males, job involvement was not significantly correlated with psychological needs excepting n-aggression. With regard to rural female teachers job involvement was not significantly correlated with any of the fifteen psychological needs. Among urban males job involvement was significantly correlated with n-nurturance, n-endurance, n-hetero sexuality and n-aggression but not significantly correlated with the remaining eleven needs.

Srivastava, Kantimohan, (1982) *Effectiveness of the Teacher Education Programme, Avadh University.*

The investigation was an attempt to find out the effectiveness of the teacher education programme of Avadh University. The main objectives of the study were (i) to study the actual position of resources, existing conditions and working of the teacher-education programme (ii) to study the quantitative and qualitative characteristics of the programmer's end-product.

The major findings were: (1) The ten colleges having teacher education department were unequal in size and facilities and not were initially opened with the intention of providing facilities for teacher education. The colleges were on the Government grant list; hence there was no problem of staff salary payment. Except SC and ST student-trainees, all others were required to pay fees. (2) The teacher-educator-student-teacher ratio was 1:14, which was higher than prescribed by the Government.

Vyas, R.P., (1982) *Relationship of Selected Factors with the Teaching Success of Prospective Teachers of Rajasthan,* Raj. University.

The main purpose of the study was to examine the relationship of certain factors (predictors) such as age, academic achievement, verbal and non-verbal intelligence, personality adjustment, self-perception, attitude towards teaching, teaching aptitude and socio-economic status of the prospective teachers with their teaching success criteria such as supervisor's ratings, self-rating, university practical marks, total practical assessment university theory marks and university total marks. Apart from this, other subsidiary objectives were, (i) to study the relationship among the proposed predictors and a teaching success of prospective teachers in the case of total sample.

The findings of the study were: (1) Age was significantly related to the criterion variables, supervisions' ratings in the case of the total sample. It was also significantly related to criterion variables, university practical marks and total practical assignment, in the case of total and male sample. But age was not significantly related to the criterion variables, self – rating, university theory and university total marks in all the categories of the sample. (2) Academic achievement was significantly related with supervision' rating, university practical marks total practical assignment, university theory marks and university total marks in the case of total, male and female samples of prospective teachers.

Gogate, S.B., (1983) *Training of Primary School Teachers in the Context of Universal Primary Education,* IIE, PUNE, (UNICEF Financed).

The objective of this scheme was to initiate a programme of training of primary teachers, especially in view of the enlarged role they would have to assume when elementary education became universal for children in the age group of 6-14. The project ultimately focused on, (i) preparation of literature for primary school teachers which could be useful in their in-service training as also in their self-training, (ii) orientation of primary school teachers, teacher educators and extension officers with the help of the literature prepared in the project.

The out comes of the project were: (1) Teachers, particularly from rural areas, were aware of the social, cultural and economic needs of rural society. (2) Teachers understood that development was possible through education. (3) Teachers understood that education was the main instrument of child development and that they had a social responsibility for achieving this development.

Rai. G., (1983), *A Study of the Self-Concept of the Prospective Teachers,* BHU, University.

The objectives of the inquiry were: (i) to study the nature and extent of self-concept of prospective teachers, (ii) to study sex, rural-urban, religious and caste differences in the self-concept of prospective teachers.

Some of the important findings were: (1) The self-concept of prospective teachers was positive. (2) Female, unmarried, post graduate and Hindu prospective teachers had significantly better self-concept than the male, married graduate and non-Hindu counterparts respectively.

Valand, J.B., (1983) *A Study of Innovative Proneness of Teachers of Primary Teacher Training Colleges in the State of Gujarat,* SPU, University.

The objectives of the study were: (i) to develop an instrument seeking to identify and quantify four aspects of innovative proneness of teacher educators, viz., teacher-educators' expressed attitude towards specific innovations, teacher-educators' general attitudes to change or their change-related values, teacher-educators' preferred behaviors in relation to their perception of attitudes of innovations, and teacher-educators' preferred behaviours in relation to their perception of the setting and circumstances in which innovations were introduced, (ii) to design and validate innovative proneness scale.

Some of these findings were: (1) The mean innovative proneness score of the teachers above 35 years of age was greater than those of teachers under that age. (2) The mean score of the female teachers was higher than that of the male teachers. (3) The mean score of the teachers having more than five years of teaching experience was greater than that of teachers having less than five years of teaching experience.

Yadav, R.A., (1983), has conducted *A Study of the Effect of Training for Classroom Questioning Behaviour on Teaching Competence and Pupil Achievement.*

The major objectives of the study were: (1) To compare the classroom questioning behaviour (CQB) in the experimental and control groups, (2) To compare the teaching competence of student teachers with and without (CQB).

The major findings of the study were: (1) the student teachers with CQB tended to increase the incidence of questions at higher books, (2) The training in CQB helped in improving the structural characteristics, namely, relevance, precision, grammatical correctness, and clarity of questioning.

Gopalacharyulu, R.V.V., (1984) *A Study of Relationship between Certain Psycho-Sociological Factors and Achievement of Student Teachers in Teacher Training Institutes of Andhra Pradesh,* SVU, University.

The objectives of the study were: (i) to find out whether differences in the psycho-sociological factors of the student teachers accounted for the significant differences in their achievement, (ii) to identify the psycho-sociological factors that significantly predicted the achievement of student-teachers, (iii) to study the contribution of psycho-sociological factors in predicting the achievement of student-teachers singly and jointly.

The major findings of the study were: (1) Socio-economic status and caste influenced all the three achievement variables, namely, theory, practical and total achievement. (2) Attitude towards profession and attitude towards training influenced theory and total achievement significantly. (3) Age and locality of student teachers were found to have significant influence on theory and total achievement. (4) None of the 16 PF factors and sex were found to have any influence on the three achievement variables.

Joshi, A.N., (1984) *A Study of Developing Performance Criteria and Testing their Efficacy in Training Student Teachers in a Teaching Skill Cluster,* Poona University.

The study focused on (i) the evaluation of the behavioral model of teaching skill programmes, (ii) the relationship between a symbolic (planning) model and a behavioural (performance) model, (iii) its bearing on planning and the critique procedures of micro-teaching, and (iv) study of efficacy of the modified planning and critique procedures.

The major findings of the study were: (1) The coefficient of stability for three forms of moves in interactive strategies of teaching (MIST) was 0.85 (2) The rates of teachers steady talk and pupils' steady talk seemed to be useful and stable for estimation of the time dimension at the time of planning. (3) The coefficients of correlation between completely translated planning (CTP) and performance varied from 0.61 to 0.83 for the skills of reacting, questioning and initiation, and response (RQI). (4) The performance scores could be predicted from CTP scores and vice versa, using appropriate regression equations.

Naik, V.V., (1984) *A Comparative Study of the Effect of Microteaching and Conventional Approaches of Teacher Training upon Pupils Achievement, Pupils Perception and General Teaching Competence of Pre-service Student Teachers,* Bombay University.

The objectives of the study were: (i) to study the differential effect of microteaching and conventional teacher training approaches in relation to the achievement of pupils, (ii) to study the pupil's perception of student-teachers trained through microteaching and conventional teacher training approaches, and (iii) to study the differential effect of microteaching and conventional teacher training approaches in relation to the general teaching competence of student teachers.

The major findings of the study were: (1) For total gain in achievement in Physics, the experimental group scored significantly higher than the control group. The results were not significantly different for gain in the achievement in Chemistry, and Physics and Chemistry together. (2) The results did not show significant differences between the experimental and control group when tested for gain in knowledge and understanding objectives of both subjects taken together or separately.

Suthar, J.N., (1987) *An Investigation into the Effect of Caste, Effectiveness, Responsibility and Sex of the Primary School Teachers upon the Pupils Achievement,* S.P. University.

The objectives of the study were : (i) to adopt a tool to measure the teacher effectiveness and to find out its reliability coefficient, (ii) to measure the teacher effectiveness of primary school teachers.

The major findings of the study were : (1) The non-backward class teachers were more effective than the backward class teachers. (2) The male teachers were more effective than the female teachers. (3) The more experienced teachers were found more effective than the less experienced teachers.

Natarajan, S., (1984), A *Competency Based Programme in Teacher Education Curriculum,* Madras University.

The major objectives of this investigation were: (i) to study the relative efficacy of competency-based teacher education in the pre-service education programme of secondary school teachers, (ii) to identify factors influencing competency achievement such as social status, economic status and level of education.

The major findings of the study were: (1) Competency-based instruction proved suitable for teaching selected units in Institutional Planning and Administration. (2) The seminar method seemed to be an effective method as it compared favorably with the competency-based approach. (3) The lecture method was effective as a group method. (4) Directed self-study did not compete well with other methods. (5) There was a significant relation between self-esteem and acquisition of competencies. (6) Attitudes towards teaching methods had a favorable correlation with acquisition of competencies. (7) The study proved that teacher education programmes could be made more effective through a competency-based approach.

Singh, Satyanarayana, (1984) *Effect of Training in Teaching Skills Using Micro-class and Real Pupils on the General Teaching Competence of Student Teachers at Elementary Level.* DSERT, Karnataka.

The objectives of the study were: (i) to compare the general teaching competency of the student-teachers ongoing student teaching programme using microteaching and the traditional approach, (ii) to study the effectiveness of microteaching under simulated and real classroom situations in respect of general teaching competence.

The major findings of the study were: (1) The student teachers trained using microteaching under the simulated conditions acquired better teaching competency than those trained under the traditional training method and (2) The student teachers trained, using microteaching under real classroom conditions acquired better teaching competency than those trained under the traditional training method.

Som, P., (1984) *Teachers Personality Pattern and their Attitudes Towards Teaching and Related Areas,* Calcutta University.

The study was an investigation into the relation between non-cognitive, personality structure type following Eysenck's teacher's attitudes towards teaching and related areas. The objectives of the study were (i) to find the structure-pattern, which is likely to suggest better attitudes towards teaching and related areas, (ii) to find the descriptive personality pattern of teachers with reference to the dimension of extroversion-introversion and the traits involved in it.

The major findings were: (1) The secondary teachers were neither extrovert nor introvert and they could be tentatively described as lacking patience but possessing sociability, sobriety, carefulness, temporal thought, introspection, concentration and mental exertion, in terms of their extroversion-introversion traits. (2) Male teachers were found to be more initiative, expressive, careful, introspective, mentally exertive and concentrated than female teachers. But there was no difference between them on extroversion, and experience had a positive effect on stoicism for either sex.

Wangoo, M.L., (1984) *Teacher Personality Correlates and Scholastic Competence as Related to Teacher Effectiveness,* Kashmir University.

The major aim of the inquiry was to study teacher personality correlates and scholastic competence as related of effective teaching.

The major finding was: personality adjustment, democratic leadership, a high degree of intelligence and emotional control were the main characteristics that went with teacher effectiveness.

Dash, J., (1985) *An Investigation into the Development of Teacher Education Programme in Orissa with reference to Motivation, Cost Structure and Quality,* Utkal University.

The objectives of the inquiry were : (i) to study the factors that motivated the authorities to set up private training colleges.(ii) to study the factors that prompted the trainees to pursue the B.Ed. course,

The findings of the study were : (1) The private training colleges were established mostly with commercial motives and parochial feelings. (2) Inadequate physical facilities, inefficient teachers, poor quality of trainees, unsuitable practice teaching and undue expansion of training colleges was reflected in the poor status of teacher-training programmes in the state.

Deo, D.S., (1985) *To Study the Practical Programme Other than Practice Teaching in Teacher Education Institutions,* Delhi University.

The objectives of the inquiry were: (i) to study the role of practical work (besides practice teaching) in a secondary teacher education programme, (ii) to survey the nature and type of practical work, other than practice teaching, that was being given to student-teachers in secondary teacher education institutions in Delhi, (iii) to study how these programmes of practical work were actually implemented,

The findings of the study were: (1) Most of the student teachers felt that 'lack of time' was major factor in not being able to achieve the objectives of the practical programme. 2. The teacher educators opined that lack of sufficient opportunities and lack of time were the causes for non-fulfillment of the objectives of practical programme.

Ahmad, Q., (1986) *Determinants of Job Involvement among Teachers,* Mag. University.

The major objectives of the study were (i) to examine the relationship between value orientation and job involvement, (ii) to study the relationship of background factors, such as length of service, family size, etc. with job involvement and job satisfaction, (iii) to investigate if job involvement and one's satisfaction with the institution where one worked were significantly correlated, (iii) to find out the relationship between job involvement and job characteristics, (v) to measure whether there was any difference between teachers belonging to constituent colleges and affiliated colleges on a number of factors such as job involvement, college satisfaction, job satisfaction and job characteristics, and (vi) to investigate the relationship between job involvement and job satisfaction. Six hypotheses were examined.

The major conclusions were: (1) Both individual and organizational factors determined job involvement of college teachers. (2) Job involvement was positively correlated with job satisfaction and college satisfaction. (3) Constituent colleges induced more job involvement, identification with institution and job satisfaction among its teachers compared to affiliated colleges. (4) Some value preferences, such as ability utilization, achievement and economic gains were negatively correlated with job satisfaction. Social relations, prestige and autonomy were positively associated with satisfaction. (5) Some job attributes, such as variety, autonomy interaction and feedback contributed to job satisfaction.

Dixit, M., (1986) *A Comparative Study of Job Satisfaction among Primary School Teachers and Secondary School Teachers,* Ludhiyana University.

The study was designed (i) to measure job satisfaction among primary and secondary school teachers, and (ii) to observe the effect of sex, teaching experience and medium of instruction on the level of satisfaction with their profession.

The main findings of the study were: (1) In Hindi medium schools, primary school teachers were more satisfied than secondary school teachers. (2) In English medium schools the level of job satisfaction among primary and secondary school teachers was the same. (3) The female teachers were more satisfied than male teachers both at the primary and the secondary levels.

Dubey, Rajeshwari, (1986) *Study of the Personality Traits of Pupil-Teachers towards Successful Integration of Instructional Skills,* Bhopal University.

The objectives of the study were: (i) to identify those male and female teacher trainees who obtained high and low scores on the component of integration of instructional skills (IIS), as measured by the Indore Teaching Assessment Scale (ITAS), in terms of their personality traits, intelligence level and attitude towards teaching, (ii) to determine the relationships between the scores on different personality factors of the teacher-trainees and their scores on the component of IIS.

The major findings of the study were: (1) Significant personality traits of the males scoring high on the IIS component as identified on the basis of the investigation were: they were suspicious, self-opinionated and hard to fool (L+) and experimenting, critical, liberal, analytical. (2) Females scoring high on the IIS components were also found to have the L+ factor.

Srivastava, Shobha, (1986) *A Study of Job Satisfaction and Professional Honesty of Primary School Teachers with Necessary Suggestions,* Avadh University.

The objectives of the study were: (i) to examine the extent of job-satisfaction and professional honesty among primary school teachers, and (ii) to make suggestions for creating a suitable environment in primary education in the above context.

The findings of the study were: (1) The primary teachers of the area were found to have high-job satisfaction and professional honesty. (2) Female teachers, as compared to male teachers, unmarried teachers as compared to married teachers, urban teachers as compared to rural teachers, and non-agricultural family occupation background teachers were significantly higher in job-satisfaction and professional honesty. (3) Physical facilities (space, equipment, etc.) problems getting arrears, exploitation by officers, etc. (4) The major factors conducive to professional honesty in primary teachers were the teacher's sincerity towards work, recognition and appreciation of the teacher's good work, a health and open environment in the school, the teacher's mental health, etc.

Bhide, L.G., (1987) *An Experimental Study of the Impact of the Teacher Education Programme on the Self-Concept of the Pupil-teachers,* Nagpur University.

The objectives of the study were (i) to evaluate the impact of a training programme in the modification of self-concept of pupil teachers at each end of their training and (ii) to compare the self-concept among pupil teachers, teachers-untrained and trained-and also post-graduate students at each commencement of the academic session,

The findings were: (1) Change in self concept due to training in education was in consequential. (2) Training could bring modification in self-concept but better results could be produced by modification in the training programme.

Butlala, M., (1987) *A Critical Inquiry into In-service Educational Programmes Conducted by Secondary Teachers Training Colleges of Gujrat State,* Gujarat University.

The objectives of the study were: (i) to study the existing position of In-service educational programmes in secondary teachers training colleges classified by types, organization, and factors affecting planning, (ii) to study the usefulness of In-service educational programmes for teachers.

Some of the major findings were : (1) The teachers were in favour of in-service training programmes being organized on working days only. The second preference was summer vacation. Working on weakends was their last preference. (2) The training colleges did not have adequate facilities for conducting the programmes. (3) Teacher participants indicated that the major achievement of in-service education was updating the teacher and the content area. The second gain of the in-service programme was developing skills for better teaching of the subject. (4) The in-service programmes were not evaluated systematically.

Dave, C.S., (1987) *Relative Effectiveness of Microteaching Having Summative Model of Integration versus Miniteaching Model in terms of General Teaching Competence, Teacher Attitude towards Teaching, Pupil Liking and Pupil Achievement,* DAVV. University.

The objectives were: (i) to compare the effectiveness of the summative model of integration (SMI), miniteaching model of integration (MMI) in terms of general teaching competence (GTC), (ii) to compare the effectiveness of the summative model of integration, miniteaching model of integration and traditional model of integration (TMI) in terms of teachers attitude towards teaching (TATT).

The findings were: (1) The miniteaching model of integration (MMI) was found superior to the summative model of integration (SMI) and traditional model of integration (TMI), in terms of development of general teaching competence in student teachers. (2) The teachers belonging to the MMI group did not attain a significantly favorable attitude towards teaching in comparison with those belonging to the SMI group and TMI group at occasion II (post-test I). (3) The teachers belonging to the MMI group produced a significant favourable attitude towards teaching in comparison with the SMI and TMI groups at occasion II (post-test II).

Donga, N.S., (1987) *A Study of the Adjustment of Trainees of Teachers Training Colleges in Gujarat,* Sau. University.

The objectives of the enquiry were: (i) to study adjustment differences among different groups according to the different levels of cultural and educational variables, viz., sex, marital status, age, teaching experience, level of teaching experience, educational qualification, faculty, residential accommodation, social status, economic status and status in family of teacher-trainees of Gujarat State, (ii) to observe the effect of interaction on income, social status and residential accommodation on adjustment.

The major findings were: (1) Female trainees were more adjusted than male trainees. (2) There was no significant effect of marital status, level of education, status in family and age on adjustment. (3) Socially backward trainees were more adjusted than non-backward trainees. (4) Trainees of different colleges differed significantly in adjustment.

Ekbote, E.R., (1987) *Development of a Strategy for Integration of Skills in Teacher Training,* MSU University, Baroda.

The objectives of the study were: (i) to develop a strategy for integrating the teaching skills acquired through microteaching practice, (ii) to determine the validity of the integration strategy in terms of content validity, student-teachers' performance in classroom teaching and their reaction to the strategy.

The major findings were: (1) The integration strategy was found effective in terms of the improvement it made in the student-teacher's performance in classroom teaching. (2) All the seven variables pertaining to the student-teachers, viz., qualification, teaching experience, availability of study time, academic achievement, skill comprehension, attitude towards teaching and attitude towards microteaching influenced the improvement in classroom teaching performance through the strategy.

Mathur, S., (1987), *Attitudes of Teachers towards Creative Learning and Teaching,* Agra University.

The objectives of the inquiry were: (i) to study attitudes of teachers of the pre higher secondary school stage towards creative learning and teaching, (ii) to make a comparative study of attitudes of teachers of pre higher secondary school stage, i.e. primary and junior high school teachers towards creative learning and teaching on the basis of age, sex, teaching experience and academic disciplines,

The following conclusions were arrived at: (1) By and large, teachers of prehigher secondary, higher secondary and post higher secondary stages tended to have favorable attitudes towards creative learning and unfavorable attitudes towards creative teaching. (2) Age, sex, teaching experience and academic disciplines did not tend to affect the attitudes of teachers of pre higher secondary, higher secondary and post higher secondary stages towards creative learning and teaching. Only teaching experience tended to affect the attitudes of teachers of the higher secondary stage towards creative teaching.

Narsogi Raw, K. (1994), *An Experiment on the Effectiveness of the Activity Based Instruction over Traditional Method of Teaching in the Primary Schools of Andhra Pradesh.*

The major objective: To study the effectiveness of activity based instructtion adopted in APPEP schools or the traditional methods of teaching.

The major finding of the study was: The activity based method is superior over the traditional methods.

Pullareddy P.V., (1994), *An Investigator into Organizational and Administrative Factors which Affect Achievement of Pupils in the Project Primary Schools of Andhra Pradesh.*

The objective : To study the organizational and administrative influence on the achievement of pupils.

The major findings were : (1) Freedom is needed for high academic achievement (2) Interference in administrative and academic matters hampers achievement.

Kentycky's star professional development network: *Perceptions of Effectiveness in Improving Student Achievement in Low Performing Schools, 1996-97.* Barlow Doris seats, Education D. University of Kentucky.

Main objective: To help schools raise student achievement and meet their accountability threshold in the next biennium and there after.

The findings were: Perception of survey respondents indicated that professional development strategies helped to improve student achievement. There was agreement that the DEs were helpful in improving students achievement, however some educators disagreed that the DEs had helped with engaging parents and the community in school activities.

Sai Babu, A. (1996) *An Institutional Study of DIET Vizanagaram – A Descriptive Presentation,* Andhra University, Visakhapatnam.

Major objectives of the study were; (i) to examine the structural aspects of Vizianagaram DIET with reference to physical, aspects, financial aspects and Human resource aspects. (ii) to examine in the functional aspects of Vizianagaram DIET with reference to pre-service and in-service training and associated activities.

The major findings were; (i) The Rural trainees vs urban trainees differed significantly. (ii) Rural teachers vs rural trainees differred significantly. (iii) Rural teachers Vs urban teachers differred significantly. (iv) Trainees of Vizianagaram vs of Bheemunipatnam differred significantly.

Pandey, R.S., (1999) *Documentation of Positive Practices in Four DIETs, Meeting Challenges,* District Primary Education Programme.

The major objectives of the study were; (i) to record the good practices in selected well functioning DIETs in the country. (ii) to identify the enabling conditions within the DIET or at the state level due to which the above good practices have got established. (iii) to share this documentation with different DIETs, SCERTs, State Government officials and others in order to generate thinking and discussion about policy, its implementation and improvement.

Major findings of the study were: (i) The states have not made use of the opportunity provided in the Guidelines to conceptualise and evolve their own state specific models of DIETs. (ii) Almost all states appear to have accepted without any modifications the organizational framework have the seven branches as suggested in the Guidelines. (iii) The situation on the ground however, reveals that many "branches" remain inactive even in the best of DIETs.

Etter, Gregg Wayne, (2000), *Perceived Effectiveness of In-Service Training of Sheriffs Deputies in Kansas : A Post-Instruction Analyses.*

The purpose of the study was: to examine the perceived effectiveness of current in service training methods of law enforcement officers in Kansas.

The major findings were: (1) over 20% of those responding personal perceived that their needs were not being met by traditional training methods. Participants wanted more choices for training topics and the ability to close their own training. (2) 29.9% reported that they had wanted their time in in-service training. (3) 22.4% report that the training was not relevant to them. (4) 23.4% report that traditional presentation techniques did not assist them in learning material. (5) 28% stated that they could not relate the training to their current job. (6) 79.4% of the deputies disagreed that each deputy should receive the same exact training. (7) 93.4% of the deputies wanted to choose their own in-service training classes. (8) 88% of the deputies wanted more classes for training law enforcement managers should consider alternative methods of training including andragogical, methods for in service training.

Forbes, Judy Ann Cason, (2000), *The Impact of Shared Decision-Making Elementary Schools on Student Performance.*

This study focused on the quality improvement council (QIC) shared decision-making model and its implementation in the Haborshan country, elementary school programme. It examined student achievement in reading and Mathematics as mentioned by subtests of the lova tests.

The major findings: There was statistically significant improvement in staff absence in all seven schools in Habersham, country, but no significant difference was noted in student absence or student discipline referrals of the office over the three-year period.

Public school Principal's perceptions in accredited and non-accredited elementary schools regarding strategies to improve student performance on the Michigan Education Assessment Program (Hampton Mattie, 2000).

Chandrasekhar, K. (2001) *Primary School Teacher Education Programme - An Evaluative Study of DIETs,* Discovery Publishing House, New Delhi.

The major objectives of the study were; (i) to study the perceptions of the student teachers of DIETs about different aspects of their training. (ii) to study the attitude of the student teachers towards teaching profession. (iii) to note the variation in the perceptions and attitudes of student teachers due to different personal and demographic variables. (iv) to study the perceptions of the teacher educators about different aspects of the DIETs.

Major findings of the study were: (i) most of student teachers have expressed that they have not been encouraged to participate in the Physical Education activities and have allotted time for them is considerably much less. (ii) Most of the student teachers are unhappy that their institution is far away from teaching practice schools. (iii) Majority of the student teachers have perceived that the present system of examinations has failed in assessing the teaching skills. Most of the student teachers are unhappy with disobedient student, non academic additional responsibilities entrusted to them and for the lack of recognition to the teaching profession.

Jennifer, Stark, (2002) *"Applying the Port Polio Process in Principal Evaluation: a Case Study"* Marsirise.

The purpose of this phenomological study was: to examine the Principal evaluation process as they impacted: leadership effectiveness, student achievement professional development of teachers and the reflective practice of the Principal. This analysis was accomplished by examining a school district utilized the Principal port folio as an evaluation process. This study contributed to the literature by examining Principal evaluation port polio process as it impacted leadership effectiveness, student achievement, professional development of teachers and the Principal.

Major findings of the Sduty: (1) communicative and open dialogue provided a common language of superintendents, Principals and teachers (2) A common version is shared with in the district (3) Ongoing self assessment helped Principals to grow professionally. (4) This process helped Principals to document actions at the campus level and gave Principals a way to showcase the campus and accomplishments. (5) Principals were more visible of individual teacher activities (6) The Principals supported professional reading and book studies.

Subba Raju D.V. and Subba Rao, K.P., (2002), *Over Crowded Classroom as a n Impediment for School Effectiveness.*

Objective: To find out various measures taken up by the Government or management to eradicate overcrowded class room situation and to suggest remedies to over come the overcrowded class room situation in primary schools, and the negative effects of overcrowded classrooms in the school effectiveness.

Major findings of the study were: (1) The primary teachers could not pay individual attention towards pupils (2) Teachers not able to conduct individual, group & whole class activities (3) Teachers could not verify students' notes and correct them (4) Teachers not able to conduct remedial teaching and dictation (5) Teachers could not correct pronunciation of pupils, (6) Teachers could not rectify pupils spelling mistakes (7) They could not give much guidance in good hand writing (8) Teachers could not train pupils in Co-curricular Activities (9) Teachers could not provide proper examination orientation to pupils.

Babu Rao Chowdary, L.K.M (2003) *Teacher Education: A Study of DIETs, CTEs and IASEs with special reference to NPE 1986: A Descriptive Study.* Andhra University, Visakhapatnam.

Major objectives of the study were: (i) To identify present conditions and point to present needs. (ii) To study immediate status of phenomenon. (iii) To examine the relationship of traits and characteristics.

Major findings of the study were: (i) The institutions are still in the process of procurement of land/constructions of buildings. (ii) Only four institutions have received grants for procurement of equipment. (iii) There are limited staff and they have not been able to conduct the programme. (iv) The majority of institutions have not been able to conduct in-service training programmes.

Das, R.C., Passi, B.K., Jangira, N.K., and Sing, A., have Studied on the *Effectiveness of Different Strategies of Integration of Teaching Skills in Developing General Teaching Competence of Student Teachers.* Deptt of Teacher Education NCERT.

The objectives of the investigation were : (1) to determine the effectiveness of non-integration strategy and summative model of integration of teaching skills in developing general teaching competence in student teachers. (2) to study the relative efficacy of non-integration strategy and addictive model of integration of teaching skills in developing general teaching competence in student teachers.

The main findings of the investigation were: (1) The integrative strategy tended to improve the teaching competence as well as the quality of integrator of the teaching skills, (2) The additive strategy of integrative of the teaching skills did not improve the general teaching competence of the student teachers but tended to improve the quality of integrator of the teaching skills.

A Study on Special Orientation Programme for Primary Teachers (SOPT) - its Impact on Teacher's Achievement. in Education, RIE, Bhubaneswar.

The objectives of the study were: (i) to study awareness achievement of primary teachers in concern of primary education before and after intervention. (ii) to study awareness achievement of primary teachers in the curricular areas and transactional approach before and after interaction.

Findings: (1) The special orientation programme for primary teachers is not effective as expected. The impact of orientations established to a small extent. (2) The awareness of teachers about the emerging concerns of primary education and curricular areas did not improve significantly due to the intervention programme provided under (SOPT).

An Inquiry into the Workload of Teachers and Conditions of Work Necessary for Quality Teaching in the Project Primary Schools of Andhra Pradesh.

Objectives: The major objectives of the investigation wake to study the work load and working conditions with reference to staff pattern pupil teacher ratio, teaching work, pupil activities, other duties, in service programmes and work relating to the building and furniture.

Findings: (1) The teachers have been attending various duties relating to teaching, assessment of pupil performance, school administration and organization of curricular activities. They were also spending a lot of time on census duties, participating in the family planning campaigns, election duties etc, which are a hurdle to their teaching work.

Dholakia. J.V., (1980) *Effects of Observers and Feedback upon Changing the Classroom Performance of Pupil Teachers.*

The major objectives of the investigation were : (1) to analyse the comments given by observers of practice lessons taught by pupil teachers, (2) to study the effects, academic qualifications, teaching methods and the status of observers upon the feedback and achievement marks of pupil teachers.

The major findings of the investigation were : (1) The observers gave more negative comments than positive; (2) The graduate observers give more comments than the post graduate observers. (3) The graduate and the postgraduate observers did not differ in their grading of the lessons.

Sharma, V.S., has studied *on Effectiveness of Pre-service Teacher Training Programmes at Elementary Level in Rajasthan.*

The purpose of the study was finding out the effectiveness of the two year teacher training programme at the elementary level in Rajasthan.

The main specific objectives of the study were : (1) to identify and analyze some of the prospective classroom behavior patterns, various perspectives and perception and intellectual and emotional equalities of teachers on the basis of the opinion of teacher educators. (2) to study the classroom behavior patterns of trained and un trained teachers working in the field of elementary education.

The major findings of the study were : (1) In almost all the aspects of preparedness of teachers, the trained teachers had a definite superiority over the untrained teachers (2) The trained teachers differed significantly from the untrained teachers in respect of cooperative aptitude and moral characters. In rotation to the rest of the teaching aptitude such as kindness, patience, wide interest fairness, discipline, optimism, scholastic taste, and enthusiasm, there was no significant difference in the aptitude of the trained and untrained teachers.

CONCLUSION

The review of related literature indicates that only few studies have been conducted on the role and performance of DIETs, and no study is designed upto date, especially DIETs in Andhra Pradesh State. Thus the present study departs from the previous investigations, in the following manner.

The present study aimed to study the structural aspects of DIETs, role and performance of DIETs, teacher training programmes of in-service as well as pre-service programmes.

The present study also aimed to findout the specific deviations from the Guidelines of MHRD and measures for improving the conditions in DIETs for improving the quality of elementary education.

3

Methodology

This chapter deals with the different procedures followed in the construction and development of data gathering instruments on different variables which are included in the study and methods adopted in the selection of sample, collection of data, method of scoring and analysis of data.

Research is directed toward the solution of a problem. The ultimate goal is to discover cause-and-effect relationships between variables, though researchers often have to settle for the useful discovery of a systematic relationship, because the evidence for a cause and effect relationship is insufficient. (John W. Best. (1995) p. 20, para 5).

Research is considered to be the more formal, systematic and intensive process of carrying on a scientific method of analysis. Scientific method in problem solving may be informal application of problem identification, hypothesis formulation, observation, analysis and conclusion. Research is a more systematic activity that is directed towards discovery and the development of an organized body of knowledge.

THE PRESENT RESEARCH

Teacher plays pivotal role in the field of education. Nothing can substitute the place of a teacher. Learning is a process between the teacher and the taught. For effective learning effective teacher is needed. For effective teacher effective teacher training is a necessary one.

The role of the teacher training institute and the teacher educator is again became very important.

In the ladder of education primary education got vital role because there the foundation for the child in different concepts is being laid, basing on which further education can only be developed gradually. Hence the primary educational institutions, the primary teachers and the primary teacher training institutions play vital role in the field of education.

There are DIETs, which give training to pre- service as well as in-service elementary teachers. The DIETs are located one in each district all over India, like wise in all the districts of Andhra Pradesh state. On the other hand there are B.Ed training colleges to train secondary school teachers in the state. Our present study is limited to DIETs in Andhra Pradesh. Moreover it is further limited to the "Role and Performance of DIETs in Andhra Pradesh State.

Three research tools are selected for the present study. They are :

1. A check list for the Principals (on the facilities provided in the DIETs)
2. A opinionnaire to pre-service trainees and
3. A opinionnaire to in-service teachers.

All the DIETs were taken up as sample. In each DIET 15 pre-service trainees were taken up totaling to 345 as sample. In the same way 15 in-service teachers were selected from each district, totaling to 345 teachers as sample.

The researcher has visited most of the DIETs personally and has talked to the Principals, staff, trainees and teachers and got filled the checklists and the opinionnaire. He personally verified the physical nature of most of the DIETs, moreover the researcher himself is also a DIET faculty member having ample of experience by working in DIETs and schools, got the advantage of knowing all the happenings and processes in DIETs.

The present study falls under descriptive survey research. A descriptive research deals with what exists. It describes and interprets what exists at present.

According to John. W. Best (2005), "It is concerned with conditions or relationships that exists, opinions that are held, processes that are going on effects that are evident, or treds that are developing. It is primarily concerned with the present, although it often considered past events and influences as they relate to current conditions." (p 114)

According to Webster and New College "get exact information by this method of gathering data from a relatively large number of cases on a particular time".

STATEMENT OF THE PROBLEM

The present study is on DIETs in Andhra Pradesh. It is to know whether the role and performance of the DIETs are appropriate according to the Guidelines by MHRD, Government of India, as envisaged by NPE 1986. It is also to know whether the teacher education programmes conducted by the DIETs are according to the Guidelines.

The present study is taken up, to know whether the independent and dependent variables have any influence on the role and performance of DIETs with respect to pre-service and in-service programmes, activities for the improvement of quality of DIETs in the state.

TITLE OF THE STUDY

"A Study on the Role and Performance of District Institutes of Education and Training of Andhra Pradesh State" with special reference to Guidelines of MHRD, Government of India.

SCOPE AND LIMITATIONS OF THE STUDY

In this study, an attempt was made to analyse the problem of the role and performance of DIETs in Andhra Pradesh State. The study was carried out throughout the state. The role and performance of DIETs was studied in terms of the opinions of both D.Ed teacher trainees and in-service teachers of the state. Apart from it an attempt was made to elicit the opinions of Principals of concerned DIETs of the state, to analyse the state-of-the-art. The present study was carried out to analyse the role and performance of the DIETs of A.P., with reference to the Guidelines of MHRD, Government of India as envisaged by national policy on education 1986.

VARIABLES STUDIED

As the present study bring out the role and performance of DIETs in the sense the elementary school teacher education programme in Andhra Pradesh on the basis of the opinions of the D.Ed teacher trainees in-service teachers and Principals.

The Dependent Variables

1. Opinions of D.Ed teacher trainees on different aspects of DIET.
2. Opinions of D.Ed teacher trainees towards the teacher educators of DIET concerned.
3. Opinions of D.Ed teacher trainees towards the different aspects of the D.Ed syllabus.
4. Opinions of the D.Ed teacher trainees towards facilities in DIET.
5. Opinions of D.Ed teacher trainees towards the training programmes conducted by DIETs.
6. Opinions of in-service teachers towards the performance of teacher educators.
7. Opinions of in-service teachers towards the facilities provided in DIETs.
8. Opinions of in-service teachers towards the utility of the training programmes.

The Independent Variables:

The independent variables considered in the study are of two kinds namely (a) The student teacher (D.Ed. teachers) trainees related personal and demographic variables and (b) The in-service teacher related personal and demographic variables. The student teacher related independent variables are age, sex, marital status, locality of DIET, nativity, general qualifications and community (social class). The in-service teacher related independent variables are age, sex, marital status, nativity, general qualifications, professional qualifications subjects teaching and experience as elementary school teacher, school location, classes teaching and community (social class).

DESIGN OF THE STUDY

The present study is essentially explorative and descriptive in nature. The study was carried on three stages. A check list was prepared to know the state-of-art-of the DIETs in the first stage. An opinionaire was administered to the D.Ed teacher trainees to know their attitudes towards the educational programmes and professional development in DIETs. In the third stage the researcher tried to elicit the opinions of in-service teachers towards the effectiveness of the in-service training programme in DIETs.

The present study is meant for the description of the institutions, by surveying the opinions of the members involved. The procedure adopted in this particular type of research may not be as scientific and technical as in the case of experimental research. An element of subjectivity is involved in the selection of sample and in the opinions of the subjects. Yet social survey method is selected for the present study in view of the constraints of distance, type and time involvement.

OBJECTIVES OF THE STUDY

The objectives of the study are:

1. To study the structural aspects of DIETs in Andhra Pradesh in terms of Guidelines issued by MHRD Government of India.
2. To study the role and performance of DIETs on the different aspects of teacher training progrmmes.
3. To study the D.Ed teacher trainees programmes and professional development.
4. To study the in-service teachers' programmes and professional development.
5. To find out the specific deviations, if any, from the Guidelines while performing the functions by the DIETs of Andhra Pradesh.
6. To suggest measures for improving the functioning of DIETs with reference to quality in elementary teacher education.

HYPOTHESES OF THE STUDY

1. The DIETs of Andhra Pradesh do not differ significantly with respect to their role and performance on the different aspects of teacher training programmes.
2. a. The DIETs in Andhra Pradesh do not differ significantly with respect to the general facilities in DIETs.

   a. The DIETs in Andhra Pradesh do not differ significantly with respect to the student welfare.

   b. The DIETs in Andhra Pradesh do not differ significantly with respect to the practice teaching and evaluation.

   c. The DIETs in Andhra Pradesh do not differ significantly with respect to in-service training programmes.

   d. The DIETs in Andhra Pradesh do not differ significantly with respect to pre-service training programme.

   e. The DIETs in Andhra Pradesh do not differ significantly with respect to research activities.
3. a. The D.Ed teacher trainees do not differ significantly in the training programmes irrespective of their personal variables.

   b. The D.Ed teacher trainees do not differ significantly in the training programmes irrespective of their demographic variables.

   c. The D.Ed teacher trainees do not differ significantly in their professional development irrespective of their personal variables.

   d. The D.Ed teacher trainees do not differ significantly in their professional development irrespective of their demographic variables.
4. a. The in-service teachers do not differ significantly in the training programmes irrespective of their personal variables.

b. The in-service teachers do not differ significantly in the training programmes irrespective of their demographic variables.

c. The in-service teachers do not differ significantly in their professional development irrespective of their personal variables.

d. The in-service teachers do not differ significantly in their professional development irrespective of their demographic variables.

SAMPLING PROCEDURE FOR THE PRESENT RESEARCH

Keeping in view the suitability and advantages the investigator adopts the following sampling methods at different stages of sampling.

The sample selected for the present study belongs to three categories.

1. The researcher has taken the whole population of DIETs in Andhra Pradesh i.e. Twenty three DIETs from all the twenty three districts of Andhra Pradesh State for collection of data from the DIET Principals by using checklist.
2. For the purpose of measuring the attitudes of D.Ed teacher trainees (pre-service) from each of the 23 DIETs systematic randomn sampling method was applied by selecting each nth trainee namely each 6th second year trainee in each DIET, as there are 100 trainees in each DIET. Like wise 15 trainees from each DIET were selected. In total 345 D.Ed teacher trainees were selected from 23 DIETs in Andhra Pradesh state.
3. In the selection of in-service teachers, area randomn sampling method was applied. From the in-service teachers gathered in District level in-service training programmes represented from all the mandals in the district, fifteen teaches from 15 mandals (one from each mandal on randomn basis) were taken for measuring their opinions, by opinionnaire. Like wise 15 in- service

teachers were selected from each of the 23 districts in the state of Andhra Pradesh. Therefore from 23 districts @ 15 in-service teachers, totaling the sample to 345 teachers.

TOOLS USED IN THE STUDY

For the collection of reliable data from the different persons in the field three tools were designed to cater to the type of data to be collected. They were :

1. A checklist was prepared for collecting data relating to the facilities and functional aspects of DIETs.
2. An opinionnaire to know the opinions of D.Ed teacher trainees (pre-service) about their course and their opinions towards the facilities and functions of DIETs.
3. An opinionnaire was prepared for collecting the opinions from the in service teachers on the in-service training programmes offered to them.

VALIDITY AND RELIABILITY OF OPINIONNAIRES

The right questions which were least ambiguous, were selected from the pilot study. The meaning of all terms were clearly defined, so the items give the same meaning to all the respondents. Suggestions from colleagues and experts in the field of inquiry revealed the ambiguities which were removed. A panel of experts rated the instruments in terms of effectiveness it samples, significant aspects of its purpose, providing estimates of content validity.

Reliability of the opinionnaires was inferred by a second administration of the instruments, comparing the responses with those of the first one.

PLAN AND PROCEDURE

After thorough review of various previous investigations and related studies from journals, periodicals, and books the researcher prepared three different tools for collecting the data for three different respondents namely (1) The Principals of 23 DIETs, (2) D.Ed teacher trainees of DIETs and (3) In-service teachers from 23 districts.

THE CHECKLIST

The checklist consists of a list of items with a place to check or mark yes (or) no. The chief purpose of the checklist is to call attention to various aspects of an object (or) situation, to see that nothing of importance is over looked. It is a sample laundry-list type of device, consisting of a prepared list of items. It systematizes and facilitates the recording of observations and helps to ensure the consideration of the important aspects of the object or act – observed.

The values for 108 items were found significant, at 0.05 level. Hence 108 items were retained from the total of 120 items for final administering of the Principals checklist.

OPINIONNAIRE FOR D.ED TEACHER TRAINEES

All necessary precautions were taken in the preparation of the opinionnaire. It was administered for D.Ed teacher trainees of 23 DIETs. Four areas were selected for preparing items of the opinionnaire. They were :

(A) Facilities and Resources available in DIETs.

(B) Instruction being given to the trainees in DIETs.

(C) Co-curricular Activities and

(D) Field work and records being turned out by the trainees.

About 60 Likert type of items were prepared in 3 point scale of agree, undecided and disagree including personal data.

A pilot study was conducted on 50 D.Ed teacher trainees of DIET, Bheemunipatnam. The responses were checked whether there was any ambiguity and misunderstanding of the items. The responses were calculated by using chi-square test. Out of sixty items 53 were found significant. Hence these 53 items were retained for final form of the opinionnaire. Fifteen trainees from each of the 23 DIETs were selected by using systematic randomn sampling method, totalling to 345 trainees. An appeal was made to the respondents to respond to all of the statements.

OPINIONNAIRE FOR IN-SERVICE TEACHERS

After taking all precautions an opinionnaire was prepared by the researcher for in-service teachers for all the 23 districts.

Mainly two areas were selected for preparing items of the opinionnaire. They were :

(a) Needs of the teachers and

(b) Guidance given by DIET faculty.

There were about 23 items prepared including personal data. The items were of closed as well as open ended. Some items were rank order type and some were Likert type with three point scale of agree, undecided and disagree.

A pilot study was conducted on 50 in-service teachers of Bheemunipatnam by the investigator. The responses were checked whether there was any ambiguity or misunderstanding with the items. The responses were calculated by using chi-square test. It was found that out of 23 items 20 items were found significant. Hence, these 20 items were got included in final opinionnaire administering in 23 districts on the sample of 345 in-service teachers. An appeal was made to the respondents to respond to all of the statements given in the opinionnaire and promised to keep the information confidential and will be used for educational purpose only. The final opinionnaire was got printed taking all necessary precautions.

ADMINISTERING THE CHECKLIST AND THE TWO OPINIONNAIRES

All the 23 DIETs Principals were consulted in advance on phone and by post, asking for their consent for giving information of DIETs on checklist, and for their co-operation in administering the opinionnaire on D.Ed teacher trainees. The Principals were also requested for administering opinionnaire on in-service teachers from different mandals of the districts, undergoing in-service training in DIETs.

The copies of opinionnaires were serial numbered starting from 1 to 345 in respect of both D.Ed teacher trainees as well as in-service teachers opinionnaires separately.

Regarding D.Ed teacher trainees out of 100 second year trainees every 6th number candidate was to be selected randomnnly for issuing the opinionnaire. If any such numbered trainee happened to be absent the next trainee was given the opinionnaire.

Regarding in-service teachers undergoing training courses in DIETs, one teacher from each manadal, totaling to 15 were area randomnnly selected for responding to the opinionnaire of in-service teachers.

The tools of ten nearby DIETs were personally taken by the investigator and he himself personally administered the checklist and opinionnaires. But to save time and expense the tools of thirteen distantly situated DIETs were mailed by registered-post.

Follow up action of contacting these thirteen DIETs Principals and acquinted faculty members was regularly done. The Principals and faculty members, of these 13 DIETs had properly administered the tools. The investigator could succeed in getting back all the 13 covers of duly filled tools mailed from the 13 DIETs.

STATISTICAL CALCULATIONS

The variables selected for the purpose of the study were sex, age, general qualifications, professional qualifications, service, nativity, locality of the school/DIET, classes teaching. The responses for the items of the opinionnaires were quantified by assigning numerical values as 3, 2, 1 for most useful, useful, less useful and agree, un-decided, disagree respectively. The qualitative responses for some items were quantified and the total responses for each item of the opinionnaires were noted and classified variable wise. The responses received against each item, variable wise were noted in a separate table. The responses thus received were put to statistical treatment, for arriving at inferences. The data was carefully analysed by employing the appropriate statistical techniques such as t-test, F-test and chi-square to test the null hypothesis.

TREATMENT OF THE DATA

D.Ed (Pre-service) Trainees Opinionnaire Containing 53 Items

Items 1-10 were of personal data – variables like sex, age, nativity, community, location of the DIET, marital status and educational qualifications.

Items 11-21 Area (A) (11 items) were regarding facilities and resources available in DIETs for D.Ed teacher trainees. Likert method of 3 point scale was used. The choices agree/undecided/ disagree were quantified as 3, 2, 1 respectively.

Items 22-30 (9 items) Area (B) were of instruction to the D.Ed trainees. Likert method of 3 point scale was used to the items agree/un decided/disagree by assigning values as 3, 2, 1 respectively.

Items 31-39 (9 Items) (Area C) were of Co-curricular and Extra-curricular Activities. Likert method of 3 point scale was used by choosing 3 alternatives of agree/un decided/disagree assigning values as 3, 2, 1 respectively. Items 40-53 (14 Items) (Area D) were of field work and records Likert Method of 3 point scale was adopted to these items by assigning alternatives of agree/un decided/disagree and assigning values of 3, 2, 1 respectively.

These four areas of items were responded by the D.Ed. trainees. These responses were taken for calculation of mean values and standard deviations. As to the number of variable factors 't' value or 'F' value was calculated. When the variable factors were two, 't' value was calculated. For example the variable 'sex' has two factors namely 'male' and 'female'.

On the other hand when the variable refers to three factors, then 'F', value (ANOVA) was calculated. eg. variable "nativity " has three factors namely urban, rural, tribal.

Taking grouping of sex, age, educational qualifications, nativity community, locality of DIET , marital status , the items were subjected to t-test and F-test and verified for significance of difference of opinions at 0.05 and 0.01 levels.

IN-SERVICE TEACHERS' OPINIONNAIRE

In this opinionnniare the items 1-12 were about personal data of in-service teachers.

The Item 13: Area (A) was asked to rank order the usefulness of the training programme with regard to different school subjects. The responses were in the form of ranks, were computed into a tabular form against each subject. The number of respondents that ranked Telugu subject I, and the number of respondents that ranked Telugu subject 2 like-wise up to 8th rank, for every subject. Then the percentages were also calculated about the number of respondents that ranked a subject in rank 1, 2 and so on and so forth. In this way for the remaining subjects as shown in table 12. analysis was given subject wise and rank-wise.

Item (14): In this item the respondents were asked to rank order the difficulty level of the methodologies from more difficult to less difficult. The number of respondents ranked a subject 1, 2, 3, 4, 5 and 6 were seen and percentages were calculated and analysed the highest number opted a rank and the least number opted which rank basis.

Item – (15): The respondents were asked to rank order the school subjects basing on difficulty level from more difficult to less difficult.

The responses were tabulated with the help of computer by segregating rank wise responses towards the six ranks regarding all the six subjects. The number of respondents opted a particular rank.

Items (16-19): The guidance given by DIET faculty was asked to respond, regarding preparation of question banks, students Hand-books teachers Hand-books and use of teaching learning material. The responses were asked in Likert method of 3-point scale of agree/undecided and disagree. The responses were tabulated choice-wise and sub-item wise and percentages were calculated Then these responses were grouped with the demographic variable of the respondents for which 't' or 'F' values were calculated as per the number of factors. If there are only two factors for the variable like, sex (male and female) 't'-value is calculated. On the other hand if there are three or more then comparables for a variable like locality of the school (rural, urban, tribal 'F' – value (ANOVA) is calculated and the level of significance was verified.

Item (20): The respondents were asked to express the usefulness of the four in-service training programmes that the respondents have undergone from most useful to less useful.

Programme-wise ranking was tabulated against the demographic variables of the respondents and against each variable grouping was done as shown in the tables from 26-29. The number of respondents opted the choices were shown in percentages also. Chi-square was used to verify its significance.

4

Analysis and Interpretation of the Data

SECTION A: CHECK-LIST FOR PRINCIPALS OF DIETS

The check-list data is about the facilities and resources available in all the 23 DIETs of Andhra Pradesh State. The opinions of Principals on certain aspects like facilities available in DIETs, self-rating about the training programmes conducted by the Principals, results of D.Ed teacher trainees, staff development and welfare, research activities conducted and self evaluation of DIETs by the Principals etc. All the 23 DIETs' check-lists were computed and the data was analysed item wise and subject wise. The interpretation and analysis of the data is as follows.

The suggested carpet area as per the MHRD Guidelines is 10,000 sft of buildings, for the administrative and classrooms for each DIET. Except seven DIETs namely Angaluru, Pallepadu, Rayachoty, Mahabubnagar, Vikarabad, Haveli ghanpur and Warangal, all the other sixteen DIETs possess one thousand or more than one thousand square feet of carpet area of buildings. Seven DIETs possess less than 1000 sft of carpet area. It is inferred that all the DIET's buildings are own. Moreover it is found that the number of rooms for DIETs vary from thirteen to twenty six in different DIETs catering to class rooms for administration and staff etc. The toilet facility is available for both male and female staff separately in all DIETs. But as for as trainees are concerned it is observed that sixteen DIETs possess toilet facility and seven DIETs namely Mynampadu, Rayachoty, Bukkapatnam, B. Thandrapadu, Adilabad, Khammam and Warangal did not provide toilet facility at all (Table 4.1).

Table 4.1. Building, Accommodation of DIETs and Toilet Facilities for Staff & Trainees

Sl. No.	*Name of the DIET*	*Carpet*	*No. of rooms*	*No. of toilets*			
				Staff		*Students*	
				Male	*Female*	*Male*	*Female*
1.	Vomaravalli, Strikakulam (Dist)	1000	20	1	1	16	8
2.	V.G. Puram, VZM (Dist)	15000	20	1	1	2	2
3.	Bheemunipatnam, VSP (Dist)	20000	23	2	1	0	10
4.	Bommuru, E.G (Dist)	12000	24	2	2	6	6
5.	Dubacheria, W.G (Dist)	10000	18	3	3	7	7
6.	Angaluru, Krishna (Dist)	7000	13	1	1	3	3
7.	Boyapalem, Guntur (Dist)	10000	19	1	1	0	1
8.	Mynampadu, Prakasam (Dist)	13000	26	3	3	0	0
9.	Pallepadu, Nellore (Dist)	8000	16	2	2	0	1
10.	Rayachoty, Cuddapah (Dist)	7023	16	2	2	0	0
11.	Karvetinagar, Chittoor (Dist)	10000	20	2	1	4	10
12.	Bukkapatnam, Ananthapur (Dist)	16000	20	1	1	0	0
13.	B. Thandrapadu, Kurnool (Dist)	10000	20	1	1	0	0

Continued

Sl. No.	*Name of the DIET*	*Carpet*	*No. of rooms*	*No. of toilets*			
				Staff		*Students*	
				Male	*Female*	*Male*	*Female*
14.	Mahabubnagar (Dist)	7000	14	2	2	1	1
15.	Neredmet, Hyderabad (Dist)	10500	21	2	1	6	3
16.	Vikarabad, Ranga Reddy (Dist)	6500	13	6	2	12	2
17.	Haveilighanapur, Medak (Dist)	9000	18	1	1	1	1
18.	LMD colony, Karimnagar (Dist)	10000	20	1	1	1	1
19.	Nagaram, Nizambad (Dist)	12000	24	2	2	4	1
20.	Adilabad (Dist)	10000	20	2	2	0	0
21.	Khammam (Distt)	10000	20	3	3	0	0
22.	Warangal (Dist)	800	15	2	2	0	0
23.	Nalgonda (Dist)	1000	20	1	1	1	0

All the twenty three DIETs are having separate Principal chamber each. The furniture like chairs and tables available vary in number from one DIET to another. This is due to availability of accommodation in the Principals' chambers and as per the interest of the present Principal. For storage of some important files and other important records shelves are provided in Principals' chambers. Only seven Principals' chambers are with out attached toilets, namely V.G. Puram, Angaluru, Rayachoty, Karvetinagar, Bukkapatnam, Neredmet and Nalgonda (Table 4.2).

As per MHRD Guidelines the DIETs should possess two land phones. But all the DIETs possess only one land phone to the office with an extension to the Principals' chambers. Recently the Government has sanctioned one mobile phone to each of the DIET Principals for facilitating school monitoring, under Sarva Siksha Abhiyan.

As per MHRD Guidelines all DIETs staff are to be provided with an intercom facility. But in no DIET in Andhra Pradesh the facility is provided so far.

All the DIETs Principals' chambers are having one computer except in four DIETs namely Vomaravalli, Pallepadu, Mynampadu and Nalgonda (Table 4.3).

The office rooms of all twenty three DIETs are furnished with tables the number vary from a minimum of five in Vikarabad to a maximum of fifteen in Rayachoty DIET. The possession of computers differ in DIETs from a minimum of three in sixteen DIETs to a maximum number of thirteen in warnagal DIET.

The possession of chairs in office rooms of different DIETs vary from a minimum of seven in DIET Chittoor to a maximum number of twenty four in Bommuru. As far as fans are concerned only three DIETs namely Bommuru, Mynampadu, and Karvetinagar possess six fans each in their offices. Whereas three DIETs namely Bukkapatnam, Vikarabad and Khammam possess only five fans in their offices. The other seventeen DIETs posses fans differing from three to five in their offices. As far as possession of almirahs are concerned Bommuru DIET office possess four. Whereas Boyapalem and Mahabubnagar DIET

Table 4.2. Furniture, Equipment and Facilities in Principals' Chambers of DIETs

Sl. No.	*Name of the DIET*	*Principal chamber*		
		Chairs	*Tables*	*Iron shelves*
1.	Vomaravalli, Strikakulam (Dist)	10	1	1
2.	V.G. Puram, VZM (Dist)	8	1	1
3.	Bheemunipatnam, VSP (Dist)	30	5	1
4.	Bommuru, E.G (Dist)	23	6	2
5.	Dubacherla, W.G (Dist)	15	1	1
6.	Angaluru, Krishna (Dist)	5	3	2
7.	Boyapalem, Guntur (Dist)	10	1	4
8.	Mynampadu, Prakasam (Dist)	11	1	1
9.	Pallepadu, Nellore (Dist)	20	1	1
10.	Rayachoty, Cuddapah (Dist)	15	8	7
11.	Karvetinagar, Chittoor (Dist)	6	1	1
12.	Bukkapatnam, ananthapur, (Dist)	15	4	3
13.	B. Thandrapadu, Kurnool (Dist)	20	3	2
14.	Mahabubnagar (Dist)	20	4	1

Continued

Sl. No.	*Name of the DIET*	*Principal chamber*		
		Chairs	*Tables*	*Iron shelves*
15.	Neredmet, Hyderabad (Dist)	26	5	4
16.	Vikarabad, Ranga Reddy (Dist)	8	2	1
17.	Haveilighanapur, Medak (Dist)	10	3	1
18.	LMD colony, Karimnagar (Dist)	20	3	3
19.	Nagaram, Nizamabad (Dist)	10	1	1
20.	Adilabad (Dist)	8	2	2
21.	Khammam (Dist)	20	2	2
22.	Warangal (Dist)	9	2	2
23.	Nalgonda (Dist)	12	1	2

Table 4.3. Furniture, Equipment and Other Facilities in Office Rooms of DIETs

		Office room						
Sl. No.	*Name of the DIET*	*Tables*	*Computers*	*Chairs*	*Fans*	*Almirahs*	*Type machines*	*Toilets*
1.	Vomaravalli, Srikakulam (Dist)	8	1	8	4	10	1	0
2.	V.G. Puram, VZM (Dist)	6	0	17	4	13	1	0
3.	Bheemunipatnam, VSP (Dist)	10	2	15	4	10	3	0
4.	Bommuru E.G (Dist)	10	1	24	6	3	2	0
5.	Dubacherla, W.G (Dist)	10	11	15	4	7	3	0
6.	Angaluru, Krishna (Dist)	10	0	10	4	4	2	1
7.	Boyapalem, Guntur (Dist)	10	3	12	6	8	2	0
8.	Mynampadu, Nellore (Dist)	15	1	15	3	10	2	0
9.	Pallepadu, Nellore (Dist)	13	0	18	5	8	2	0
10.	Rayachoty, Cuddapah (Dist)	15	1	15	3	10	2	0
11.	Karvetinagar, Chittoor (Dist)	6	0	7	6	6	2	0
12.	Bukkapatnam, Ananthapur (Dist)	6	1	10	2	5	1	0
13.	B. Thandrapadu, Kurnool (Dist)	12	6	15	4	10	1	0

Continued

Sl. No.	Name of the DIET	Office room						
		Tables	Computers	Chairs	Fans	Almirahs	Type machines	Toilets
14.	Mahabubnagar (Dist)	10	0	10	4	15	2	0
15.	Neredmet, Hyderabad (Dist)	12	2	12	5	12	3	0
16.	Vikarabad, Ranga Reddy (Dist)	5	1	5	2	5	5	0
17.	Haveilighanapur, Medak (Dist)	8	2	12	3	14	2	0
18.	LMD colony, Karimnagar (Dist)	13	0	15	4	8	2	0
19.	Nagaram, Nizamabad (Dist)	8	0	12	4	11	2	0
20.	Adilabad (Dist)	8	0	11	4	8	1	1
21.	Khammam (Dist)	8	1	8	2	6	2	0
22.	Warangal (Dist)	6	18	10	5	12	1	1
23.	Nalgonda (Dist)	10	0	15	4	8	2	1

offices possess fifteen almirahs each and all the twenty three DIETs in the state are equipped with a minimum number of one type machine each. In seven DIETs namely Vomaravalli, Venugopalapuram, Boyapalem, Bukkapatnam, B.Thandrapadu,, Adilabad and Warangal there is one type machine each. In Vikarabad only there are five type machines. In the remaining fifteen DIETs the number of machines vary from two to four (Table 4.3) .

The availability of attached toilet facility to DIET office is for only four DIETs namely Angaluru, Adilabad, Warangal and Nalgonda one each.

As suggested in the MHRD Guidelines all the seven departments are established in each of the twenty three DIETs, constituting separate departmental rooms.

As per the observations of the researcher there are only two tables in Bukkapatnam and there are 30 tables in Rayachoty. In all the other twenty one DIETs the possession of tables vary from seven to twenty in each DIET.

The availability of chairs in departments again is varied in number. In four DIETs namely Vomaravalli, Bommuru, Dubacherla, Khammam and Warangal there are only seven chairs for seven departments. Whereas in B.Thandrapadu there are about forty chairs for seven departments, and in the other seventeen DIETs the availability of number of chairs vary from thirty five to ten.

The computers allotted to departmental rooms again vary from twelve in Mynampadu and eleven in Rayachoty which are at the maximum. In fifteen DIETs departments there are no computers at all. In Bommuru there is only one computer. In five more DIETs they vary from four to nine.

In two DIETs departments namely Karvetinagar and Mahabubnagar there are no almirahs at all. Whereas the least number of two almirahs are possessed by Bommuru and Khammam. The maximum number of almirahs available in DIETs are thirty in Rayachoty. Whereas the number vary from twenty four to three in about nineteen DIETs departments.

Table 4.4. Furniture, Equipment and Facilities Rooms of Branches and in Women's waiting Halls of DIETs

Sl. No.	Name of the DIET	Departmental particulars						Separate waiting half for women		
		Tables	Computers	Chairs	Almirahs	Fans	Toilets	Available	Attached Toilets	Requirement of furniture
1.	Vomaravalli, Strikakulam (Dist)	7	5	7	7	1	0	0	0	0
2.	V.G. Puram, VZM (Dist)	14	0	30	9	9	1	0	0	0
3.	Bheemunipatnam, VSP (Dist)	20	4	30	20	15	1	0	0	0
4.	Bommuru, E.G (Dist)	7	1	7	2	2	0	0	0	0
5.	Dubacherla, W.G (Dist)	9	9	7	3	1	0	1	1	1
6.	Angaluru, Krishna (Dist)	10	0	10	8	7	0	0	0	0
7.	Boyapalem, Guntur (Dist)	20	0	20	15	15	2	1	1	1
8.	Mynampadu, Prakasam (Dist)	15	12	15	12	10	0	0	0	0
9.	Pallepadu, Nellore (Dist)	7	0	12	8	8	8	0	0	0
10.	Rayachoty, Cuddapah (Dist)	30	11	30	30	10	0	0	0	0
11.	Karvetinagar, Chittoor (Dist)	20	0	20	0	10	0	0	0	0

Continued

Sl. No.	Name of the DIET	Departmental particulars						Separate waiting half for women		
		Tables	Computers	Chairs	Almirahs	Fans	Toilets	Available	Attached Toilets	Requirement of furnitur
12.	Bukkapatnam, Ananthapur (Dist)	2	4	15	7	4	0	0	0	0
13.	B. Thandrapadu, Kurnool (Dist)	20	0	40	20	20	0	0	0	0
14.	Mahabubnagar (Dist)	20	0	20	0	5	0	0	0	0
15.	Neredmet, Hyderabad (Dist)	18	5	18	24	7	0	0	0	0
16.	Vikarabad, Ranga Reddy (Dist)	17	0	17	18	18	5	0	0	0
17.	Haveilighanapur, Medak (Dist)	14	0	35	16	7	0	0	0	0
18.	LMD colony, Karimnagar (Dist)	14	0	28	3	7	0	1	1	1
19.	Nagaram, Nizamabad (Dist)	14	0	20	14	9	0	1	1	1
20.	Adilabad (Dist)	8	0	10	10	10	0	0	0	0
21.	Khammam (Dist)	10	0	7	2	1	0	0	0	0
22.	Warangal (Dist)	14	0	7	5	2	2	0	0	0
23.	Nalgonda (Dist)	10	0	20	15	8	0	0	0	0

There are fans available in all 23 DIETs departments but it varies from one in Vomaravalli, Dubacherla and Khammam and twenty in B.Thandrapadu (the maximum number). In the other nineteen DIETs the number is increased from two to eighteen in different DIETs.

The facility of attached toilets to departmental rooms is available in only six DIETs namely one each for Venugopalazpuram and Bheemunipatnam, two each for Boyapalem and Warangal and five in Vikarabad and eight the maximum number in Pallepadu.

The availability of a separate waiting hall for women in DIETs is a question. It is observed that the hall is not available in nineteen DIETs and there is a separate waiting hall in four DIETs namely Dubacherla, Boyapalem, LMD Colony and Nagaram. All these four DIETs women waiting halls where attached toilet facility is provided. Moreover, required furniture is also provided in these four DIETs in women waiting halls (Table (4.4).

The facility of availability of computer in the library is made possible in DIETs of Angaluru, Bukkapatnam, Neredmet and Adilabad only (Table 4.5).

The number of reference books possessed in the library is at the minimum three hundred in Karimnagar and Rayachoty. Whereas it is noted that in Mahabubnagar there are all about six thousand seven hundred books and fourteen thousand books at the maximum. By and large all the DIETs are in possession of required books.

As far as the general books are concerned the availability of number of general books is again has great variability from DIET to DIET. Vomaravalli DIET possess the maximum number of general books which is about 10,000 whereas the minimum number of general books are possessed in DIET Bommuru is 749 only. All the other twenty one DIETs possess varying number of general books which range from seven thousand to one thousand (Table 4.6).

As far as the contribution of journals is concerned it is observed that two hundred journals are available in Mynampadu and the least number available is two journals in Mahabubnagar. The rakhs to keep books in the libraries vary in number from a maximum of one in Nagaram to twenty four in Karvetinagar. There is a great variability in possession of number of rakhs for the libraries.

The facility of fans to library vary from one in Angaluru to ten in Boyapalem and Neradmet. The availability of fans to library is one each in Angaluru, Rayachoty and Bukkapatnam. The availability of a separate library building is observed in twenty DIETs except in three DIETs, namely Vomaravalli, Venugopalapuram and Warangal.

As per the MHRD Guidelines a separate reading hall to be established in each DIET for faculty as well as trainees for their academic as well as professional development with at least ten professional journals, periodicals and news papers.

The number of tables vary from two in Nagaram to twenty in Neredmet DIET. In eleven DIETs namely vomaravalli, Venugopalapuram, Bommuru, Boyapalem, Pallepadu, Rayachoty Karvetinagar, Bukkapatnam, B.Thandrapadu, L.M.D. Colony and Adilabad, there are no tables at all in reading hall.

As far as the possession of chairs in reading hall is concerned there are 60 in Neredmet the maximum number and in eight DIETs there are no chairs at all, namely in all most all DIETs where there are no tables. But in Dubacherla 50 chairs in Bheemunipatnam and Havelighanapur there are 30 chairs each and the least number is six chairs each in Boyapalem, Mynampadu, and Pallepadu DIETs' reading halls (Table 4.6).

It is observed that fans are not possessed by almost the same ten DIETs where there are no tables or chairs. But in Bheemunipatnam, Mynampadu and Vikarabad they possess a minimum number of two fans each where as Khammam and Neredmet possess the maximum number of six fans each.

It is observed that there are no tubelights at all in the reading halls of Bommuru, Rayachoty, Bukkapatnam, B.Thandrapadu and LMD Colony where as the maximum number of 17 tube lights are found in Neredmet and in eight DIETs a minimum number of two fans are possessed in each (Table 4.6).

Table 4.5. Availability of Books and Facilities in Libraries of DIETs

Sl. No.	Name of the DIET	Facilities in the library						
		No. using Computers	Reference books	General books	Text books	Journals	Shelves	Fans
1.	Vomaravalli, Strikakulam (Dist)	0	1000	10000	300	10	5	2
2.	V.G. Puram, VZM (Dist)	0	2000	1500	400	40	18	2
3.	Beemunipatnam, VSP (Dist)	0	2870	995	1345	5	20	2
4.	Bommuru, E.G (Dist)	0	413	749	156	14	6	4
5.	Dubacherla, W.G. (Dist)	0	1000	7000	200	10	10	4
6.	Angaluru, Krishna (Dist)	1	400	2000	440	5	13	1
7.	Boyapalem, Guntur (Dist)	0	3500	2800	700	4	4	10
8.	Mynampadu, Prakasam (Dist)	0	800	1000	3000	200	10	2
9.	Pallepadu, Nellore (Dist)	0	1485	1485	200	3	6	2
10.	Rayachoty, Cuddapah (Dist)	0	300	3000	300	100	15	1
11.	Karvetinagar, Chittoor (Dist)	0	1500	4000	1500	25	24	9
12.	Bukkapatnam, Ananthapur (Dist)	1	2000	3000	1000	10	12	1

Continued

Sl. No.	*Name of the DIET*	*Facilities in the library*						
		No. using Computers	*Reference books*	*General books*	*Text books*	*Journals*	*Shelves*	*Fans*
13.	B. Thandrapadu, Kurnool (Dist)	0	2000	1000	100	0	20	6
14.	Mahabubnagar (Dist)	0	6714	1000	100	2	15	4
15.	Neredmet, Hyderabad (Dist)	1	3212	2121	3456	8	23	10
16.	Vikarabad, Ranga Reddy (Dist)	0	2000	1000	100	4	10	2
17.	Haveilighanapur, Medak (Dist)	0	1000	8000	1000	4	20	3
18.	LMD colony, Karimnagar (Dist)	0	300	3200	1200	3	10	4
19.	Nagaram, Nizamabad (Dist)	0	2000	1500	600	10	1	2
20.	Adilabad (Dist)	1	1000	1500	1000	10	10	4
21.	Khammam (Dist)	0	500	1000	200	100	6	5
22.	Warangal (Dist)	0	1000	1000	100	4	4	3
23.	Nalgonda (Dist)	0	3000	2000	4000	3	2	8

Table 4.6. Availability of Books and Facilities in Reading Halls of DIETs

Sl. No.	Name of the DIET	Reading hall facilities							
		Tables	Chairs	Fans	Tube lights	Daily News papers	Weekly journals	Fortnightly journals	Monthly journals
1.	Vomeravalli, Strikakulam (Dist)	0	0	0	2	4	0	1	5
2.	V.G. Puram, VZM (Dist)	0	0	0	2	2	2	1	1
3.	Bheemunipatnam, VSP (Dist)	4	30	2	2	4	4	1	1
4.	Bommuru, E.G. (Dist)	0	0	0	0	2	1	1	1
5.	Dubacherla, W.G (Dist)	4	50	4	4	4	1	0	1
6.	Angaluru, Krishna (Dist)	4	15	4	2	4	0	0	0
7.	Boyapalem, Guntur (Dist)	0	6	2	2	4	0	0	1
8.	Mynampadu, Prakasam, (Dist)	3	6	2	2	4	0	0	1
9.	Pallepadu, Nellore (Dist)	0	6	0	3	3	0	0	3
10.	Rayachoty, Cuddapah (Dist)	0	0	0	0	5	0	3	6
11.	Karvetinagar, Chittoor (Dist)	0	8	0	2	3	0	2	8
12.	Bukkapatnam, Ananthapur (Dist)	0	0	0	0	5	7	2	2
13.	B. Thandrapadu, Kurnool (Dist)	0	0	0	0	3	0	0	0

Continued

Sl. No.	*Name of the DIET*	*Reading hall facilities*							
		Tables	*Chairs*	*Fans*	*Tube lights*	*Daily News papers*	*Weekly journals*	*Fortnightly journals*	*Monthly journals*
14.	Mahabubnagar (Dist)	3	8	4	5	6	0	0	14
15.	Neredmet, Hyderabad (Dist)	20	60	6	17	6	0	4	4
16.	Vikarabad, Ranga Reddy (Dist)	4	20	2	4	2	0	0	0
17.	Haveilighanapur, Medak (Dist)	3	30	4	2	4	15	10	8
18.	LMD colony, Karimnagar (Dist)	0	0	0	0	5	4	10	0
19.	Nagaram, Nizamabad (Dist)	2	20	1	2	6	10	2	2
20.	Adilabad (Dist)	0	0	0	0	6	4	0	0
21.	Khammam (Dist)	6	15	5	4	4	5	2	10
22.	Warangal (Dist)	4	10	0	6	6	1	0	0
23.	Nalgonda (Dist)	3	20	0	8	4	10	0	2

It is inquired that the availability of all DIETs are contributory for daily news papers a maximum of six in three DIETs namely Nagaram, Adilabad and Warangal whereas a minimum of two newspapers are contributed by three DIETs namely, Venugapalapuram, Bommuru and Vikarabad.

As per the MHRD Guidelines a minimum of ten journals are to be subscribed for DIET reading hall. But it is found that the total of weekly, fortnightly and monthly journals subscribed by DIETs for their reading halls are minimal. It is found that eight DIETs have contributed ten or above journals and thirty three by Haveli̇ghanapur. The other fifteen DIETs contributed less than ten and B.Thandrapadu and Neredmet not at all contributed for journals (Table 4.6).

As per MHRD Guidelines there should be a separate provision for construction of an auditorium for each DIET. But there is no separate auditorium constructed in DIETs. Many DIETs have been managing to use some hall as meeting hall and for all such purposes. But a few DIETs have not such facility for example Vanugopalapuram, Pallepadu, Karvetinagar, B.Thandrapadu, Havelighanapur and Khammam.

It is found that the number of chairs possessed in the meeting hall vary from forty in Bommuru and Angaluru to a maximum of two hundred and eighty in Neredmet. In the same way the possession of tube lights and fans also vary from DIET to DIET. Two fans are possessed by Angaluru and a maximum number of fans are noticed in DIETs Neredmet and Vikarabad. The facility of tube lights vary from two in Bommuru, Boyapalem and one in Mahabubnagar where as the maximum number of twelve are possessed in Neredmet and Vikarabad (Table 4.7).

As per the MHRD Guidelines the possession of addressing system is suggested but it is possessed by only eleven DIETs namely Bheemunipatnam, Bommuru, Dubacherla, Angaluru, Boyapalem, Rayachoty, Neredmet, Vikarabad, LMD Colony, Warangal and Nalgonda.

As per the suggestion given in the MHRD Guidelines the following equipment is to be possessed by all DIETs and proper discharge of their function as suggested.

Table 4.7. Availability of Furniture and Equipment in the Meeting Halls of DIETs

Sl. No.	Name of the DIET	Meeting hall facilities			
		Chairs	Fans	Tube lights	Public addressing system
1.	Vomeravalli, Strikakulam (Dist)	40	6	3	0
2.	V.C. Puram, VZM (Dist)	0	0	0	0
3.	Bheemunipatnam, VSP (Dist)	130	8	10	1
4.	Bommuru, E.G (Dist()	40	3	2	1
5.	Bubacherla, W.G (Dist)	50	4	4	1
6.	Angaluru, Krishna (Dist)	40	2	2	1
7.	Boyapalem, Guntur (Dist)	150	7	5	1
8.	Mynampadu, Prakasam (Dist)	40	6	6	0
9.	Pallepadu, Nellore (Dist)	0	0	0	
10.	Rayachoty, Cuddapah (Dist)	80	3	10	1
11.	Karvetinagar, Chittoor (Dist)	0	0	0	0
12.	Bukkapatnam, Ananthapur (Dist)	40	5	3	0

Contiued

Sl. No.	Name of the DIET	Meeting hall facilities			
		Chairs	Fans	Tube lights	Public addressing system
13.	B. Thandrapadu, Kurnool (Dist)	0	0	0	0
14.	Mahabubnagar (Dist)	100	9	1	0
15.	Neredmet, Hyderabad (Dist)	280	10	12	1
16.	Vikarabad, Ranga Reddy (Dist)	250	10	12	1
17.	Haveilighanapur, Medak (Dist)	0	0	0	0
18.	LMD colony, Karimnagar (Dist)	100	8	6	1
19.	Nagaram, Nizamabad (Dist)	50	3	6	0
20.	Adilabad (Dist)	40	3	4	0
21.	Khammam (Dist)	0	0	0	0
22.	Warangal (Dist)	100	8	6	1
23.	Nalgonda (Dist)	1505	7	8	1

Table 4.8. Availability of Equipment and Furniture in Educational Technology Branch of DIETs

Sl. No.	Name of the DIET	Information of Educational Technology Department										
		Dish Antenna	*No. of working televisions available*	*Computers*	*OHPs*	*16mm Films-trip Projectors*	*Slide projectors*	*Two-in-ones*	*Radios*	*DVD/VCD/VCR*	*Video cassettes*	*Audio cassettes*
1.	Vomaravalli, Strikakulam (Dist)	1	1	2	1	1	1	1	0	1	35	60
2.	V.G. Puram VZM (Dist)	1	2	7	2	0	0	0	0	0	57	50
3.	Bheemunipatnam, VSP (Dist)	1	2	5	2	2	1	2	2	3	60	25
4.	Bommuru, E.G (Dist)	1	2	6	1	1	1	1	1	1	10	4
5.	Dubacherla, W.G (Dist)	0	2	5	1	2	2	1	1	0	20	20
6.	Angaluru, Krishna (Dist)	1	1	3	0	0	0	1	1	0	10	9
7.	Boyapalem, Guntur (Dist)	0	1	18	2	0	1	1	0	1	30	10
8.	Mynampadu, Prakasam (Dist)	1	1	12	2	0	1	2	0	1	20	20
9.	Pallepadu, Nellure (Dist)	0	1	1	0	0	0	0	0	0	18	40
10.	Rayachoty, Cuddapah (Dist)	1	2	11	3	1	2	2	1	1	50	5
11.	Karvetinagar, Chittor (Dist)	1	2	10	0	0	0	1	4	1	50	70

Continued

Sl. No.	Name of the DIET	Information of Educational Technology Department										
		Dish Antenna	*No. of working televisions available*	*Computers*	*OHPs*	*16mm Filmstrip Projectors*	*Slide projectors*	*Two-in-ones*	*Radios*	*DVD/ VCD/ VCR*	*Video casset-*	*Audio casset*
12.	Bukkapatnam, Ananthapur (Dist)	0	2	4	0	1	1	3	2	2	16	10
13.	B. Thandrapadu, Kurnool (Dist)	0	2	4	0	1	1	3	2	2	16	10
14.	Mahabubnagar (Dist)	1	5	7	6	1	1	4	4	2	80	20
15.	Neredmet, Hyderabad (Dist)	1	2	14	2	2	1	2	2	2	30	50
16.	Vikarabad, Ranga Reddy (Dist)	1	2	8	2	1	2	2	2	1	70	20
17.	Haveilighanapur, Medak (Dist)	1	4	22	6	1	2	1	2	2	100	5
18.	LMD colony, Karimnagar (Dist)	1	4	12	2	1	1	1	1	1	30	10
19.	Nagaram, Nizamabad (Dist)	1	2	5	2	1	1	1	1	2	60	30
20.	Adilabad (Dist)	0	2	10	1	1	2	1	1	1	50	20
21.	Khammam (Dist)	1	2	10	0	1	0	1	2	3	15	15
22.	Warangal (Dist)	1	2	18	2	1	2	2	1	1	20	20
23.	Nalgonda (Dist)	1	3	10	2	1	1	2	1	3	40	12

The possession of dish antenna is a minimum for getting educational channels and lessons through the T.V. programmes. All the DIETs except six DIETs namely Dubacharla, Boyapalem, Pallepadu, Bukkapatnam, B.Thandrapadu and Adilabad possess dish antennae for getting educational channels.

But it is observed that even though some DIETs possess dish antenna, five DIETs did not get educational channels due to shadow area such as Vomaravalli, Rayachoty, Karvetinagar, Vikarabad and Nalgonda. In this way although seventeen DIETs possess dish antennae only twelve DIETs do get educational channels.

Though the MHRD Guidelines suggest two colour T.Vs for each DIET is necessary, four DIETs possess two colour T.Vs each, and five DIETs namely Vomaravalli, Angaluru, Boyapalem, Mynampadu, Pallepadu possess only one colour T.V. each whereas four DIETs possess more than suggested number of two colour T.V.s i.e. five in Mahabubnagar, four each in Heveligharapur and LMD colony and three in Nalgonda. As per the MHRD Guidelines three audio cassette players and one two-in-one are suggested for each DIET educational technology department. Eight DIETs namely Bheemunipatnam, Mynampadu, Rayachoty, Bukkapatnam four each whereas Mahabubnagar possess four, and B. Thandrapadu possess three a few DIETs namely Venugopalapuram and Pallepadu possess no two-in-ones at all. The rest of the eleven DIETs possess one each as per MHRD Guidelines. Except five DIETs namely Vamaravalli, Venugopalapuram, Boyapalem, Mynampadu and Pallepadu which did not possess radio sets, all the other eighteen DIETs possess one or more radio sets.

As per MHRD Guidelines each DIET should have one VCP. But four DIETs namely Venugopalapuram, Dubacharla, Angaluru and Pallepadu did not possess them. But the remaining DIETs procured one or more (up to three also) VCPs.

As far as the possession of cassettes are concerned MHRD Guidelines suggests possession of some cassettes. All the DIETs possess both video and audio cassettes in varying number for use.

As per MHRD Guidelines one slide projector is to be possessed by each DIET. Eighteen DIETs possess one or more slide projectors but five DIETs did not posses slide projectors namely Venugopalapuram, Angaluru, Pallepadu, Karvetinagar and Khammam.

As per MHRD Guidelines one 16 mm filmstrip projector to be equipped to each DIET. Seventeen DIETs possess one or more filmstrip projectors but six DIETs namely Venugopalapuram, Angaluru, Boyapalem, Mynampadu, Pallepadu and Karvetinagar did not possess filmstrip projectors.

As far as OHPs are concerned MHRD Guidelines suggest two OHPs for each DIET for use in training courses as well in regular pre-service classes. Thirteen DIEPs posses two or more up to six OHPs in their E.T. department equipment, namely Venugopalapuram, Bheemunipatnam, Boyapalem, Mynampadu, Rayachoty, Mahabubnagar, Neredmet, Vikarabad, Havelighanapur, L.M.D. Colony, Nagaram, Warangal, and Nalgonda. But it is in Augalore, Pallepadu, Karvetinagar, B.Thandrapadu and Khammam there is not even one OHP. In the remaining five DIETs they possess only one OHP in each.

DIET Guidelines suggest three computers and out of them one computer with dot-matrix printer for the use of educational technology department; Twenty one DIETs possess three or more up to twenty two computers, but two DIETs possessed only one and two computers.

The MHRD Guidelines suggest regarding hostel facility about 150-200 seats are to be accommodated in the hostel. In about seven DIETs the hostel is not running, namely Pallepadu, Bukkapatnam, Nagaram, Adilabad, Khammam, Warangal and Nalgonda. All the other eighteen DIETs run the hostel with 150-200 trainees.

The number of useful cots owned by the hostels vary from DIET to DIET Only eleven DIETs namely Bommuru, Dubacherla, Mynampadu, Rayachoty, Karvetinagar, B.Thadrapadu, Neredmet, Vikarabad, Havelighanapur, Adilabad and Nalgonda. The remaning twelve DIETs hostels do not possess any cots.

Table 4.9. Availability of Trainees Strength, Cots and Water Facility in the Hostels of DIETs

Sl. No.	*Name of the DIET*	*Trainees hostel facility*		
		Strength of hostel	*Number of cots*	*Mode of water supply*
1.	Vomeravalli, Strikakulam (Dist)	200	0	Bore well
2.	V.C. Puram, VZM (Dist)	156	0	Bore well
3.	Bheemunipatnam, VSP (Dist)	180	0	Bore well
4.	Bommuru, E.G (Dist()	186	49	Bore well
5.	Bubacherla, W.G (Dist)	200	20	Bore well
6.	Angaluru, Krishna (Dist)	200	0	General tank
7.	Boyapalem, Guntur (Dist)	123	0	Bore well
8.	Mynampadu, Prakasam (Dist)	110	110	Bore well
9.	Pallepadu, Nellore (Dist)	0	0	General tank
10.	Rayachoty, Cuddapah (Dist)	200	50	General tank
11.	Karvetinagar, Chittoor (Dist)	140	180	Bore well
12.	Bukkapatnam, Ananthapur (Dist)	0	0	Bore well
13.	B. Thandrapadu, Kurnool (Dist)	105	40	Bore well

Continued

Sl. No.	Name of the DIET	Trainees hostel facility		
		Strength of hostel	Numbe" of cots	Mode of water suppl
14.	Mahabubnagar (Dist)	200	0	Bore well
15.	Neredmet, Hyderabad (Dist)	165	120	Bore well
16.	Vikarabad, Ranga Reddy (Dist)	201	90	Bore well
17.	Haveilighanapur, Medak (Dist)	200	100	Bore well
18.	LMD colony, Karimnagar (Dist)	200	0	General tank
19.	Nagaram, Nizamabad (Dist)	0	0	Bore well
20.	Adilabad (Dist)	0	50	Bore well
21.	Khammam (Dist)	0	0	Bore well
22.	Warangal (Dist)	0	0	Bore well
23.	Nalgonda (Dist)	0	28	Bore well

Table 4.10. Area C (Achievement) Table First and Second Year Results of D.Ed Teacher Trainees

Sl. No.	*Name of DIET*	*Results in percentages of D.Ed. teacher trainees*									
		First Year					*Second Year*				
		2000-01	*2001-02*	*2002-03*	*2003-04*	*2004-05*	*2000 01*	*2001-02*	*2002-03*	*2003-04*	*2004-05*
1.	Vomaravalli, Strikakulam (Dist)	100	93	93	92	100	100	93	92	82	95
2.	V.G. Puram, VZM (Dist)	100	100	100	100	100	100	97	96	100	91
3.	Bheemunipatnam, VSP (Dist)	100	100	100	100	100	97	100	100	100	99
4.	Bommuru, E.G (Dist)	98	95	95	96	94	100	100	99	100	100
5.	Dubacherla, W.G (Dist)	95	100	100	100	93	100	100	100	100	89
6.	Angaluru, Krishna (Dist)	100	100	100	100	100	100	100	100	100	100
7.	Boyapalem, Guntur (Dist)	100	100	100	92	100	100	100	100	100	100
8.	Mynampadu, Prakasam (Dist)	100	100	100	100	100	100	97	100	90	100
9.	Pallepadu, Nellore (Dist)	100	100	100	100	100	100	96	100	92	100
10.	Rayachoty, Cuddapah (Dist)	93	100	100	100	93	66	100	98	100	99
11.	Karvetinagar, Chittoor (Dist)	100	100	100	100	100	100	100	100	100	100
12.	Bukkapatnam, Ananthapur (Dist)	100	100	100	100	100	100	100	100	100	100

Continued

Sl. No.	Name of DIET	Results in percentages of D.Ed. teacher trainees									
		First Year					Second Year				
		2000-01	2001-02	2002-03	2003-04	2004-05	2000 01	2001-02	2002-03	2003-04	2004-05
13.	B. Thandrapadu, Kurnool (Dist)	100	100	100	100	100	100	100	100	100	100
14.	Mahabubnagar (Dist)	97	100	100	100	100	97	100	100	100	100
15.	Neredmet, Hyderabad (Dist)	100	100	100	100	100	100	100	100	100	93
16.	Vikarabad, Ranga Reddy (Dist)	100	100	100	100	99	100	100	97	100	93
17.	Haveilighanapur, Medak (Dist)	73	99	100	97	99	100	100	100	100	100
18.	LMD colony, Karimnagar (Dist)	96	97	94	98	100	95	95	96	95	98
19.	Nagaram, Nizamabad (Dist)	100	100	100	100	100	100	100	99	100	97
20.	Adilabad (Dist)	92	99	100	99	98	99	100	100	99	96
21.	Khammam (Dist)	100	100	97	100	100	97	95	97	100	99
22.	Warangal (Dist)	93	100	100	100	100	100	100	100	100	100
23.	Nalgonda (Dist)	99	100	99	100	100	99	100	99	100	100

It is suggested DIETs should run hostels for trainees. All most all DIETs own a bore well for water in the hostel. But only four DIETs namely Angaluru, Pallepadu, Mynampadu and LMD. Colony are getting drinking water from general tanks.

It is noticed that during the last five academic years (2000-01 to 2004-05) five DIETs achieved 100 per cent results both in I and II year examinations. They are Angaluru, Boyapalem, Karvetinagar, Bukkapatnam and B.Thandrapadu.

Three DIETs namely Venugopalapuram, Nagaram and Khammam achieved 100 per cent result in I year examinations.

On the other hand three DIETs namely Bommuru, Havelighanapur and Warangal achieved 100 per cent result in second year examinations.

The least percentage of result is the 66 per cent achieved by Rayachoty DIET by the II year trainees.

All the other DIETs have achieved between 100 per cent and 66 per cent respectively during 2000-01 to 2004-05 by the I and II year trainees.

The involvement of the trainees in the games and sports for the all round development of the teacher consequently the children at schools showed a very good sign.

The maximum number of games participated by DIETs in the state is eight by only one DIET namely Bheemunipatnam. The next highest number of games participated by DIETs is the seven by nine DIETs namely Venugopalapuram, Dubacherla, Karvetinagar, Mahabubnagar, Neredmet, Vikarabad , Havelighanapur and Nagaram.

Two DIETs namely Bommuru and Mynampadu participated in only two games.

On the other hand the common games participated by most DIETs are chess, volleyball, kabaddi and kho-kho i.e. 19 DIETs have participated whereas the least participating games are shuttle, ring tennis and throw ball. Six or seven DIETs only do participate in these games. This may be due to costliness of shuttle cock and the ladies are not encouraged to play ring tennis.

The MHRD Guidelines suggested a work shed, and garden/ farm for Work-Experience activities. And also furniture and equipment for education in visual & performance arts, and garden development.

Adilabad DIET performing eight activities out of ten and Bheemunipatnam and LMD.Colony are performing six activities out of ten. Thirteen DIETs have been performing less than half i.e. four activities only out of ten, namely Vomaravally, Venugopalapuram, Bommuru, Dubacheral, Angaluru, Boyapalem, Pallepadu, Rayachoty, Karvetinagar, B.Thandrapadu, Vikarabad, Havelighanapur and Nalgonda.

All the twenty three DIETs have been conducting gardening, clean and green, teaching learning material preparation and phenol preparation. But only a few DIETs have conducting activities regarding book binding (Mynampadu, Bukkapatnam, Mahabubnagar, LMD.Colony, Nagaram, Khammam and Warangal) three DIETs only conducting file pad preparation namely Mynampadu, LMD.Colony and Adilabad.

Only two DIETs namely Bheemunipatnam and Mynampadu have been conducting Red cross and Scouts & Guides activities.

Very few DIETs namely Bheemunipatnam and Mynampadu have been training D.Ed teacher trainees in Scouting and Red-cross.

It is interesting to note that all the twenty three DIETs in the state are conducting Extra-curricular Activities like quiz competitions, essay writing, elocutions, debates and participating in Science Fairs, encouraging cultural activities among trainees.

But only two DIETs namely Venugopalapuram and Adilabad conducting field trips. It is also observed that only two DIETs namely Venugopalapuram and Mynampadu have conducted excursions. Only four DIETs namely Vomaravalli, Mynampadu, Rayachoty and Adilabad are organizing seminars in the DIET regularly.

On the other hand it is evidenced that out of the nine Co-curricular Activities three DIETs namely Venugopalapuram, Mynampadu and Adilabad have participating in eight activities and all the remaining DIETs have organizing at least six activities out of ten activities.

Table 4.11. Area D Table Showing Availability and Participation by D.Ed Teacher Trainees in Different Games and sports (both in-door and out-door)

Sl. No.	Name of the DIET	Games and sports										
		Table Tennis	Caroms	Chess	Shuttle	Volley ball	Kabadi	Cricket	Kho-kho	Ring tennis	Throw ball	Total
1	Vomaravalli, srikakulam (Dist)	1	1	0	0	1	1	1	0	0	0	5
2	V.G.puram, VZM(Dist)	0	1	1	1	1	1	0	1	1	0	7
3	Bheemunipatnam, VSP (Dist)	0	1	1	0	1	1	1	1	1	1	8
4	Bommuru, E.G (Dist)	0	0	1	0	1	0	0	0	0	0	2
5	Dubacherla, W.G (Dist)	1	0	1	0	1	1	1	1	0	1	7
6	Angaluru, Krishna (Dist)	0	1	1	0	1	1	0	1	1	0	6
7	Boyapalem, Guntur (Dist)	0	1	1	0	1	1	0	1	1	0	6
8	Mynampadu, Prakasam (Dist)	0	0	1	1	0	0	0	0	0	0	2
9	Pallepadu, Nellore (Dist)	0	0	0	0	0	1	1	1	1	0	4
10	Rayachoty, Cuddapah (Dist)	0	1	1	0	1	0	1	1	0	1	6
11	Karvetinagar, Chittoor (Dist)	0	1	1	1	1	1	1	0	0	1	7
12	Bukkapatnam, Ananthapur (Dist)	1	0	0	0	1	0	1	1	0	0	4
13	B.Thandrapadu, Kurnool (Dist)	0	0	1	0	1	0	0	0	1	1	4

Sl. No.	*Name of the DIET*	*Games and sports*										
		Table Tennis	*Caroms*	*Chess*	*Shuttle*	*Volley ball*	*Kabadi*	*Cricket*	*Kho-kho*	*Ring tennis*	*Throw ball*	*Total*
14	Mahabubnagar (Dist)	0	1	1	1	1	1	0	1	0	1	7
15	Neredmet, Hyderabad (Dist)	1	1	1	0	1	1	1	1	0	0	7
16	Vikarabad, Ranga Reddy (Dist)	1	1	1	0	1	1	1	1	0	0	7
17	Haveilighanapur, Medak (Dist)	1	1	1	1	1	1	0	1	0	0	7
18	LMD colony, Karimnagar (Dist)	1	1	1	0	1	1	1	1	0	0	7
19	Nagaram, Nizamabad (Dist)	0	1	1	0	1	1	1	1	0	1	7
20	Adilabad (Dist)	1	1	1	0	1	1	0	1	0	0	6
21	Khammam (Dist)	0	1	1	0	0	1	0	1	0	0	4
22	Warangal (Dist)	0	0	0	1	0	1	0	1	0	0	3
23	Nalgonda (Dist)	1	1	1	0	1	1	0	1	0	0	6
	Total	9	16	19	6	19	18	16	18	6	7	134

Please note: 1 - indicates positive answer
0 - indicates negative answer

The latest trend in the pedagogy is the activity oriented and child centered approach. It requires small class size and equipment and material for each class. This approach ensures participation of most of the children in the class.

All the faculty members of 23 DIETs preferred Activity Method as the best among the seven methods. It is also observed that the second place is chosen for two methods the lecture demonstration method and demonstration method equally.

They have preferred lecture method as the third one. Fourth place is given to discussion method and fifth is to project method and the sixth and least preference is given to seminar method.

It is observed that seventeen DIETs excepting Mynampadu, Karvetinagar, Bukkapatnam, Mahabubnagar, Vikarabad and LMD.Colony conducted seminars and participated in seminars.

The number of seminars conducted by these seventeen DIETs is ranging form one to ten. Regarding the organization of workshops all the twenty three DIETs have conducted workshops, but the number of workshops differ from DIET to DIET. Dubacherla DIET organized only one workshop whereas Angaluru DIET organized seventeen workshops.

As far as organization of conferences are concerned only ten DIETs namely Venugopalapuram, Bheemunipatnam, Bommuru, Angaluru, Mynampadu, Rayachoty, Mahabubnagar, Neredmet, Havelighanapur and Adilabad organized conferences. The organization of conferences also vary from DIET to DIET. The number vary from one to sixteen in Venugopalapuram and Bheemunipatnam, respectively Bommuru has conducted sixteen.

As per MHRD Guidelines as far as teaching staff is concerned along with Principal seven Senior Lecturers, and seventeen Lecturers shall be appointed for each DIET, catering to the seven branches in the DIET. Due to some changes like destruction of non-formal education of DRU and change in the PSTE course from one year TTC course to two year D.Ed course the number of Lecturer posts is reduced to sixteen. There is one Craft Teacher post in Work-Experience Branch, as per MHRD Guidelines.

Table 4.12. Area D

Table Showing Availability and Participation of D.Ed Teacher Trainees in some Extra-curricular Activities and Work Experience Activities

S.No	Name of the DIET	Extra-Curricular		Work-Experience activities						
		Red-Cross	Scouts & Guides	Gardening	Clean & Green	TLM preparations	Phenol preparation	Book binding	File pad preparation	Food items preparation
1	Vomaravalli, srikakulam (Dist)	0	0	1	1	1	1	0	0	1
2	V.G.puram, VZM(Dist)	0	0	1	1	1	1	0	0	0
3	Bheemunipatnam, VSP (Dist)	1	1	1	1	1	1	0	0	1
4	Bommuru, E.G (Dist)	0	0	1	1	1	1	0	0	0
5	Dubacherla, W.G (Dist)	0	0	1	1	1	1	0	0	0
6	Angaluru, Krishna (Dist)	0	0	1	1	1	1	0	0	0
7	Boyapalem, Guntur (Dist)	0	0	1	1	1	1	0	0	0
8	Mynampadu, Prakasam (Dist)	1	1	1	1	1	1	1	1	0
9	Pallepadu, Nellore (Dist)	0	0	1	1	1	1	0	0	0
10	Rayachoty, Cuddapah (Dist)	0	0	1	1	1	1	0	0	0
11	Karvetinagar, Chittoor (Dist)	0	0	1	1	1	1	0	0	0
12	Bukkapatnam, Ananthapur (Dist)	0	0	1	1	1	1	1	0	0

S.No	*Name of the DIET*	*Extra-Curricular*		*Work-Experience activities*						
		Red-Cross	*Scouts & Guides*	*Gardening*	*Clean & Green*	*TLM preparations*	*Phenol preparation*	*Book binding*	*File pad preparation*	*Food items preparation*
13	B.Thandrapadu, Kurnool (Dist)	0	0	1	1	1	1	0	0	0
14	Mahabubnagar (Dist)	0	0	1	1	1	1	1	0	0
15	Neredmet, Hyderabad (Dist)	0	0	1	1	1	1	0	0	0
16	Vikarabad, Ranga Reddy (Dist)	0	0	1	1	1	1	0	0	0
17	Haveilighanapur, Medak (Dist)	0	0	1	1	1	1	0	0	0
18	LMD colony, Karimnagar (Dist)	0	0	1	1	1	1	1	1	0
19	Nagaram, Nizamabad (Dist)	0	0	1	1	1	1	1	0	0
20	Adilabad (Dist)	0	0	1	1	1	1	1	1	1
21	Khammam (Dist)	0	0	1	1	1	1	1	0	0
22	Warangal (Dist)	0	0	1	1	1	1	1	0	0
23	Nalgonda (Dist)	0	0	1	1	1	1	0	0	0
	Total	2	2	23	23	23	23	8	3	3

Please note : 1 - Indicates positive answer
0 - Indicates negative answer

It is also observed that the number of lecturers working in the seven branches of DIET also vary from DIET to DIET. There are fifteen lectures in Bommuru and Boyapalem, four lecturers in Khammam five lecturers in Adilabad three lecturers in Havalighanapur and four in Mynampadu, working.

The Craft teacher post in the Work Experience department of DIETs is filled in four DIETs only namely in Pallepadu, B.Thandrapadu, LMD.Colony and Nagaram.

The teacher pupil ratio in DIETs is varying from 1:10 in Bommuru to 1:37 in Havelighanapur. In majority of DIETs the ratio is fluctuating from 1:10 to 1:25

It is observed that nineteen DIETs are functioning with regular Principals whereas four DIETs namely Angaluru, Mynampadu, Karvetinagar and LMD.Colony are with acting Principals.

As far as the information on the vacancy position of Senior Lecturers is concerned out of seven posts as per MHRD Guidelines four DIETs namely Bheemunipatnam, Mahabubnagar, Warangal and Nalgonda possess no vacancy whereas all the other nineteen DIETs possess one or more i.e up to six vacancies Vomaravalli possess six vacancies, Bukkaaptnam possess five vacancies and Bommuru, B.Thandrapadu, Vikarabad, Nagaram possess only one vacancy each.

As far as the vacancy position of Lecturer posts are concerned the MHRD Guidelines suggested that at least sixteen lecturer posts are required at, present but due to various reasons like retirements and non-filling of direct recruitment quota some posts fell vacant. All the twenty three DIETs suffering from varying number of vacancies from two to thirteen. For example Havelighanapur is with thirteen vacancies, Mynampadu, Adilabad and Khammam possess twelve vacancies each and very few vacancies in DIET Bommuru and Boyapalem.

It is found that all the DIETs have Craft Teacher except only few like pallepedu, B.Thanddrapadu, LMD.Colony and Nagaram.

Table 4.13. Table Showing Participation of D.Ed Teacher Trainees in certain Co-curricular Activities

S.No	*Name of the DIET*	*Co-curricular Activities*									
		Quiz	*Essay Writing*	*Elocution*	*Seminars*	*Debates*	*Field visits*	*Excursions*	*Science fairs*	*Cultural activities*	*Total*
1	Vomaravalli, srikakulam (Dist)	1	1	1	1	1	0	0	1	1	7
2	V.G.puram, VZM(Dist)	1	1	1	0	1	1	1	1	1	8
3	Bheemunipatnam, VSP (Dist)	1	1	1	0	1	0	0	1	1	4
4	Bommuru, E.G (Dist)	1	1	1	0	1	0	0	1	1	6
5	Dubacherla, W.G (Dist)	1	1	1	0	1	0	0	1	1	6
6	Angaluru, Krishna (Dist)	1	1	1	0	1	0	0	1	1	6
7	Boyapalem, Guntur (Dist)	1	1	1	0	1	0	0	1	1	6
8	Mynampadu, Prakasam (Dist)	1	1	1	1	1	0	1	1	1	8
9	Pallepadu, Nellore (Dist)	1	1	1	0	1	0	0	1	1	6
10	Rayachoty, Cuddapah (Dist)	1	1	1	1	1	0	0	1	1	7
11	Karvetinagar, Chittoor (Dist)	1	1	1	0	1	0	0	1	1	6
12	Bukkapatnam, Ananthapur (Dist)	1	1	1	0	1	0	0	1	1	6
13	B.Thandrapadu, Kurnool (Dist)	1	1	1	0	1	0	0	1	1	6
14	Mahabubnagar (Dist)	1	1	1	0	1	0	0	1	1	6

S.No	Name of the DIET	*Co-curricular Activities*									
		Quiz	*Essay Writing*	*Elocution*	*Seminars*	*Debates*	*Field visits*	*Excursions*	*Science fairs*	*Cultural activities*	*Total*
15	Neredmet, Hyderabad (Dist)	1	1	1	0	1	0	0	1	1	6
16	Vikarabad, Ranga Reddy (Dist)	1	1	1	0	1	0	0	1	1	6
17	Haveilighanapur, Medak (Dist)	1	1	1	0	1	0	0	1	1	6
18	LMD colony, Karimnagar (Dist)	1	1	1	0	1	0	0	1	1	6
19	Nagaram, Nizamabad (Dist)	1	1	1	0	1	0	0	1	1	6
20	Adilabad (Dist)	1	1	1	1	1	1	0	1	1	8
21	Khammam (Dist)	1	1	1	0	1	0	0	1	1	6
22	Warangal (Dist)	1	1	1	0	1	0	0	1	1	6
23	Nalgonda (Dist)	1	1	1	0	1	0	0	1	1	6
	Total	23	23	23	4	23	2	2	23	23	146

Table 4.14. Area E (Staff development and welfare)

Table Showing Preference out of the Seven Teaching Methods Serial Umbered as 1, 2, 3, 4, 5, 6 and 7 in the Opinionnaire in the Order of Preference by DIET Faculty Members for their Teaching Purpose in the Regular Course as Rated by Principals of DIETs

S.No	Name of the DIET	Order of preference from 1-7						
		Lecture method	Lecture demonstration method	Demonstration method	Activity Method	Project method	Discussion method	Seminar method
1	Vomaravalli, srikakulam (Dist)	3	5	6	1	7	2	4
2	V.G.puram, VZM(Dist)	7	5	4	1	2	3	6
3	Bheemunipatnam, VSP (Dist)	4	3	2	1	7	5	6
4	Bommuru, E.G (Dist)	1	4	5	2	6	3	7
5	Dubacherla, W.G (Dist)	1	4	5	2	6	3	7
6	Angaluru, Krishna (Dist)	1	2	3	4	5	6	7
7	Boyapalem, Guntur (Dist)	4	2	3	1	6	7	5
8	Mynampadu, Prakasam (Dist)	7	2	3	1	6	4	5
9	Pallepadu, Nellore (Dist)	5	2	1	6	4	7	3
10	Rayachoty, Cuddapah (Dist)	3	1	4	7	5	2	6
11	Karvetinagar, Chittoor (Dist)	3	1	4	7	5	2	6

S.No	Name of the DIET	Order of preference from 1-7						
		Lecture method	*Lecture demonstration method*	*Demonstration method*	*Activity Method*	*Project method*	*Discussion method*	*Seminar method*
12	Bukkapatnam, Ananthapur (Dist)	2	3	4	1	7	6	5
13	B.Thandrapadu, Kurnool (Dist)	2	3	4	1	7	6	5
14	Mahabubnagar (Dist)	4	3	7	5	6	1	2
15	Neredmet, Hyderabad (Dist)	5	4	3	1	2	6	7
16	Vikarabad, Ranga Reddy (Dist)	1	7	2	3	4	5	6
17	Haveilighanapur, Medak (Dist)	5	3	4	1	2	6	7
18	LMD colony, Karimnagar (Dist)	7	4	5	1	3	2	6
19	Nagaram, Nizamabad (Dist)	7	6	5	1	2	4	3
20	Adilabad (Dist)	5	2	3	4	6	1	7
21	Khammam (Dist)	6	3	2	1	5	4	7
22	Warangal (Dist)	7	2	3	1	4	5	6
23	Nalgonda (Dist)	3	5	4	2	7	1	6

Table 4.15. Table Showing the Number of Academic Activities Organized by the DIETs

S.No	*Name of the DIET*	*Number of activities*		
		Seminars	*Workshops*	*Conferences*
1	Vomaravalli, srikakulam (Dist)	1	6	0
2	V.G.puram, VZM(Dist)	1	4	1
3	Bheemunipatnam, VSP (Dist)	2	13	1
4	Bommuru, E.G (Dist)	2	6	16
5	Dubacherla, W.G (Dist)	5	1	0
6	Angaluru, Krishna (Dist)	10	17	10
7	Boyapalem, Guntur (Dist)	1	3	0
8	Mynampadu, Prakasam (Dist)	0	12	6
9	Pallepadu, Nellore (Dist)	3	6	0
10	Rayachoty, Cuddapah (Dist)	5	13	2
11	Karvetinagar, Chittoor (Dist)	0	8	0
12	Bukkapatnam, Ananthapur (Dist)	0	2	0
13	B.Thandrapadu, Kurnool (Dist)	3	2	0
14	Mahabubnagar (Dist)	0	6	2
15	Neredmet, Hyderabad (Dist)	6	5	5
16	Vikarabad, Ranga Reddy (Dist)	0	2	0
17	Haveilighanapur, Medak (Dist)	5	5	5
18	LMD colony, Karimnagar (Dist)	0	13	0
19	Nagaram, Nizamabad (Dist)	1	9	0
20	Adilabad (Dist)	2	6	0
21	Khammam (Dist)	2	7	6
22	Warangal (Dist)	2	6	0
23	Nalgonda (Dist)	1	10	0

It is observed that the position of non-teaching posts in DIETs is more or less the same.

Except three DIETs namely Rayachoty, Neredmet and haveliighanapur all the other twenty DIETs working with the Superintendent in office.

As per the MHRD Guidelines one Senior Assistant post shall be sanctioned for each DIET. Except two DIETs namely Angaluru and Haveliighanapur all the other twenty one DIETs remained with Senior Assistant post.

As per the MHRD Guidelines nine Junior Assistant posts are sanctioned for each DIET. But no DIET positioned the any posts. Twelve DIETs namely Venugopalapuram, Bheemunipatnam, Dubacherla, Angaluru, Mahabubnagar, Vikarabad, Haveliighanapur, LMD.Colony, Nagaram, Khammam, Warangal and Nalgonda positioned nine posts each at the maximum number. Whereas DIET Karvetinagar positioned two posts only. It is further inferred that as per the MHRD Guidelines a Steno-cum-Typist post is sanctioned to the Vice Principal. But it is not positioned by a few DIETs namely Vomaravalli, Dubacherla, Angaluru, Karvetinagar, Neredmet, Vikarabad, Havelighanapur, Adilabad, Warangal and Nalgonda. All the other thirteen DIETs did position the post.

Table 4.16. Table Showing the Number of Faculty Posts Filled and Working in DIETs

S.No	Name of the DIET	Number of teaching staff working			
		Senior lecturers	Lecturers	Craft teachers	Teacher people ratios in DIETs
1	Vomaravalli, srikakulam (Dist)	1	8	0	1:20
2	V.G.puram, VZM(Dist)	4	12	0	1:11
3	Bheemunipatnam, VSP (Dist)	7	8	0	1:13
4	Bommuru, E.G (Dist)	6	15	0	1:10
5	Dubacherla, W.G (Dist)	4	5	0	1:25
6	Angaluru, Krishna (Dist)	3	11	0	1:14
7	Boyapalem, Guntur (Dist)	3	15	0	1:16
8	Mynampadu, Prakasam (Dist)	4	4	0	1:25
9	Pallepadu, Nellore (Dist)	3	9	1	1:23
10	Rayachoty, Cuddapah (Dist)	4	9	0	1:23
11	Karvetinagar, Chittoor (Dist)	5	13	0	1:11
12	Bukkapatnam, Ananthapur (Dist)	2	9	0	1:18
13	B.Thandrapadu, Kurnool (Dist)	6	12	1	1:15
14	Mahabubnagar (Dist)	7	9	0	1:20
15	Neredmet, Hyderabad (Dist)	3	13	0	1:20
16	Vikarabad, Ranga Reddy (Dist)	6	14	0	1:15
17	Haveilighanapur, Medak (Dist)	5	3	0	1:37
18	LMD colony, Karimnagar (Dist)	4	10	1	1:20
19	Nagaram, Nizamabad (Dist)	6	8	1	1:20
20	Adilabad (Dist)	4	5	0	1:20
21	Khammam (Dist)	5	4	0	1:22
22	Warangal (Dist)	7	14	0	1:15
23	Nalgonda (Dist)	7	10	0	1:12

MHRD Guidelines suggests one Steno-cum-Typist post for each DIET (for Vice-Principal, which in not designated in Andhra Pradesh DIETs). Thirteen DIETs have Steno post and the other ten DIETs do not have the post.

MHRD Guidelines suggested one technician post for the maintenance of Educational Technology equipment for each DIET. It is noticed that the only DIET Bhimunipatnam has positioned the technician post in the state.

The MHRD Guidelines suggested one Librarian post for each DIET. It is observed that no DIET in the state has the Librarian post, got filled so far.

As per the MHRD Guidelines two Laboratory Assistant posts are provisioned for every DIET. But it is observed that, the posts are positioned by only very few DIETs namely Mynampadu and Adilabad, whereas Mahabubnagar, LMD.Colony and Khammam have positioned one laboratory assistant post one each, out of two laboratory assistant posts sanctioned as per MHRD Guidelines.

MHRD Guidelines suggests there shall be ten Attender posts for each DIET. It is evidenced that only one DIET namely Nalgonda positioned all the ten Attender posts. B.Thandrapadu positioned only three Attender posts. All the other DIETs positioned in varying number from four to nine.

As per the MHRD Guidelines there is one Superintendent post, one Senior Assistant (accountant) post, nine Junior Assistant posts, one Typist-cum-Steno post and one Steno post one Technician post, one Librarian post, two Laboratory Assistant posts and ten Attender posts, for each DIET

It is also observed that Angaluru and Havelighanapur DIETs did not fill the Senior Assistant posts. The vacancy position of Lecturer posts is held by different DIETs of Andhra Pradesh differently as the maximum number of seven vacancies are in DIET Karvetinagar no vacancies by eleven DIETs namely Venugopalapuram, Bheemunipatnam, Dubacherla, Angaluru, Mahabubnagar, Vikarabad, Havelighanapur, LMD.Colony, Nagaram, Khammam and Nalgonda.

It is also informed that ten DIETs namely Vomaravalli, Dubacherla, Angaluru, Karvetinagar Neredmet, Vikarabad, Havelighanapur, Adilabad, Warangal and Khammam did not fill the Typist-cum-Steno post. But as far as Steno post is concerned no DIET in Andhra Pradesh attempted to fill the post.

Excepting Bheemunipatnam all the other twenty two DIETs possess vacancy of Technician post. No DIET in Andhra Pradesh filled the post of Librarian nineteen DIETs possess two

Table 4.16a. Table Showing Vacancy Position in DIETs

S.No	Name of the DIET	Number of teaching vacancies			
		Principal	Senior lecturers	Lecturers	Craft teachers
1	Vomaravalli, srikakulam (Dist)	0	6	8	1
2	V.G.puram, VZM(Dist)	0	3	5	1
3	Bheemunipatnam, VSP (Dist)	0	0	8	1
4	Bommuru, E.G (Dist)	0	1	2	1
5	Dubacherla, W.G (Dist)	0	3	11	1
6	Angaluru, Krishna (Dist)	1	4	6	1
7	Boyapalem, Guntur (Dist)	0	4	2	1
8	Mynampadu, Prakasam (Dist)	1	3	12	1
9	Pallepadu, Nellore (Dist)	0	4	8	0
10	Rayachoty Cuddapah (Dist)	0	3	7	1
11	Karvetinagar, Chittoor (Dist)	1	2	4	1
12	Bukkapatnam, Ananthapur (Dist)	0	5	8	1
13	B.Thandrapadu, Kurnool (Dist)	0	1	5	0
14	Mahabubnagar (Dist)	0	0	8	1
15	Neredmet, Hyderabad (Dist)	0	4	4	1
16	Vikarabad, Ranga Reddy (Dist)	0	1	3	1
17	Haveilighanapur, Medak (Dist)	0	2	13	1
18	LMD colony, Karimnagar (Dist)	1	3	6	0
19	Nagaram, Nizamabad (Dist)	0	1	9	0
20	Adilabad (Dist)	0	3	12	1
21	Khammam (Dist)	0	2	12	1
22	Warangal (Dist)	0	0	3	1
23	Nalgonda (Dist)	0	0	7	1

Laboratory Assistant posts vacant and three DIETs namely Mahabubnagar, Nagaram, and Khammam posses one vacant Laboratory Assistant post each whereas Mynampadu and Adilabad did not possess any vacancy of Laboratory Assistant posts.

As far as the vacancy position of Attenders are concerned it is observed that only Nalgonda possess no vacancy where as B.Thandrapadu possess seven Attender posts vacant. All the other DIETs maintain one or more (usually upto six) vacancies of Attender posts.

All the DIETs in the state have conducted almost similar training programmes.

Among them content enrichment programme rated by Principals as high calculating to 53/69 at the first rank, the preparation of TLM and its use scored 49/69 and second place,

Table 4.17. Table Showing Number of Non-Teaching Posts Filled and Persons Working in DIETs

Sl.No.	*Name of the DIET*	*No. of posts in which working*								
		Office Superintendent	*Senior assts*	*Junior assts*	*Typists*	*Steno*	*Technicians*	*Librarians*	*Lab assts*	*Attenders*
1	Vomaravalli, srikakulam (Dist)	1	1	5	0	0	0	0	0	8
2	V.G.puram, VZM(Dist)	1	1	9	1	0	0	0	0	5
3	Bheemunipatnam, VSP (Dist)	1	1	9	1	0	1	0	0	4
4	Bommuru, E.G (Dist)	1	1	8	1	0	0	0	0	8
5	Dubacherla, W.G (Dist)	1	1	9	0	0	0	0	0	6
6	Angaluru, Krishna (Dist)	1	0	9	0	0	0	0	0	6
7	Boyapalem, Guntur (Dist)	1	1	8	1	0	0	0	0	4
8	Mynampadu, Prakasam (Dist)	1	1	8	1	0	0	0	2	8
9	Pallepadu, Nellore (Dist)	1	1	8	1	0	0	0	0	5
10	Rayachoty, Cuddapah (Dist)	0	1	8	1	0	0	0	0	5
11	Karvetinagar, Chittoor (Dist)	1	1	2	0	0	0	0	0	5
12	Bukkapatnam, Ananthapur (Dist)	1	1	5	1	0	0	0	0	4
13	B.Thandrapadu, Kurnool (Dist)	1	1	5	1	0	0	0	0	3
14	Mahabubnagar (Dist)	1	1	9	1	0	0	0	1	6
15	Neredmet, Hyderabad (Dist)	0	1	8	0	0	0	0	0	6
16	Vikarabad, Ranga Reddy (Dist)	1	1	9	0	0	0	0	0	5
17	Haveilighanapur, Medak (Dist)	0	0	9	0	0	0	0	0	8
18	LMD colony, Karimnagar (Dist)	1	1	9	1	0	0	0	0	5
19	Nagaram, Nizamabad (Dist)	1	1	9	1	0	0	0	1	7
20	Adilabad (Dist)	1	1	8	0	0	0	0	2	7
21	Khammam (Dist)	1	1	9	1	0	0	0	1	7
22	Warangal (Dist)	1	1	9	0	0	0	0	0	5
23	Nalgonda (Dist)	1	1	9	0	0	0	0	0	10

Methodology development occupied third place by scoring 46/69 i.e. third rank where as the fourth place is occupied by two programmes namely developing positive attitude and action research and finally the motivation and innovative practices programme score 37 and secured fifth rank.

It is also analysed that ranking of DIET wise training programmes by the Principals concerned, which depicts the level of quality of the training programmes conducted in DIETs.

The traning programmes conducted in DIET Venugopalapuram scored highest score of 16/18, Boyapatem and Neredmet scored next highest i.e. 15/18th whereas Bukkapatnam, B.Thandrapadu and Nagaram scored the least i.e. 8.18 each in quality of training programmes.

All the 23 DIETs have been conducting in-service training programmes from centrally sponsored schemes and DPEP/SSA in one month or other in the same pattern as specified uniformly as per the common schedule. The programmes namely content enrichment training programme, Work-Experience Training Programme, training on foundations, children language improvement programme, quality improvement programme, preparation of teaching learning material, class I.II Mathematics text books preparation, action research for teachers and orientation on school complex meetings.

It is observed that the DIET Warangal, Bheemunipatnam and Nagaram encouraged and facilitated faculty members to the maximum possible extent to do eight and six M.Phil degrees respectively. Whereas a few DIETs did not encourage their faculty at all namely Angaluru, Mynampadu, Rayachoty, Mahabubnagar and Khammam. The number of other DIETs faculty who did M.Phil degrees vary from one to five members per DIET.

While with regards to Ph.D degree four DIETs namely Bheemunipatnam, B.Thandrapadu, Neredmet and Nagaram encouraged faculty members to prosecute three research degrees each. Whereas ten DIETs did not encourage even one faculty member for Ph.D degree, namely Angaluru, Boyapalem, Mynampadu, Rayachoty, Bukkapatnam, Mahabubnagar, Havelighanapur, Adilabad, Khammam and Nalgonda. The other DIETs vary in possessing faculty members with Ph.D degree from one to two members each.

In some DIETs a few faculty members' research work is in progress the number vary from four to one. Bheemunipatnam and Neredmet posses four members each and seven DIETs did not possess any such faculty members namely Venugopalapuram, Angaluru, Boyapalem, Rayachoty, Nagaram, Adilabad and Khammam.

As a whole DIET Bheemunipatnam encouraged thirteen research degrees Neredmet twelve research degrees and Nagaram nine research degrees. The other DIETs vary in possessing faculty members with Ph.D degrees from one to two members each.

Table 4.17a. Table Showing Vacancy Position of Non-Teaching Posts in DIETs

Sl. No	*Name of the DIET*	*Number of non-teaching vacancies*								
		Office Superintendent	*Senior assts*	*Junior assts*	*Typists*	*Technicians*	*Librarians*	*Lab assts*	*Attenders*	*Steno*
1	Vomaravalli, srikakulam (Dist)	0	0	4	1	1	1	2	2	1
2	V.G.puram, VZM(Dist)	0	0	0	0	1	1	2	5	1
3	Bheemunipatnam, VSP (Dist)	0	0	0	0	0	1	2	6	1
4	Bommuru, E.G (Dist)	0	0	1	0	1	1	2	2	1
5	Dubacherla, W.G (Dist)	0	0	0	1	1	1	2	4	1
6	Angaluru, Krishna (Dist)	0	1	0	1	1	1	2	4	1
7	Boyapalem, Guntur (Dist)	0	0	1	0	1	1	2	6	1
8	Mynampadu, Prakasam (Dist)	0	0	1	0	1	1	0	2	1
9	Pallepadu, Nellore (Dist)	0	0	1	0	1	1	2	5	1
10	Rayachoty, Cuddapah (Dist)	1	0	1	0	1	1	2	5	1
11	Karvetinagar, Chittoor (Dist)	0	0	7	1	1	1	2	5	1

Sl. No	Name of the DIET	Number of non-teaching vacancies								
		Office Superintendent	Senior assts	Junior assts	Typists	Technicians	Librarians	Lab assts	Attenders	Steno
15	Neredmet, Hyderabad (Dist)	1	0	1	1	1	1	2	4	1
16	Vikarabad, Ranga Reddy (Dist)	0	0	0	1	1	1	2	5	1
17	Haveilighanapur, Medak (Dist)	1	1	0	1	1	1	2	3	1
18	LMD colony, Karimnagar (Dist)	0	0	0	0	1	1	2	5	1
19	Nagaram, Nizamabad (Dist)	0	0	0	0	1	1	1	2	1
20	Adilabad (Dist)	0	0	1	1	1	1	0	3	1
21	Khammam (Dist)	0	0	0	0	1	1	1	3	1
22	Warangal (Dist)	0	0	5	1	1	1	2	5	1
23	Nalgonda (Dist)	0	0	0	1	1	1	2	0	1

The DIET faculty also participated in many research training programmes the number vary from DIET to DIET. The maximum number of six programmes attended by DIET staff of Mynampadu, Mahabubnagar, and Neredmet. Whereas the least number of training programmes were attended i.e. one each by the staff of Bukkapatnam and LMD.Colony.

It is noticed that the number of research training programmes organized by DIETs also vary from DIET to DIET. One programme each by Venugopalapuram, Boyapalem, Bukkapatnam, LMD.Colony and Khammam the maximum number of programmes organized is about six by DIET Mahabubnagar. The other DIETs vary in number from two to five programmes.

It is also computed that the number of school teachers trained in research training programmes greatly vary from DIET to DIET. The maximum number was 342 by DIET nagaram and the minimum number is twenty by DIET Adilabad. The other DIETs vary in involvement from twenty four to three hundred.

The number of action researches done by faculty and teachers is also vary in number from DIET to DIET. The maximum number encouraged is 154 by DIET Bheemunipatnam. The minimum number is ten by DIET Angaluru.

The National Council for teacher education has set forth certain norms incorporated in the MHRD Guidelines about the quality, physical and human resources to be provided for DIETs. The state Government provided the resources differently for different DIETs due to local variations and local needs and existing conditions. This is based on the self rating by the Principals of the DIETs. The details are discussed below:

Keeping 23 DIETs together it is noted that out of the maximum 69 value points, if any item scores 34.5, it can be viewed asper NCTE norms. If the score is < 34.5 it is below norms and if it is > 34.5 above norms.

It is inferred from the table about the strengths of teaching staff, all the DIETs rating put together, scored upto 35/69 secured the least score, whereas the qualifications of the staff scoring 53/69 and ranked first among the twelve items.

Table 4.18. Table Showing In-service Training Programmes Conducted in DIETs and Self Rated by Principals as Excellent, above Average and Average and Quantified as 3,2,1 Respectively

SI.No	*Name of the DIET*	*Content enrichment*	*Methodology development*	*Developing Positive attitude*	*Preparation of TLM and its use*	*Action Research orientation*	*Motivation & innovative practices*
1	Vomaravalli, srikakulam (Dist) III	3	2	2	2	2	2
2	V.G.puram, VZM(Dist) II	3	3	3	3	2	2
3	Bheemunipatnam, VSP (Dist) III	3	2	2	2	3	1
4	Bommuru, E.G (Dist)	2	2	1	2	1	1
5	Dubacherla, W.G (Dist)	1	2	1	3	3	1
6	Angaluru, Krishna (Dist) II	3	2	2	3	2	2
7	Boyapalem, Guntur (Dist) I	3	2	2	2	3	3
8	Mynampadu, Prakasam (Dist) III	3	2	2	3	1	2
9	Pallepadu, Nellore (Dist)	2	1	2	2	1	1
10	Rayachoty, Cuddapah (Dist)	2	2	2	1	1	1
11	Karvetinagar, Chittoor (Dist)	3	3	1	2	2	1
12	Bukkapatnam, Ananthapur (Dist)	1	1	2	1	1	2

Sl.No	*Name of the DIET*	*Content enrichment*	*Methodology development*	*Developing Positive attitude*	*Preparation of TLM and its use*	*Action Research orientation*	*Motivation & innovative practices*
13	B.Thandrapadu, Kurnool (Dist)	2	1	1	1	1	2
14	Mahabubnagar (Dist) II	3	2	3	2	2	2
15	Neredmet, Hyderabad (Dist) I	3	3	2	3	2	2
16	Vikarabad, Ranga Reddy (Dist) III	2	2	1	3	3	2
17	Haveilighanapur, Medak (Dist)	2	2	2	2	2	2
18	LMD colony, Karimnagar (Dist)	2	2	2	2	2	1
19	Nagaram, Nizamabad (Dist)	2	2	1	1	1	1
20	Adilabad (Dist)	2	2	1	2	1	1
21	Khammam (Dist)	2	2	2	2	2	1
22	Warangal (Dist) III	2	2	2	3	2	2
23	Nalgonda (Dist)	2	2	1	2	1	2

Table 4.19. Area F

Table Showing In-service Training Programmes Organized by DIETs

Sl. No	Name of the DIET	Content enrichment	Work-Experience	Foundation	CLIP	QIP	TLM workshop	Class I, II Mathematics books	Action research	School complex
1	Vomaravalli, srikakulam (Dist)	1	1	1	1	1	1	1	1	1
2	V.G.puram, VZM(Dist)	1	1	1	1	1	1	1	1	1
3	Bheemunipatnam, VSP (Dist)	1	1	1	1	1	1	1	1	1
4	Bommuru, E.G (Dist)	0	0	0	1	1	0	0	0	0
5	Dubacherla, W.G (Dist)	0	0	0	0	0	0	0	0	0
6	Angaluru, Krishna (Dist)	0	0	0	0	0	0	0	0	0
7	Boyapalem, Guntur (Dist)	0	0	0	1	0	0	0	0	1
8	Mynampadu, Prakasam (Dist)	1	1	0	0	0	0	0	0	0
9	Pallepadu, Nellore (Dist)	0	0	0	1	1	0	0	0	0
10	Rayachoty, Cuddapah (Dist)	0	1	0	1	0	0	0	0	1
11	Karvetinagar, Chittoor (Dist)	0	0	0	0	0	0	0	0	0
12	Bukkapatnam, Ananthapur (Dist)	0	1	0	0	0	0	0	0	0

Sl. No	Name of the DIET	Content enrichment	Work-Experience	Foundation	CLIP	QIP	TLM workshop	Class I, II Mathematics books	Action research	School complex
13	B.Thandrapadu, Kurnool (Dist)	0	1	0	0	0	0	0	0	1
14	Mahabubnagar (Dist)	0	0	0	0	0	0	0	0	0
15	Neredmet, Hyderabad (Dist)	0	1	0	0	0	0	0	0	1
16	Vikarabad, Ranga Reddy (Dist)	0	0	0	1	0	0	0	0	0
17	Haveilighanapur, Medak (Dist)	0	0	0	0	0	0	0	0	0
18	LMD colony, Karimnagar (Dist)	0	1	0	1	0	0	0	0	1
19	Nagaram, Nizamabad (Dist)	0	0	0	0	0	0	0	0	0
20	Adilabad (Dist)	0	0	0	1	1	0	1	0	0
21	Khammam (Dist)	0	0	0	1	1	1	0	0	0
22	Warangal (Dist)	0	0	0	1	0	0	0	0	0
23	Nalgonda (Dist)	0	0	0	0	1	0	0	0	0

Please Note: 1 – indicates positive answer
0 – indicate negative answere

Table 4.20. Table Showing Research Work done by DIET Faculty, Training Programmes Attended and Conducted by Faculty for Action Research by Teachers

SI. No	*Name of the DIET*	*M.Phil.*	*Ph.D.*	*Still doing research*	*Research training programmes participated by faculty*	*Organized research programs*	*Teachers trained*	*Action research done and guided by the staff*
1	Vomaravalli, srikakulam (Dist)	4	1	1	2	2	200	56
2	V.G.puram, VZM(Dist)	2	2	0	4	1	43	21
3	Bheemunipatnam, VSP (Dist)	6	3	4	4	2	300	154
4	Bommuru, E.G (Dist)	3	2	2	2	3	96	68
5	Dubacherla, W.G (Dist)	2	1	1	2	2	150	50
6	Angaluru, Krishna (Dist)	0	0	0	2	2	100	10
7	Boyapalem, Guntur (Dist)	2	0	0	5	1	77	34
8	Mynampadu, Prakasam (Dist)	0	0	3	6	4	100	25
9	Pallepadu, Nellore (Dist)	2	1	2	2	2	100	100
10	Rayachoty, Cuddapah (Dist)	0	0	0	5	4	150	115
11	Karvetinagar, Chittoor (Dist)	1	2	1	2	3	120	93
12	Bukkapatnam, Ananthapur (Dist)	1	0	1	1	1	100	110
13	B.Thandrapadu, Kurnool (Dist)	1	3	2	2	2	100	27

SI. No	*Name of the DIET*	*M.Phil.*	*Ph.D.*	*Still doing research*	*Research training programmes participated by faculty*	*Organized research programs*	*Teachers trained*	*Action research done and guided by the staff*
14	Mahabubnagar (Dist)	0	0	3	6	6	150	100
15	Neredmet, Hyderabad (Dist)	5	3	4	6	2	84	28
16	Vikarabad, Ranga Reddy (Dist)	2	1	1	4	2	60	60
17	Haveilighanapur, Medak (Dist)	3	0	2	4	2	70	40
18	LMD colony, Karimnagar (Dist)	3	2	3	1	1	24	28
19	Nagaram, Nizamabad (Dist)	6	3	0	4	4	342	56
20	Adilabad (Dist)	1	0	0	5	2	20	14
21	Khammam (Dist)	0	0	0	3	1	150	23
22	Warangal (Dist)	8	1	1	2	2	180	100
23	Nalgonda (Dist)	1	0	1	2	3	130	36

Table 4.21. Area H

Table Showing Developmental Aspects of DIETs as Self Rated by Principals

Sl. No	Name of the DIET	Man Power		Physical facilities					Equipment				
		Teaching Staff	*Qualifications of staff*	*Administrative accommodation*	*Academic accommodation*	*Hostel accommodation*	*Science labs*	*Physical Education accommodation*	*Educational technology*	*Work-Experience / work shops / Craft*	*Art Education*	*Games / sports*	*Furniture*
1	Vomaravalli, srikakulam (Dist)	b	a	b	c	c	b	c	c	c	c	c	b
2	V.G.puram, VZM(Dist)	b	b	b	b	b	b	b	b	b	b	b	b
3	Bheemunipatnam, VSP (Dist)	b	a	b	b	b	b	b	b	b	c	b	b
4	Bommuru, E.G (Dist)	c	b	c	c	c	b	c	c	c	c	c	c
5	Dubacherla, W.G (Dist)	b	b	b	b	b	c	c	c	b	c	b	c
6	Angaluru, Krishna (Dist)	c	b	b	b	b	b	b	b	b	b	b	b
7	Boyapalem, Guntur (Dist)	c	a	b	b	b	b	b	b	b	b	b	b
8	Mynampadu, Prakasam (Dist)	c	b	b	b	b	b	b	b	b	b	b	b
9	Pallepadu, Nellore (Dist)	b	b	a	b	b	b	b	a	b	b	b	b
10	Rayachoty, Cuddapah (Dist)	c	b	b	b	b	c	b	a	a	c	c	b
11	Karvetinagar, Chittoor (Dist)	c	b	b	b	c	b	c	c	c	c	c	c
12	Bukkapatnam, Ananthapur (Dist)	c	b	c	c	c	c	c	b	c	c	c	c

Sl. No	Name of the DIET	Man Power		Physical facilities					Equipment				
		Teaching Staff	Qualifications of staff	Administrative accommodation	Academic accommodation	Hostel accommodation	Science labs	Physical Education accommodation	Educational technology	Work-Experience / work shops / Craft	Art Education	Games / sports	Furniture
13	B.Thandrapadu, Kurnool (Dist)	c	b	b	b	b	b	b	b	b	c	c	b
14	Mahabubnagar (Dist)	b	a	a	b	b	b	b	a	b	b	b	b
15	Neredmet, Hyderabad (Dist)	c	b	b	b	b	b	b	b	b	b	b	b
16	Vikarabad, Ranga Reddy (Dist)	b	a	a	a	a	a	a	a	a	a	a	a
17	Haveilighanapur, Medak (Dist)	c	b	b	b	b	b	b	b	b	b	b	b
18	LMD colony, Karimnagar (Dist)	b	a	b	c	b	b	b	b	b	c	b	b
19	Nagaram, Nizamabad (Dist)	c	b	c	c	c	c	c	c	c	c	c	c
20	Adilabad (Dist)	c	b	b	c	c	b	c	b	b	b	b	b
21	Khammam (Dist)	b	b	b	b	b	b	b	b	b	c	b	c
22	Warangal (Dist)	a	a	b	b	b	b	b	b	b	b	b	b
23	Nalgonda (Dist)	b	b	b	b	b	b	c	b	b	c	c	b

Please note: a – indicates more than NCTE norms
b – indicates as per NCTE norms
c – indicates less than NCTE norms

Considering the physical facilities (accommodation for different purposes) administrative accommodation ranked 2nd, scoring 46/69 value points. The Science laboratory accommodation occupied the next place i.e. 4th rank by scoring 43/69 value points. The academic accommodation achieved 5th rank by scoring 41/69 value points. Hostel accommodation achieved 6th rank by scoring 41/69 value points. The Physical Education accommodation achieved 7th rank by scoring 39/69 value points.

Considering the equipment available in the institutions, the Educational Technology equipment achieved 3rd rank by scoring 45/69 value points. On the other hand Work Experience and Craft securea 4th rank by scoring 43/69 value points. The availability of institute furniture secured 6th rank by scoring 41/69 value points. The games sports equipment secured 7th rank by scoring 39/69 value points and ultimately Art education secured 8th rank by scoring 35/69 value points.

Considering the individual DIETs ranking by the Principals DIETs, when 18/36 being the normal score (as per the NCTE norms) keeping all reasources of a DIET together, DIET Vikarabad scored high of all the twenty three DIETs scoring 35/36 the highest score whereas Pallepadu and Mahabubnagar scoring 26/36 and 27/36 respectively. Bukkapatnam secured 14/36 the least score among the 23 DIETs.

SECTION – B

ANALYSIS AND INTERPRETATION OF OPINIONS OF THE D.ED (PRE-SERVICE) TEACHER TRAINEES

The following is the analysis and interpretation of the calculations of the opinions collected from D.Ed teacher trainees of 23 DIETs of Andhra Pradesh (Sample 345). The opinions of the trainees are computed and mean, standard deviation values are arrived. The 't' test and ANOVA are used to find out the difference of significance of the opinions of D.Ed teacher trainees, with reference to the independent variables.

Table 4.1. Sex-wise Distribution of Sample D.Ed Teacher Trainees

Sl.No.	*Sex*	*Frequency*	*Percent*
1	**Male**	183	53.0
2	**Female**	162	47.0
	Total	345	100.0

Table 1 shows that majority respondents are male i.e. 183(53%) and female 162 (47%) constituted, from the sample.

Table 4.2. Table Showing Age-wise Distribution of D.Ed Teacher Trainees

Sl.No.	*Age group*	*Frequency*	*Percent*
1	**Below 20 years**	230	66.7
2	**Above 20 years**	115	33.3
	Total	345	100.0

Table 2 indicates that there are 230 (66.7%) respondents, who are below 20 years age group and the rest of the respondents 115 (33.3%) belong to above 20 years age group. The below 20 years respondents are more than above 20 years respondents.

Table 4.3. Table Showing Nativity Wise Distribution of D.Ed Teacher Trainees

Sl.No.	*Nativity*	*Frequency*	*Percent*
1	**Rural**	235	68.1
2	**Urban**	102	29.6
3	**Tribal**	8	2.3
	Total	345	100.0

As per the table 3 out of 345 respondents majority 235 (68.1%) belong to rural area, and 102 (29.6%) belong to urban area whereas 08 (2.3%) belong to tribal area.

Table 4.4. Table Showing Community wise Distribution of Sample of D.Ed Teacher Trainees

Sl.No.	*Community*	*Frequency*	*Percent*
1	**Open category (OC)**	**109**	**31.6**
2	**Backward class (BC)**	**175**	**50.7**
3	**Other backward class (OBC)**	**9**	**2.6**
4	**Scheduled castes (SC)**	**36**	**10.4**
5	**Scheduled tribes (ST)**	**16**	**4.6**
	Total	**345**	**100.0**

Table 4 reveals the community classification of the respondents. The majority of the respondents (i.e.) 175 (52.13%) belong to backward class and the second place occupied by open category (OC) (i.e.) 109 (31.6%), whereas 36 (10.4%) belonging to scheduled castes, and the rest 16(4.6%) belonging to scheduled tribes.

Table 4.5 Table Showing Locality Wise Distribution of DIETs in the State

Sl.No.	*Locality of the DiETs*	*Frequency of DIETs*	*Percent*
1	**Rural**	**14**	**60.94**
2	**Urban**	**6**	**26.04**
3	**Sub-urban**	**3**	**13.02**
	Total	**23**	**100.0**

Table 5 shows the location of the 23 DIETs in the state. They are located in three areas such as 14(60.94%) in rural areas, 6(26.04%) in urban areas and 3(13.02%) in sub-urban areas.

Table 4.6. Table Showing Marital Status-Wise Distribution of D.Ed Teacher Trainees

Sl.No.	*Marital status*	*Frequency*	*Percent*
1	**Unmarried**	**326**	**94.5**
2	**Married**	**19**	**5.5**
	Total	**345**	**100.0**

According to table 6 there are 326 (94.5%) respondents who are unmarried and 19(5.5%) married out of the total 345 respondents.

Table 4.7. Table Showing Educational Qualifications Wise Distribution of D.Ed and Trainees

Sl.No.	*Educational qualification (general)*	*Trainees frequency*	*Percent of trainees*
1	**Intermediate**	285	82.6
2	**Degree**	58	16.8
3	**Post-graduation**	2	0.6
	Total	345	100.0

Table 7 speaks about the educational qualifications of the respondents. The majority of the respondents (i.e.) 285 (82.6%) possess the general qualification of intermediate, whereas 58(16.6%) possess degree and 02(0.6%) got post graduation out of 345 sample teacher trainees.

Table 4.8. Table Showing the Mean Difference of the Opinions of Male and Female D.Ed Teacher Trainees and the Level of Significance of Difference of Opinions

Grouping: Sex Group 1:Male (183) Group 2:Female (162)					
Area of activities	*Male*		*Female*		*t value*
	Mean	*Standard deviation*	*Mean*	*Standard deviation*	
A. Facilities and resources	25.27	5.24	27.36	3.99	4.13**
B. Instruction	21.35	3.61	22.72	3.07	3.76**
C. Co-curricular and Extra curricular Activities	20.90	3.78	22.68	3.46	4.55**
D. Field work and Records	37.90	4.23	39.25	3.63	3.16**

**Significant at 0.01 level.

The table 8 explains the mean variations between male and female teacher trainees opinion on the different areas of activities.

To find out the levels of difference of significance between male and female trainees on these areas. It is employed a statistical tool called 't'-test, with the help of which we can find out the level of significance of difference in their opinion. According to the above table, the opinion on facilities and resources, the mean score of males is 25.27 and of the females is 27.36, which is higher than the male. The standard deviations of male and female trainees are 5.24 and 3.99 respectively. And the 't'-value 4.13 shows to be significant at 0.01 level. Hence the null hypothesis is rejected. This shows that the female trainees opinion on facilities and resources is significantly more than the male trainees opinion. This may be due to female trainees spend more time towards academic aspects and study than the male trainees.

In the instruction area the means of the male and female trainees are 21.35 and 22.72 respectively and the standard deviations are 3.619 and 3.07, respectively. The obtained 't' value 3.76 is significant at 0.01 level. Hence the null hypothesis is rejected. This shows that female trainees' opinion on instructional activities is significantly favourable than that of the male trainees. This may be due to female trainees paying more attention towards classroom instruction and other academic activities.

Regarding the area Co-curricular and Extra-curricular Activities the mean scores of female trainees is 22.68, whereas the males is 20.90. The standard deviations are 3.46 and 3.78 respectively. The employed 't' value 4.55 is significant at 0.01 level. Hence the null hypothesis is rejected. This shows that the opinion of female trainees in respect to Co-curricular and Extra curricular Activities is significantly better than the male trainees. Why because generally the females show more interest in Co-curricular and Extra-curricular Activities which are one way or other linked to their cultural background.

In the same way the opinions regarding the area fieldwork and records the derived mean scores of male and female trainees are 37.90 and 39.25 respectively. And the standard deviations are 4.23 and 3.63. The generated 't'-value 3.16 is significant at 0.01 level. Hence the null hypothesis is rejected. This shows that the female trainees are better in the activities of fieldwork and records than male trainees. This may be because the female trainees prepare records more neatly than males. Moreover the female trainees prepare more carefully for fieldwork than male trainees. Moreover female trainees hand writing in plans and records is more neat and legible than that of males.

In all the above four areas the opinions of the female trainees is far more significantly better than the male trainees. This may be because the female trainees put more sincere efforts than male trainees. Females generally do not go out frequently for visiting new places and movies. Hence females find more time to concentrate on studies and writing lesson plans records, and notes.

Fig. 4.1. Graph Showing the Mean Difference of the Opinions of Male and Female D.Ed Teacher Trainees and the Level of Significance of Difference of Opinions

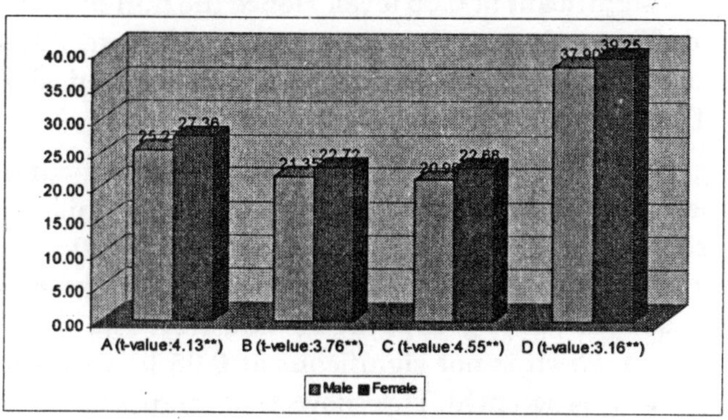

Table 4.9. Table Showing Mean, Mean Difference of Opinions of Below 20 Years and Above 20 Years Aged Trainees, on the Four Areas of DIET Activities

Grouping: Age *Group 1: Below 20 years (230)* *Group 2:Above 20 years (115)*					
Area of activities	*Below 20 years*		*Above 20 years*		*t value*
	Mean	*Standard deviation*	*Mean*	*Standard deviation*	
A. Facilities and resources	26.50	4.15	25.74	5.88	1.40
B. Instruction	22.11	3.40	21.75	3.49	0.93
C. Co-curricular and Extra curricular Activities	21.84	3.50	21.52	4.17	0.74
D. Field work and Records	38.41	4.13	38.77	3.78	0.77

The above table explains about the mean difference of different areas between the two age groups. In the facilities and resources area the opinion of below 20 aged trainees mean score is 26.50 and that of above 20 years aged trainers is 25.74 and the standard deviations of the above two groups are 4.15 and 5.88 respectively. The obtained 't' value 1.40 is not significant at both levels. Hence the null hypothesis is accepted. This shows that there is no significant difference between the above two age groups in their opinions regarding the area.

As far as instructional activities are concerned the mean scores of below 20 years aged trainees and above 20 years aged trainees are 21.11 and 21.75 respectively. And the standard deviations are 3.40 and 3.49 whereas the calculated 't' value 0.93 is not significant at 0.05 level. Hence the null hypothesis is accepted. This indicates the there is no significant difference between the opinions of the trainees of below and above 20 years of age.

Regarding the area Co-curricular and Extra-curricular Activities is concerned the mean scores of the opinions of the below 20 years age group of trainees and above 20 years age group of trainees are 21.84 and 21.52 respectively. The standard deviations of the above groups are 3.5 end 4.17. The obtained 't' value is 0.74 which is not significant at 0.05 level. Hence the null hypothesis is accepted. This shows that there is no significant difference between the opinions regarding the area Co-curricular and Extra-curricular Activities of below 20 years aged trainees and above 20 years aged trainees.

As far as the area field work and records is concerned the mean scores of the opinions of the below 20 years age group of trainees and above 20 years age group of trainees are 38.41 and 38.77 respectively. The standard deviations of the above groups are 4.13 and 3.78. The calculated 't' value 0.77, is not significant at 0.05 level. Hence the null hypothesis is accepted. This indicates that there is no significant difference between the opinions regarding the area field work and records of below 20 years age group trainees and above 20 years age group trainees.

Figure 4.2. Graph Showing Mean, Mean Difference of Opinions of below 20 years and Above 20 years Aged Trainees, on the four Areas of DIET Activities

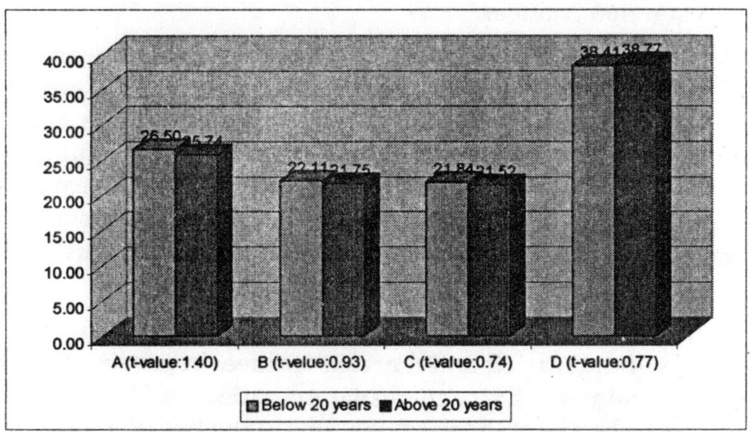

Table 4.10. Table Showing Mean Difference and the Level of Significance of the Opinions of Un-married and Married D.Ed Teacher Trainees on the four Areas of DIET Activities

Grouping: Marital Status *Group 1:Unmarried (326)* *Group 2:Married (19)*					
Area of activities	*Unmarried*		*Married*		*t value*
	Mean	*Standard deviation*	*Mean*	*Standard deviation*	
A. Facilities and resources	26.17	4.86	27.68	3.46	1.34
B. Instruction	21.91	3.44	23.32	2.96	1.74
C. Co-curricular and Extra curricular Activities	21.62	3.77	23.63	2.50	2.29*
D. Field work and Records	38.49	4.06	39.26	3.18	0.82

*Significant at 0.05 level

The above table explains about the mean difference of scores of different areas between the two groups about the marital status.

Regarding the area facilities and resources the mean scores of opinions of unmarried trainees and married trainees are 26.17 and 27.68 respectively. The standard deviations are 4.86 and 3.46. Whereas the calculated 't' value 1.34 is not significant at

0.05 level. Hence the null hypothesis is accepted. This infers that there is no significant difference between the opinions of the two groups regarding facilities and resources of unmarried and married trainees.

As far as the instruction area is concerned the mean scores of the opinions of unmarried and married trainees are 21.91 and 23.32 respectively. And the standard deviations are 3.44 and 2.96. The calculated 't' value 1.74 is not significant at 0.05 level. Hence the null hypothesis is accepted. This indicates that there is no significant difference between the opinions of the two groups of unmarried and married trainees regarding the area instruction.

As regards to the mean scores of the opinions of the two groups of unmarried and married trainees regarding the area Co-curricular and Extra curricular Activities are 21.62 and 23.63 respectively. The standard deviations of the two groups are 3.77 and 2.50. The obtained 't' value 2.29 is significant at 0.05 level. Hence the null hypothesis is rejected. This indicates that there is significant difference between the opinions of the two groups. This indicates that the married trainees opined more better than unmarried trainees. This may be due to their more responsibility and responsiveness towards participating in these activities. Moreover they may have more flair to perform and learn than unmarried ones towards Co-curricular and Extra curricular Activities which may be because of the influence of their spouses/children.

As regards to the area field work and records the mean scores of the opinions of the unmarried and married trainees are 38.49 and 39.26 respectively. The standard deviations of these two groups are 4.06 and 3.18. The obtained 't' value 0.82 is not significant at 0.05 level. Hence the null hypothesis is accepted. This indicates the there is no significant difference between the opinions of married and unmarried trainees towards field work and records.

As a whole in all the above four variables the opinions of married trainees are a little bit better than unmarried trainees. The married group expressed better opinions than the unmarried group in Co-curricular and Extra curricular Activities.

But in the other three areas the opinions of both the groups are more or less similar. This may be due to lack of much age difference between married and unmarried groups of teacher trainees.

Fig. 4.3. Graph Showing Mean Difference and the Level of Significance of the Opinions of Un-Married and Married D.Ed Teacher Trainees on the Four Areas of DIET Activities

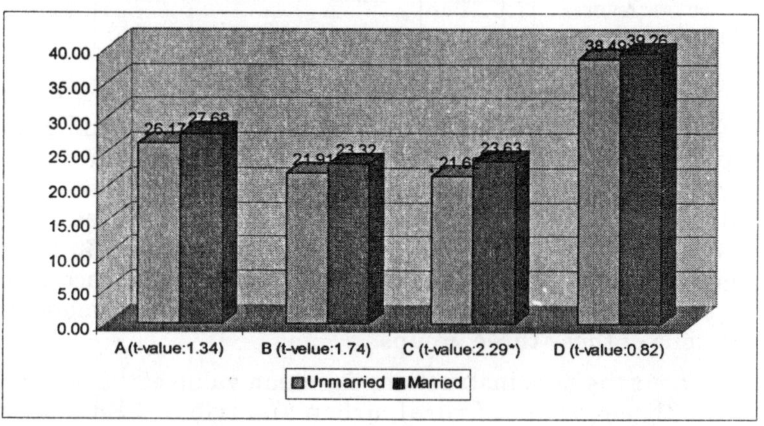

Table 4.11. Table Showing Mean Difference and the Level of Significance of the Opinions of the Different Nativity D.Ed Teacher Trainees About the Four Areas of Activities

Nativity / *Areas of activities*	*Rural N=235*		*Urban N=102*		*Tribal N=8*		*Aggregate N=345*	
	Mean	*SD*	*Mean*	*SD*	*Mean*	*SD*	*Mean*	*SD*
A. Facilities and resources	26.31	4.92	26.34	4.46	23.25	5.31	26.25	4.80
B. Instruction	22.03	3.38	21.99	3.49	20.88	4.32	21.99	3.43
C. Co-curricular and Extra curricular Activities	21.83	3.71	21.80	3.60	18.13	4.79	21.73	3.74
D. Field work and Records	38.79	3.73	38.02	4.47	37.38	5.45	38.53	4.01

*Significant at 0.05 level.

The above table shows that, with regards to Nativity of the respondents the mean difference of the scores among the different groups of rural, urban and tribal nativity with regard to the different areas of activities.

Table 4.11a. Table Showing ANOVA Values of Rural. Urban and Tribal Trainees Regarding the Four Areas of Activities

Area of activities	*Sum of squares*		*Mean square*		*F*
	Between	*Within*	*Between*	*Within*	
A. Facilities and resources	73.75	7860.81	36.87	22.98	1.60
B. Instruction	10.32	4034.66	5.16	11.80	0.44
C. Co-curricular and Extra curricular Activities	106.67	4692.80	53.33	13.72	3.89*
D. Field work and Records	53.31	5490.62	26.66	16.05	1.66

In the facilities and resources the mean values of the opinions of the three different groups of rural, urban and tribal, are 26.31, 26.34 and 23.25 respectively. The standard deviations of the above groups are 4.92, 4.46 and 5.31. The aggregate mean value of these three groups is 26.25 and the aggregate standard deviation value is 4.80. The calculated 'F' value 1.60 is not significant at 0.05 level. Hence the null hypothesis is accepted. This indicates that there is no significant difference among the opinions of these three groups.

About the area instruction, the mean value of the opinions of the three groups of rural, urban and tribal D.Ed teacher trainees are 22.03, 21.99 and 20.88 respectively. And the standard deviation values of the above three groups are 3.38, 3.49 and 4.32 respectively. The 'F' value of these three groups, 0.44 is not significant at 0.05 level. Hence the null hypothesis is accepted. This indicates that there is no, much difference among the opinions of the three groups opinions regarding the area instruction.

As to the area Co-curricular and Extra curricular Activities the mean values of the opinions of the three different groups of teacher trainees of rural, urban and tribal areas are 21.83, 21.80 and 18.13 respectively. The standard deviations are 3.71, 3.60 and 4.79. The aggregate mean value of the three groups is 21.73 and the aggregate standard deviation is 3.74. The calculated (ANOVA) 'F' value 3.89, is significant at 0.01 level. Hence the null hypothesis is rejected. This indicates that there is significant difference among the opinions of the three groups of trainees towards Co-curricular and Extra curricular Activities. This may be due to the higher opinions by urban and rural trainees than the Tribal ones may be because, the urban and rural trainees are more exposed than tribal trainees to participate more in

Co-curricular and Extra-curricular Activities. This infers that good exposure during school and college education develops better attitudes in the later life of the individual.

With regards to the field-work and records, mean values of the opinions of the three groups of trainees of rural, urban and tribal localities are 38.79, 38.02 and 37.38 respectively. The standard deviation values of the three groups are 3.73, 4.47 and 5.45. The aggregate mean values and standard deviations of these three groups are 38.53 and 4.01 respectively. The (ANOVA) 'F' value of the three groups 1.66, is not significant at 0.05 level. Hence the null hypothesis is accepted. This shows that there is no significant difference among the opinions of the three groups with regards to the fieldwork and records.

As a whole the (ANOVA) 'F' values of the three groups of the rural, urban and tribal nativities regarding the four areas, except Co-curricular and Extra curricular Activities, are not significant at 0.05 level. This shows that the opinions of the three nativity groups are more or less similar except in Co-curricular Extra curricular and Activities.

Fig. 4.4 Graph Showing Mean Difference and the Level of Significance of the Opinions of the Different Nativity Teacher Trainees About the Four Areas of Activities

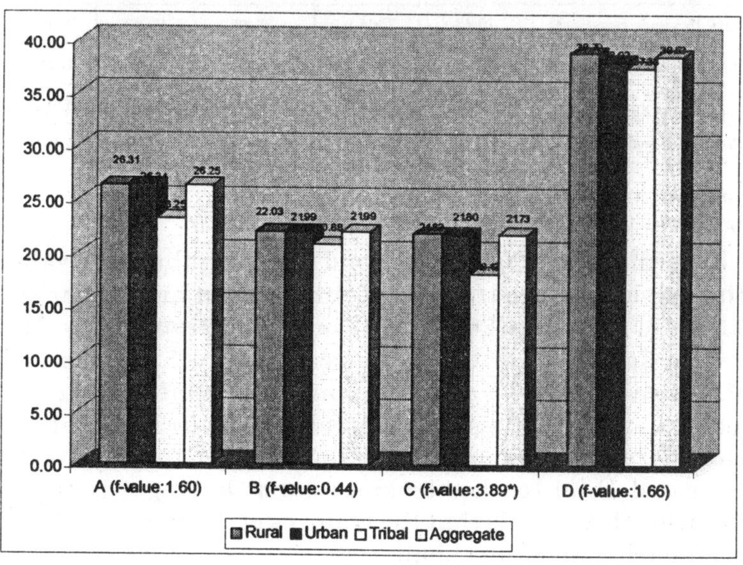

Table 4.12. Table Showing Significance of Mean Difference of Opinions of D.Ed Teacher Trainees of the Three Different Localities of DIETs

Locality / *Area of activity*	*Rural N=206*		*Urban N=86*		*Sub-urban N=53*		*Aggregate N=345*	
	Mean	*SD*	*Mean*	*SD*	*Mean*	*SD*	*Mean*	*SD*
A. Facilities and resources	26.53	5.00	26.19	4.28	25.25	4.76	26.25	4.80
B. Instruction	22.18	3.53	21.23	3.40	22.49	2.87	21.99	3.43
C. Co-curricular and Extra curricular Activities	22.27	3.79	20.88	3.51	21.04	3.56	21.73	3.74
D. Field work and Records	38.89	3.88	38.69	3.75	36.89	4.59	38.53	4.01

The above table shows the mean difference of opinions among the different groups of locality of the institutions (DIETs) situated in the districts in rural, urban and sub-urban localities.

Table 4.12a. Table Showing the ANOVA Values of the Opinions of D.Ed Teacher Trainee about the four Activities of three Localities of DIETs

Area of activity	*Sum of squares*		*Mean square*		*F*
	Between	*Within*	*Between*	*Within*	
A. Facilities and resources	70.47	7864.10	35.23	22.99	1.53
B. Instruction	70.03	3974.95	35.01	11.62	3.01*
C. Co-curricular and Extra curricular Activities	146.39	4653.08	73.19	13.61	5.38**
D. Field work and Records	171.65	5372.28	85.83	15.71	5.46**

*Significant at 0.05 level.
**Significant 0.01 level.

Regarding the area facilities and resources the mean value of the opinions of the trainees of rural, urban and sub-urban localities of DIETs are 26.53, 26.19 and 25.25 respectively. The standard deviations of the three localities are 5.00, 4.28 and 4.76. The calculated 'F' value 1.53 is not significant at 0.05 level. Hence the null hypothesis is accepted. This indicates that the mean difference of opinions among the three groups of the three localities of D.Ed teacher trainees is not having significant difference. This reveals that the trainees of the three localities have opined more or less similarly.

With regard to the area instruction, the three locality group means of the trainees opinions are 22.18, 21.23, and 22.49 respectively. The standard deviations of the groups are 3.53, 3.40 and 2.87. The calculated 'F' value of the three groups, 3.01 is significant at both the levels. Hence the null hypothesis is rejected. This infers that there is significant difference between the means of the opinions of the three groups of the three localities of teacher trainees. This tells that the sub-urban DIETs trainees are opining better than the rural and urban trainees. This may be due to the mixed environment of the social setting which gives better exposure to the individuals than the rural or urban atmosphere.

Regarding the area Co-curricular and Extra-curricular Activities, the means of the opinions of the three groups of trainees belonging to the DIETs of the three localities namely rural, urban and sub-urban, are 22.27, 20.88 and 21.04 respectively. The standard deviations are 3.79, 3.51 and 3.56. The calculated 'F' value 5.38 is significant at both the levels. Hence the null hypothesis is rejected. This indicates that the rural DIETs teacher trainees have better opined than trainees of sub-urban DIETs and the sub-urban teacher trainees have better opined than urban DIETs trainees. This may be due to better cultural and traditional background in rural DIETs than those of sub-urban and urban DIETs.

As to the area fieldwork and records is concerned the difference in the means of the opinions of the D.Ed teacher trainees. Hence the null hypothesis is the rejected of the three localities namely rural, urban and sub-urban are 38.89, 38.69 and 36.89 respectively. The standard deviations of the three groups are 3.88, 3.75 and 4.59. The calculated 'F' value 5.46 is significant at both levels.

This tells that there is significant difference among the opinions of the sub-urban, rural and urban localities of DIETs trainees. This indicates that the locality influences the DIET trainees in their opinions regarding all the four areas activities. This may be due to the local environment that was surrounding the DIET, DIET hostels, the surrounding public, the schools where the trainees practise their teaching and other factors that influence trainees opinions.

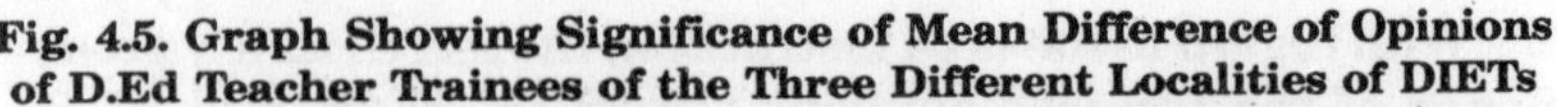

Fig. 4.5. Graph Showing Significance of Mean Difference of Opinions of D.Ed Teacher Trainees of the Three Different Localities of DIETs

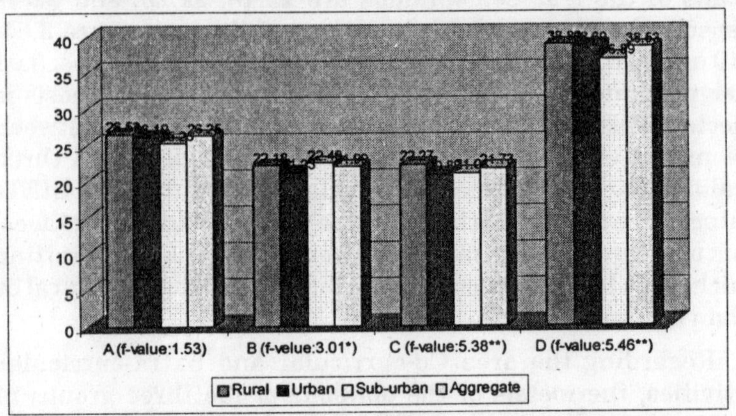

Table 4.13. Table Showing Mean Difference of Opinions of the four Social Class Groups of D.Ed Teacher Trainees on the Four Areas of Activities

Social Class / *Area of activities*	*OC N=109*		*BC N=184*		*SC N=36*		*ST N=16*		*Aggregate N=345*	
	Mean	*SD*	*Mean*	*SD*	*Mean*	*SD*	*Mean*	*SD*	*Mean*	*SD*
A. Facilities and resources	25.82	4.42	26.99	4.95	24.81	4.43	23.88	4.92	26.25	4.80
B. Instruction	21.81	3.56	22.29	3.41	21.53	2.94	20.88	3.59	21.99	3.43
C. Co-curricular and Extra curricular Activities	21.59	3.89	22.27	3.38	19.83	4.16	20.81	4.25	21.73	3.74
D. Field work and Records	38.88	3.39	38.74	3.97	37.17	5.14	36.75	4.86	38.53	4.01

The above table depicts the mean difference of the opinions of the different groups of social class like open category (OC), backward class (BC), scheduled caste (SC) and scheduled tribe (ST), of D.Ed. (pre-service) teacher trainees.

Table 4.13a. Table Showing ANOVA Values of Opinions of the Four Groups of D.Ed Teacher Trainees on the Four Areas of Activities

Area of activities	*Sum of squares*		*Mean square*		*F*
	Between	*Within*	*Between*	*Within*	
A. Facilities and resources	287.85	7646.71	95.95	22.42	4.28*
B. Instruction	47.56	3997.41	15.85	11.72	1.35
C. Co-curricular and Extra curricular Activities	199.19	4600.27	66.40	13.49	4.92**
D. Field work and Records	139.49	5404.44	46.50	15.85	2.93*

*Significant at 0.05 level.
**Significant at 0.01 level.

Regarding the area facilities and resources the ANOVA values of opinions of trainees of O.C, B.C, S.C and S.T categories are 25.82, 26.99, 24.81 and 23.88 respectively. The standard deviations are 4.42, 4.95, 4.43 and 4.92. The aggregate mean value is 26.25 and the aggregate standard deviation is 4.80. The calculated 'F' value 4.28 is significant at 0.01 level. Hence the null hypothesis is rejected. This indicates that there is significant difference among the opinions of the three groups regarding the facilities and resources. This may be due to the difference in the social class OC, BC, SC and ST of the trainees.

With regards to the area instruction, the four groups of the social class namely O.C, B.C, S.C and S.T, the mean values are, 21.81, 22.29, 21.53 and 20.88 respectively. The standard deviations are 3.56, 3.41, 2.94 and 3.59. The aggregate mean value is 21.99 and the aggregate standard deviation is 3.43. The calculated 'F' value 1.35 is not significant at 0.05 level. Hence the null hypothesis accepted. This indicates that there is no significant difference among the mean values of the four social classes of teacher trainees regarding the opinions of the area instruction.

Regarding the area Co-curricular and Extra curricular Activities, the mean values of the opinions of the four social class groups of O.C, B.C, S.C and S.T are 21.59, 22.27, 19.83 and 20.81 respectively. The standard deviations are 3.89, 3.38, 4.16 and 4.25. The aggregate mean value is 21.73 and the aggregate standard deviation is 3.74. The obtained 'F' value 4.92 is significant at 0.01 level. Hence the null hypothesis is rejected. This shows that there is significant difference among the opinions of the four social class groups regarding the area Co-curricular and Extra curricular Activities. This may be due to the variation in the exposure among the four social classes.

Regarding the area fieldwork and records the mean values of opinions of four social class groups of D.Ed teacher trainees are 38.88, 38.74, 37.17, and 36.75 respectively. The standard deviations are 3.39, 3.97, 5.14 and 4.86. The aggregate mean value is 38.53 and the aggregate standard deviation is 4.01. The arrived 'F' value 2.93 is significant at 0.01 level. Hence the null hypothesis is rejected. This indicates that there is significant difference among the mean values of the four social groups in their opinions regarding the area fieldwork and records. This may be due to the difference in their education at school and college levels.

Fig. 4.6. Graph Showing Mean Difference of Opinions of the Four Social Class Groups of D.Ed Teacher Trainees on the Four Areas of Activities

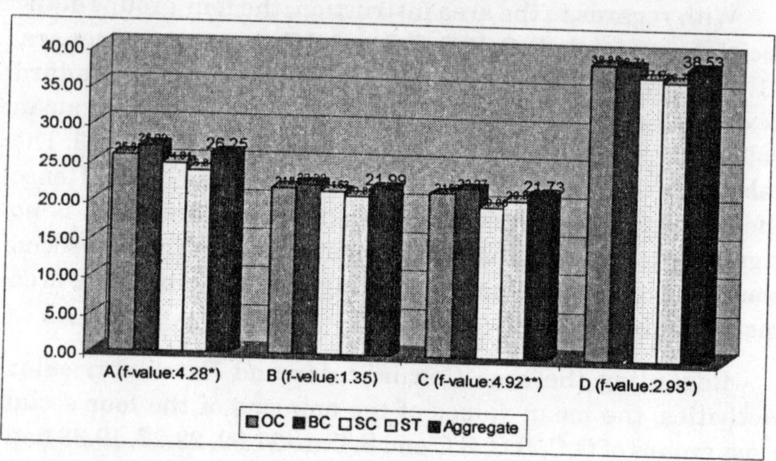

Table 4.14. Table Showing Mean Difference of Opinions of D.Ed Teacher Trainees Possessing Different General Qualifications

Qualifications / *Area of activities*	*Intermediate N=285*		*Degree N=58*		*Post graduation N=2*		*Aggregate N=345*	
	Mean	*SD*	*Mean*	*SD*	*Mean*	*SD*	*Mean*	*SD*
A. Facilities and resources	26.32	4.81	25.91	4.89	26.00	1.41	26.25	4.80
B. Instruction	22.05	3.34	21.66	3.89	24.00	1.41	21.99	3.43
C. Co-curricular and Extra curricular Activities	21.85	3.73	21.17	3.77	21.00	2.83	21.73	3.74
D. Field work and Records	38.65	3.94	37.88	4.41	40.50	0.71	38.53	4.01

The above table shows that the mean difference of opinions among the different groups of D.Ed. teacher trainees possessing different general qualifications like intermediate, graduation and post graduation.

Table 14a. Table Showing ANOVA Values of Opinions of D.Ed Teacher Trainees Possessing Different General Qualifications on the Four Areas of Activities

Area of activities	*Sum of squares*		*Mean square*		*F*
	Between	*Within*	*Between*	*Within*	
A. Facilities and resources	8.05	7926.51	4.02	23.18	0.17
B. Instruction	15.46	4029.51	7.73	11.78	0.66
C. Co-curricular and Extra curricular Activities	23.38	4776.09	11.69	13.97	0.84
D. Field work and Records	36.36	5507.57	18.18	16.10	1.13

Regarding the area, facilities and resources the mean values of the opinions of the D.Ed teacher trainees of intermediate, graduation and post graduation are 26.32, 25.91 and 26.00 respectively. The standard deviation values are 4.81, 4.89 and 1.41 respectively. The calculated 'F' value 0.17 is not significant at 0.05 level. Hence the null hypothesis is accepted. This shows that the difference in general qualifications of the differently qualified trainees has caused no difference in the opinions of the trainees. This shows that all, the trainees opined more or less similarly from all the DIETs of Andhra Pradersh.

With regards to the area instruction the mean values of the opinions of the trainees possessing three different general qualifications are 22.05, 21.66 and 24.00 respectively. The calculated 'F' value 0.66 is less than the table value. This indicates that the mean difference of opinions of the trainees possessing different general qualifications is not significant. Hence the null hypothesis is accepted. Almost all the trainees of DIETs possessing different general qualifications opined more or less similarly.

Regarding the area Co-curricular and Extra-curricular Activities the mean values of opinions of trainees possessing different general qualifications are 21.85, 21.17 and 21.00 respectively. The generated 'F' value 0.84 is less than the table value. This indicates that the difference in the opinions of the trainees possessing different general qualifications is not significant. Hence the null hypothesis is accepted. This infers that almost all the trainees of all the DIETs opined more or less similarly in Co-curricular and Extra-curricular Activities.

On the other hand regarding the area fieldwork and records the mean values of the opinions of the trainees possessing different general qualifications are 38.65, 37.88 and 40.50 respectively. The calculated 'F' value 1.13 is less than the table value. This indicates that it is not significant at both levels. Hence the null hypothesis is accepted. This infers that there is no significant difference in the opinions of the trainees possessing different general qualifications from all DIETs. This infers that the trainees of all DIETs opined more or less similarly regarding fieldwork and records.

Fig. 4.7. Graph Showing Mean Difference of Opinions of D.Ed Teacher Trainees Possessing Different General Qualifications

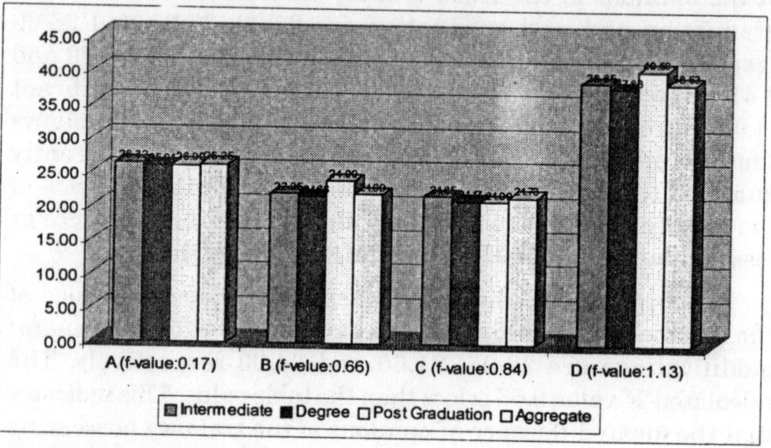

CONCLUSIONS

As a whole we can assess that the opinions of D.Ed teacher trainees from rural DIETs differed from the opinions of trainees from urban DIETs and inturn the urban differed from the sub-urban DIETs in respect of facilities and resources and fieldwork and records, whereas those of the sub-urban DIETs have differed from the urban DIETs in respect of instruction, Co-curricular, and Extra curricular Activities.

This may be because of the rural atmosphere the fresh air, spacious play ground, garden, calm atmosphere of rural DIETs may influence the trainees towards better opinions, whereas the urban DIETs trainees may lack pollution free atmosphere, peaceful climate, spacious play ground and garden which may influence their opinions supporting this the sub-urban DIETs trainees were better in instruction and Co-curricular and Extra curricular Activities than the urban ones because their via-media betterment in the atmosphere and fresh and pollution free climate. Hence differed in their opinions over the urban DIETs trainees.

This leads to the implication that it is better to establish DIETs in rural climate or sub-urban climate than urban climate for yielding better opinions of the trainees, there by better performance.

SECTION – C

ANALYSIS AND INTERPRETATION OF OPINIONS OF IN-SERVICE TEACHERS

The following is the analysis and interpretation of the opinions of the in-service teachers towards the in-service training programmes conducted by the DIETs in Andhra Pradesh. Fifteen in-service teachers from each district were area randomnly selected for a sample of 345 teachers from all 23 districts for collecting opinions about in-service training programmes conducted by DIETs. The opinions were quantified and computed to find out the difference of opinions with reference to the independent variables by using 't'-test, 'F'-test and 'chi'-square tests.

Table 4.1. Table Showing Age-wise Distribution of In-service Teachers

Sl.No.	*Age group*	*Frequency*	*Percent*
1	Below 30 yrs	58	16.8
2	31 to 45 yrs	213	61.7
3	Above 45 yrs	74	21.4
	Total	345	100.0

Out of 345 in-service teachers 61.7% respondents belong to 31 to 45 years age group. There are 21.4% of above 45 years aged and 16.8% are below 30 years aged teachers.

Table 4,.2. Table Showing Sex-Wise Distribution of In-service Teachers

Sl.No.	*Sex*	*Frequency*	*Percent*
1	Male	174	50.4
2	Female	171	49.6
	Total	345	100.0

It is known that both sexes of the respondents are almost equal and equal probability of sexes proved in reality. The male teachers are 174 (50.4%) and the female teachers are 171 (49.6%) responded.

Table 4.3. Table Showing Social Class wise Distribution of In-service Teachers

Sl.No.	*Social Class*	*Frequency*	*Percent*
1	Open category (OC)	165	47.8
2	Backward class (BC) / Other Backward class (OBC)	126	36.5
3	Scheduled castes (SC)	45	13.0
4	Scheduled tribes (ST)	9	2.6
	Total	345	100.0

There are 165 (47.8%) respondents belonging to open category, 126 (36.5%) belonging to backward classes and 45 (13%) belonging to scheduled castes and 9 (2.6%) belonging to scheduled tribes teachers.

Table 4.4. Table Showing Nativity wise Distribution of In-service Teachers

Sl.No.	*Nativity*	*Frequency*	*Percent*
1	Rural	203	58.8
2	Urban	133	38.6
3	Tribal	9	2.6
	Total	345	100.0

As per the nativity of the in-service teachers on the classification of rural, urban and tribal areas, among the 345 teachers 208 (58.8%) are from rural background. 133 (38.6%) are from urban background and 9 (2.6%) are from tribal areas.

Table 4.5. Table Showing the Marital Status wise Distribution of In-service Teachers

Sl.No.	*Marital status*	*Frequency*	*Percent*
1	Unmarried	22	6.4
2	Married	323	93.6
	Total	345	100.0

Among the 345 teachers, 323 (93.6%) are married and 22 (6.4%) are un-married.

Table 4.6. Table Showing School Location Wise Distribution of the In-Service Teachers (i.e) Place of Working

Sl.No.	*School location*	*Frequency*	*Percent*
1	Rural	197	57.1
2	Urban	123	35.7
3	Sub-urban	10	2.9
4	Tribal	15	4.3
	Total	345	100.0

Among the 345 sample, there are 197 (57.1%) rural teachers; 123 (35.7%) are working in urban located schools, 10 (2.9%) are sub-urban located school teachers and 15 (4.3%) are working in tribal located schools.

Table 4.7. Table Showing General Qualifications-wise Distribution of In-service Teachers

Sl.No.	*General qualifications*	*Frequency*	*Percent*
1	Intermediate	44	12.8
2	Bachelor degree	185	53.6
3	Post graduation	116	33.6
	Total	345	100.0

The general qualifications of the in-service teachers fall under three categories namely intermediate, bachelors degree and post graduates which represent in number 44 (12.8%), 185 (53.6%) and 116 (33.6%) respectively. This reveals that more than 87% of the in-service teachers procured higher general qualifications which are more than required for their post i.e. elementary teacher post.

Table 4.8. Table Showing Professional Qualifications-wise Distribution of In-service Teachers of the Sample

Sl.No.	*Professional qualifications*	*Frequency*	*Percent*
1	Teacher Training Certificate (T.T.C)	108	31.6
2	Diploma in Education (D.Ed)	207	60.0
3	Bachelor of Education (B.Ed)	30	8.7
	Total	345	100.0

Among the 345 sample there are 108 (31.6%) in-service teachers who possess teacher training certificate (T.T.C) and there are 207 (60%) in-service teachers who possess diploma in education (D.Ed) which is also equal to T.T.C and there are 30 (8.7%) in-service teachers who possess bachelor of education (B.Ed) as professional qualifications.

This indicates that the working teachers are able to procure degree/post graduation general qualifications more profusely than acquiring professional qualifications, because the professional qualifications are more restricted in offering to the in-service teachers through distance mode. Hence 91.6 of in-service teachers remain unimproved regarding professional qualifications.

Table 4.9. Table Showing Teaching Experience-wise Distribution of In-service Teachers

Sl.No.	*Teaching experience*	*Frequency*	*Percent*
1	Up to 10 years	158	45.8
2	11 to 20 years	115	33.3
3	Above 20 years	72	20.9
	Total	345	100.0

The teachers who responded are categorized into three types basing on their length of service rendered. Among the 345 teachers sample many fall under the minimum service of ten years (i.e.) 158 (46.1%), whereas those with above 20 years of service are very less i.e., 71 (20.6%). Those with 11 to 20 years of service are 115 (33.3%) represents 1/3 of the sample.

Table 4.10. Table Showing Classes Handing-wise Distribution of In-service Teachers

Sl.No.	*Classes teaching*	*Frequency*	*Percent*
1	1-2 classes	80	23.2
2	3-5 classes	183	53.0
3	6-7 classes	82	23.8
	Total	345	100.0

Those who teach 1,2 classes and those who teach 6,7 classes represent equal number (i.e.) 80 (23.2%) and 82 (23.8%) respectively, where as the number of teachers who teach 3,4,5 classes are comparatively more than half of the sample (i.e.) 183 (53%) teachers.

Table 4.11. Table Showing Subjects Teaching-wise Distribution of In-service Teachers

Sl.No.	*Subjects teaching*	*Frequency*	*Percentage*
1	Telugu	235	68.10
2	English	193	55.90
3	Mathematics	227	65.80
4	Sciences	221	64.10
5	Social Studies	192	55.50

Generally in primary and upper primary schools class-master system is in vogue, in which a single used to teach teaches all subjects of one class completely. Hence each and every elementary teacher is expected to teach all subjects like Telugu, English, Hindi, Mathematics, Social Studies (Environmental Studies I) and Sciences (Environmental Studies II).

Table 4.12. Table Showing Rank Ordering Subjects in the Order of their usefulness from More useful to Less useful of In-Service Training Programmes

Sl. No	*Subject*	*Rank*								*Total*
		1	2	3	4	5	6	7	8	
1	Telugu	202 (58.55)	41 (11.88)	22 (6.38)	25 (7.25)	16 (4.64)	16 (4.64)	14 (4.06)	9 (2.61)	345 (100.0)
2	English	31 (8.99)	45 (13.04)	89 (25.80)	53 (15.36)	37 (10.72)	43 (12.46)	28 (8.12)	19 (5.51)	345 (100.0)
3	Hindi	20 (5.78)	18 (5.22	13 (3.77)	33 (9.57)	28 (8.12)	29 (8.41)	61 (17.68)	143 (41.45)	345 (100.0)
4	Mathematics	53 (15.36)	162 (46.96)	44 (12.75)	30 (8.70)	26 (7.54)	18 (5.22)	7 (2.03)	5 (1.45)	345 (100.0)
5	Physical Sciences	6 (1.74)	31 (8.99)	36 (10.43)	59 (17.10)	51 (14.78)	81 23.48)	54 (15.65)	27 (7.83)	345 (100.0)
6	Biological Sciences	10 (2.90)	15 (4.35)	48 (13.91)	48 (13.91)	82 (23.77)	67 (19.42)	54 (15.65)	21 (6.09)	345 (100.0)
7	Social Studies	10 (2.90)	21 (6.09)	37 (10.72)	56 (16.23)	68 (19.71)	50 (14.49)	64 (18.55)	39 (11.30)	345 (100.0)
8	Work Experience	18 (5.22)	17 (4.93)	57 (16.52)	45 (13.04)	34 (9.86)	38 (11.01)	62 (17.97)	74 (21.45)	345 (100.0)
	Total	345 (100.0)	345 (100.0)	345 (100.0)	345 (100.0)	345 (100.0)	345 (100.0)	345 (100.0)	345 (100.0)	

But it is exhibited that 235 (68.10%) teachers teach Telugu, 193 (55.90%) teachers teach English, 227 (65.8%) teachers teach Mathematics, 221 (64.10%) teachers teach Sciences and 192 (55.50%) teachers teach Social Studies. The variations in the percentages may be due to certain specializations and interest of teachers in teaching certain subjects. (each teacher used to teach one or more subjects).

The responses of the in-service teachers towards the school subjects of in-service training programmes are noticed from the data source subject-wise.

A. For Telugu subject the highest number of 202 (58.55%) teachers expressed it first rank as most useful and a least number of 9 (2.61%) teachers have given eighth rank. Among the remaining respondents 41 (11.88%), 22 (6.38%), 25 (7.25%), 16 (4.64%), 16 (4.64%) and 14 (4.06%) have opted for second, third, fourth, fifth, sixth and seventh ranks respectively.

B. For English the highest number of teachers 89 (25.80%) have expressed third rank whereas the least number of teachers 19 (5.51%) have expressed eighth rank. Among the remaining respondents 31 (8.94%), 45 (13.04%), 53 (15.35%), 37 (10.72%), 43 (12.46%) and 28 (8.12%) have ranked the subject first, second, fourth, fifth, sixth and seventh respectively.

C. Regarding Hindi language the highest number of teachers 143 (41.45%) have expressed it as eighth rank whereas the least number of teachers 13 (3.77%) have expressed third rank and the same percentage of teachers also expressed it third rank. The remaining respondents 20 (7.78), 18 (5.22), 33 (9.57), 28 (8.12), 29 (8.41) and 61 (17.68) have ranked the subject first, second, fourth, fifth, sixth and seventh respectively.

D. As regards to Mathematics the highest number of 162 (46.96%) respondents opted for second rank whereas the least number of 5 (1.45%) have ranked it eighth. The remaining respondents 53 (15.36%), 44 (12.75), 30 (8.70), 26 (7.50), 18 (5.22) and 7 (2.03%) have ranked first, third, forth, fifth, sixth and seventh respectively.

E. With regards to Physical Sciences the highest number of 81 (23.48%) respondents have given the subject as fourth rank and the least number of respondents 6 (1.74%) have opted it for the first rank. The rest of them namely 31 (8.99), 36 (10.43), 59 (17.01), 51 (14.78), 54 (15.65) and 27 (7.83) have opted second third, fifth, sixth, seventh and eigth ranks respectively.

F. With respect to Biological Science the highest number of 82 (23.77%) respondents have ranked the subject as fifth and the least number 10 (2.90%) have ranked it as first. Among the remaining respondents 15 (4.25), 48 (13.91), 48 (13.91), 67 (19.42), 54 (15.65) and 21 (6.09) have opted second, third, fourth, sixth, seventh and eigth ranks respectively.

G. Regarding the ranking of the Social Studies the highest number of respondents 68 (19.71%) have ranked it fifth and the least number of respondents 10 (2.90%), have ranked it first. The rest of the respondents 21 (6.09%), 37 (10.72%), 56 (16.23%), 50 (14.49%), 64 (18.55%), 39 (11.30%) have opted second, third, fourth, sixth, seventh and eigth ranks respectively.

H. With regards to the subject Work Experience is concerned the highest number of 74 (21.45%) teachers have opted it eigth rank and the least number of 17 (4.93%) teachers have opted it second rank. The remaining respondents 18 (5.22%), 57 (16.52%), 45 (13.04%), 34 (9.86%), 38 (11.01%), 62 (17.97%) have opted it first, third, fourth, fifth, sixth and seventh ranks respectively.

The above table shows the ranking for the different methodologies as to their difficulty level from more difficult to less difficult ranging up to six ranks. The first rank denotes most difficult and the last rank indicates least difficult in teachers' opinion.

1. Regarding Telugu Methodology the highest number of 80 (23.19%) respondents have opted fifth rank and the least number of 41 (11.88%) respondents have opted for second rank. The remaining respondents 56 (16.23%), 54 (15.65%), 45 (13.04%) and 69 (20.00%) have opted first, third, fourth, and sixth ranks respectively.

2. With regard to Hindi Methodology among the 345 respondents the highest number of 148 (42.90%) respondents have opted for sixth rank and the least number of 36 (10.43%)

Table 4.13. Table Showing Rank Ordering the Methodologies Basing on the Difficulty Level from More Difficult to Less Difficult by the In-service Teachers

Sl.No.	*Subject*	*Rank*						*Total*
		1	*2*	*3*	*4*	*5*	*6*	
1	Telugu	56 (16.23)	41 (11.88)	54 (15.65)	45 (13.04)	80 (23.19)	69 (20.00)	345 (100.0)
2	Hindi	39 (11.30)	36 (10.43)	36 (10.43)	36 (10.43)	50 (14.49)	148 (42.90)	345 (100.0)
3	English	82 (23.77)	88 (25.51)	57 (16.52)	62 (17.97)	29 (8.41)	27 (7.83)	345 (100.0)
4	Mathematics	116 (33.62)	70 (20.29)	63 (18.26)	45 (13.04)	33 (9.57)	18 (5.22)	345 (100.0)
5	Science	27 (7.83)	61 (17.68)	75 (21.74)	93 (26.96)	67 (19.42)	22 (6,38)	345 (100.0)
6	Social Studies	25 (7.25)	50 (14.49)	63 (18.26)	64 (18.55)	85 (24.64)	58 (16.81)	345 (100.0)
	Total	345 (100.0)	345 (100.0)	345 (100.0)	345 (100.0)	345 (100.0)	345 (100.0)	

respondents have chosen second, third and fourth ranks. The rest of the respondents 39 (11.30%) and 50 (14.49%) have ranked the methodology first and fifth ranks respectively.

3. As regards to English Methodology, the highest number of respondents 88 (25.51%) have chosen second rank and the least number of respondents 27 (7.83%) have opted sixth rank. Among the remaining respondents 82 (23.77%), 57 (16.52%), 62 (17.97%) and 29 (8.41%) have chosen first, third, fourth and fifth ranks respectively.

4. As far as the Methodology of Mathematics is concerned the highest number of respondents 116 (33.62%) have accorded first rank and the least number of respondents 18 (5.22%) have given sixth rank. Out of the remaining respondents 70 (20.29%), 63 (18.26%), 45 (13.04%) and 33 (9.57%) have opted second, third, fourth, and fifth ranks respectively.

5. With regard to Science Methodology the highest number of respondents 345 93 (26.96%) have chosen fourth rank and the least number of respondents 22 (6.38%) have opted sixth rank. The remaining respondents 27 (7.83%), 61 (17.68%), 75 (21.74%) and 67 (19.42%) have opted first, second, third and fifth ranks respectively.

6. Regarding the Methodology of Social Studies among the respondents the highest number of 85 (24.64%) have opted fifth rank, and the least number of 25 (7.25%) have chosen first rank. Out of the remaining respondents 50 (14.49%), 63 (18.26%), 64 (18.55%) and 58 (16.81%) have opted second, third, fourth and sixth ranks respectively.

The above table depicts the ranking of the school subjects from more difficult to less difficult starting from one to sixth ranks by all the 345 in-service teachers.

1. Regarding Telugu, among the 345 respondents the highest number of 110 (31.88%) respondents have opted sixth rank and 33 (9.57%) teachers have chosen second rank. Among the remaining respondents 45 (13.04%) 38 (11.01%), 53 (15.36%) and 66 (19.13%) have chosen first , third, fourth and fifth ranks respectively.

Table 4.14. Table Showing Rank Ordering the School Subjects from More Difficult to Less Difficult by the In-service Teachers

Sl.No.	*Subject*	*Rank*						*Total*
		1	*2*	*3*	*4*	*5*	*6*	
1	Telugu	45 (13.04)	33 (9.57)	38 (11.01)	53 (15.36)	66 (19.13)	110 (31.88)	345 (100.0)
2	Hindi	14 (4.06)	40 (11.59)	38 (11.01)	46 (13.33)	55 (15.94)	152 (44.06)	345 (100.0)
3	English	70 20.29)	110 (31.88)	78 (22.61)	48 (13.91)	29 (8.41)	10 (2.90)	345 (100.0)
4	Mathematics	183 (53.04)	79 (22.90)	38 (11.01)	17 (4.93)	18 (5.22)	10 (2.90)	345 (100.0)
5	Science	18 (5.22)	67 (19.42)	107 (31.01)	90 (26.09)	45 (13.04)	18 (5.22)	345 (100.0)
6	Social Studies	16 (4.64)	18 (5.22)	47 (13.62)	89 (25.80)	129 (37.39)	46 (13.33)	345 (100.0)
	Total	345 (100.0)	345 (100.0)	345 (100.0)	345 (100.0)	345 (100.0)	345 (100.0)	

2. In respect of Hindi out of 345 respondents the highest number of 152 (44.06%) have opted sixth rank and the least number 14 (4.08%) have chosen first rank. Among the remaining 40 (11.59%), 38 (11.01%), 46 (13.33%) and 55 (15.94%) have opted second, third, fourth and fifth ranks respectively.

3. With regards to English subject, among the 345 respondents the highest number of 110 (31.88%) respondents have chosen second rank and the least number of 10 (2.90%) respondents have opted sixth rank. Among the remaining respondents 70 (20.29%), 78 (22.61%), 48 (13.91%) and 29 (8.41%) have opted first, third, fourth and fifth ranks respectively.

4. Regarding Mathematics subject among the 345 respondents, the highest number of 183 (53.04%) have opted first rank and the least number of of 10 (2.90%) respondents have chosen the least rank of sixth. Among the remaining respondents 79 (22.90%), 38 (11.01%), 17 (4.93%) and 18 (5.22%) have opted second, third, fourth, and fifth ranks respectively.

5. With regards to the Science subject, out of 345 respondents, the highest number of 107 (31.04%) respondents have opted the subject third rank, whereas the least number of respondents 18 (5.52%) have opted first and sixth ranks. The rest of the respondents 67 (19.42%), 90 (26.09%) and 45 (13.04%) have chosen second, fourth and fifth ranks respectively.

6. Regarding the subject Social Studies the highest number of 129 (37.39%) have opted it fifth rank and the least number of 16 (4.64%) respondents have chosen first rank. Among the remaining respondents 18 (5.22%), 47 (13.62%), 89 (25.80%) and 46 (13.33%) have opted second, third, fourth and sixth ranks respectively.

The above table shows the guidance given by DIET faculty to in-service teachers towards preparation of question banks, student Hand-books, teachers Hand-books and in the use of teaching learning material.

1. Regarding preparation of question banks, the mean values of male and female teachers are 2.59 and 2.70. The obtained 't' value 1.645, is less than the table value. Hence it is not significant. Hence the null hypothesis is accepted. This

Table 4.15. Table Showing Mean Deference of Opinions and its Significance of Male and Female In-service Teachers about the Guidance by DIETs Faculty

Grouping: SEX (df-343) *Group 1: Male(174)* *Group 2: Female(171)*						
Activities	*Male*		*Female*		*t-value*	*Significance*
	Mean	*Std.Dev.*	*Mean*	*Std.Dev.*		
The guidance given by lecturers in the preparation of question banks is satisfactory	2.59	0.71	2.70	0.58	-1.645	0.101
The guidance given by lecturers in the preparation of student Hand-books is satisfactory	2.54	0.71	2.60	0.61	-0.872	0.384
The guidance given by lecturers for the preparation of teachers Hand-books is satisfactory	2.65	0.59	2.50	0.65	2.190	0.029
The use of teaching learning material during classroom transaction by lecturers is satisfactory.	2.75	0.53	2.69	0.61	1.026	0.306
TOTAL	10.53	1.70	10.50	1.72	0.172	0.864

*Significant at 0.05 level.

indicates that there is no significant difference between the male and female teachers opinions.

2. With regard to the guidance in the preparation of student Hand-books, the mean values of male and female teachers are 2.54 and 2.60 respectively. The obtained 't' value 0.872, is less than the table value. Hence it is not significant. Hence the null hypothesis is accepted. This indicates that there is no significant difference between the opinions of male and female teachers, regarding the guidance towards the preparation of student Hand-books.

3. Regarding guidance given towards preparation of teachers Hand-books, the mean values of male and female teachers are 2.65 and 2.50 respectively. the calculated 't' value 2.190, is more than the table value. Hence it is significant at 0.05 level. Hence the null hypothesis is rejected. It can be inferred that this may be due to more attention paid by male teachers than female teachers towards preparation of teachers' Hand-books.

4. Regarding the use of TLM, the mean values of male and female teachers are 2.75 and 2.69 respectively. The calculated 't' value 1.026, is less than the table value. Hence it is not significant. Hence the null hypothesis is accepted. This indicates that there is no sifnificance difference between that opinion of the male and female respondents regarding the guidance towards the use of TLM during classroom transaction.

Fig. 4.8. Graph Showing Mean Deference of Opinions and its Significance of Male and Female In-service Teachers about the Guidance by DIETs Faculty

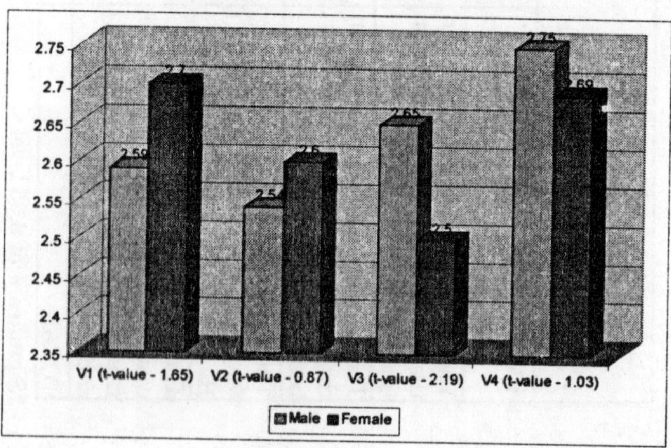

Table 4.16. Table Showing Mean Difference and Significance of Difference between the Opinions of Married and Unmarried In-Service Teachers about the Guidance given by DIETs Faculty

Grouping: Marital Status (df-343) *Group 1: Married (323)* *Group 2: Unmarried (22)*						
Activities	*Married*		*Unmarried*		*t-value*	*p*
	Mean	*Std.Dev.*	*Mean*	*Std.Dev.*		
The guidance given by lecturers in the preparation of question banks is satisfactory	2.65	0.64	2.55	0.80	0.726	0.468
The guidance given by lecturers in the preparation of student Hand-books is satisfactory	2.58	0.65	2.45	0.86	0.853	0.394
The guidance given by lecturers for the preparation of teachers Hand-books is satisfactory	2.57	0.63	2.64	0.58	-0.462	0.645
The use of teaching learning material during classroom transaction by lecturers is satisfactory.	2.71	0.57	2.86	0.47	-1.210	0.227
TOTAL	10.51	1.71	10.50	1.71	0.037	0.971

CONCLUSION

From the above table it is learnt that the opinions of female teachers are better than male teachers regarding the preparation of question banks and student Hand-books, where as the opinions of male teachers are better than female teachers regarding the preparation of teachers Hand-books and the use of teaching learning material during class room transaction.

1. Regarding preparation of question banks the mean values of male and female teachers are 2.65 and 2.55 respectively. The calculated 't' value 0.726 is less than the table value. Hence it is not significant. Hence the null hypothesis is accepted. This indicates that, there is no significant difference between guidance given to married and un-married teachers.

2. In case of preparation of student Hand-books the mean values of married and un-married teachers are 2.58 and 2.45 respectively. The calculated 't' value 0.853, is less than the table value. Hence it is not significant. Hence the null hypothesis is accepted. This indicates that there is no significant difference between the opinions of married and un-married teachers.

3. With regard to the preparation of teachers Hand-books, the mean values of married and un-married teachers are 2.57 and 2.64 respectively. The calculated 't' value 0.462, is less than the table value. Hence it is not significant. Hence the null hypothesis is accepted. This indicates that there is no significant difference in the opinion of married and un-married teachers.

4. Regarding the use of TLM the mean values of the married and un-married teachers are 2.71 and 2.86 respectively. The calculated 't' value 1.210, is less than the table value. Hence it is not significant. Hence the null hypothesis is accepted. This indicates that there is no significant difference in the opinions of married and un-married teachers in the use of TLM during class room transaction.

CONCLUSION

The above table depicts from the above analysis, the marital status of the teachers did not cause much difference in their opinion.

Fig. 4.9. Graph Showing Mean Difference and Significance of Difference between the Opinions of Married and Unmarried In-service Teachers about the Guidance by DIETs Faculty

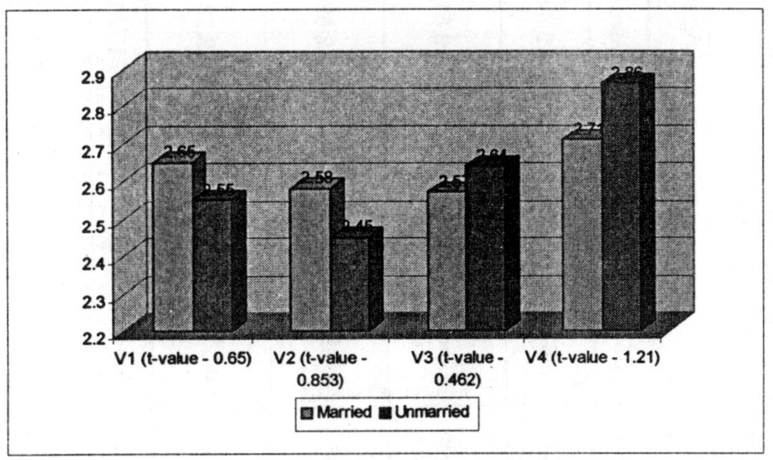

As the variable of age is divided into three groups, ANOVA (F value) is calculated to know the difference of opinion among the three age groups of teachers.

1. Regarding the preparation of question banks the means of opinions of below 30 years, 31 to 45 and above 45 years age groups are 2.60, 2.63 and 2.72 respectively. The calculated 'F' value 0.62, is less than the table value. Hence it is not significant. Hence the null hypothesis is accepted. This shows that there is no significant difference in the opinions of the three age groups of teachers.

2. With regard to the preparation of students Hand-books the mean values of three age groups of teachers are 2.45, 2.61, 2.57, respectively. The calculated 'F' value 1.29, is less than the table value. Hence it is not significant. Hence the null hypothesis is accepted. This indicates that the opinions of the teachers of the three age groups do not differ significantly.

3. Regarding teachers Hand-books the mean values of the three age groups are 2.60, 2.56 and 2.59 respectively. The calculated 'F' value 0.13, is less than the table value. Hence it is not significant. Hence the null hypothesis is accepted. Hence it

Table 4.17. Table Showing Mean Difference of Opinions of three Age Groups of In-Service Teachers on the Guidance given by DIETs Faculty

Activities / *Age*	*Below 30 N=58*		*30-45 N=213*		*Above 45 N=74*		*Aggregate N= 345*	
	Mean	*SD*	*Mean*	*SD*	*Mean*	*SD*	*Mean*	*SD*
The guidance given by lecturers in the preparation of question banks is satisfactory	2.60	0.7	2.63	0.67	2.72	0.56	2.64	0.65
The guidance given by lecturers in the preparation of student Hand-books is satisfactory	2.45	0.71	2.61	0.65	2.57	0.66	2.57	0.66
The guidance given by lecturers for the preparation of teachers Hand-books is satisfactory	2.60	0.67	2.56	0.62	2.59	0.59	2.58	0.62
The use of teaching learning material during classroom transaction by lecturers is satisfactory.	2.66	0.69	2.72	0.55	2.77	0.51	2.72	0.57
Total	10.31	1.73	10.52	1.69	10.65	1.75	10.51	1.71

Table 4.17a. Table Showing ANOVA of Opinions of three Differently Aged Groups of In-Service Teachers on the Guidance by DIETs Faculty

Activities	*Sum of squares*		*Mean square*		*F*
	Between	*Within*	*Between*	*Within*	
The guidance given by lecturers in the preparation of question banks is satisfactory	0.53	146.62	0.26	0.43	0.62
The guidance given by lecturers in the preparation of student Hand-books is satisfactory	1.13	149.38	0.57	0.44	1.29
The guidance given by lecturers for the preparation of teachers Hand-books is satisfactory	0.10	134.11	0.05	0.39	0.13
The use of teaching learning material during classroom transaction by lecturers is satisfactory.	0.43	110.86	0.22	0.32	0.67
Total	3.76	998.43	1.88	2.92	0.64

is arrived that there is no significant difference among the opinion of these three age groups.

4. With regard to the use of TLM, the mean values of the three age groups are 2.66, 2.72 and 2.77 respectively. The calculated 'F' value 0.67 is less than the table value. Hence it is not significant. Hence the null hypothesis is accepted. Hence it is indicated that there is no significant deference in the opinions of the three groups in the use of TLM during classroom transaction.

CONCLUSION

From the above table it is concluded that regarding the opinions of the teachers in the above four aspects, age of the teachers has little impact in the opinions of the teachers.

Fig. 4.10 . Graph Showing Mean Difference of Opinions of three Age Groups of In-service Teachers on the Guidance by DIETs Faculty

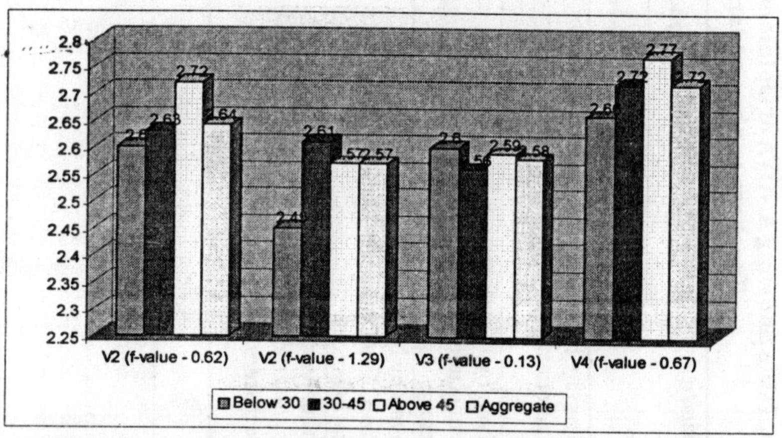

The above table shows the opinions of the teachers belonging to four different social classes towards the four activities on which the guidance given by DIET faculty.

1. Regarding preparation of question banks the mean values of teachers belonging to O.C, B.C, S.C and S.T social classes are 2.68, 2.58, 2.64 and 2.89 respectively. The calculated 'F' value 0.99, is less than the table value.

Table 4.18. Table Showing Mean Difference of Opinions of four Groups of Teachers of In-Service on the basis of Social Class on the Guidance by DIET Faculty

Social Class / *Activities*	*Open category N=165*		*Backward caste N=126*		*Scheduled caste N=45*		*Scheduled tribe N=9*		*Aggregate N=345*	
	Mean	*SD*	*Mean*	*SD*	*Mean*	*SD*	*Mean*	*SD*	*Mean*	*SD*
The guidance given by lecturers in the preparation of question banks is satisfactory	2.68	0.62	2.58	0.70	2.64	0.68	2.89	0.33	2.64	0.65
The guidance given by lecturers in the preparation of student Hand-books is satisfactory	2.54	0.69	2.60	0.66	2.53	0.59	3.00	0.00	2.57	0.66
The guidance given by lecturers for the preparation of teachers Hand-books is satisfactory	2.55	0.62	2.62	0.64	2.51	0.63	2.78	0.44	2.58	0.62
The use of teaching learning material during classroom transaction by lecturers is satisfactory.	2.67	0.61	2.75	0.55	2.78	0.52	3.00	0.00	2.72	0.57
Total	10.44	1.76	10.54	1.71	10.47	1.56	11.67	0.71	10.51	1.71

Table 4.18a. Table Showing ANOVA of Different Groups of In-Service Teachers of Social Class on the Guidance by DIETs Faculty

Activities	*Sum of squares*		*Mean square*		*F*
	Between	*Within*	*Between*	*Within*	
The guidance given by lecturers in the preparation of question banks is satisfactory	1.27	145.88	0.42	0.43	0.99
The guidance given by lecturers in the preparation of student Hand-books is satisfactory	1.96	148.55	0.65	0.44	1.50
The guidance given by lecturers for the preparation of teachers Hand-books is satisfactory	0.89	133.33	0.30	0.39	0.76
The use of teaching learning material during classroom transaction by lecturers is satisfactory.	1.31	109.98	0.44	0.32	1.35
Total	12.99	989.21	4.33	2.90	1.49

Hence it is not significant. Hence the null hypothesis is accepted. This indicates that there is no significant difference among the opinions of the different social classes of teachers.

2. As to the preparation of students Hand-books, the means of teachers of different social classes are 2.54, 2.60, 2.53 and 3.00 respectively The calculated 'F' value 1.50, is less than the table value. Hence it is not significant. Hence the null hypothesis is accepted. This indicates that there is no significant difference among the opinions of the teachers of four social classes.
3. In the case of preparation of teachers Hand-books the mean values of the opinions of the teachers of O.C, B.C, S.C and S.T social classes are 2.55, 2.62, 2.51 and 2.78 respectively. The calculated 'F' value 0.76, is less than the table value. Hence it is not significant. Hence the null hypothesis is accepted. This shows that there is no significant difference in the opinions of the four social classes of teachers.
4. Regarding the use of TLM during class room transaction, the means of opinions of four social classes of teachers are 2.67, 2.75, 2.78 and 3.00 respectively. The calculated 'F; value 1.35, is less than the table value. Hence it is not significant. Hence the null hypothesis is accepted. This indicates that there is no significant difference among the opinions of the four social classes of teachers regarding the use of TLM.

CONCLUSION

The above analysis depicts that the teachers of different social classes have responded more positively and there is not much difference in the opinions of the teachers on the guidance given by DIET faculty.

The above table shows that the opinions of the teachers belonging to three nativities of rural, urban and tribal areas.

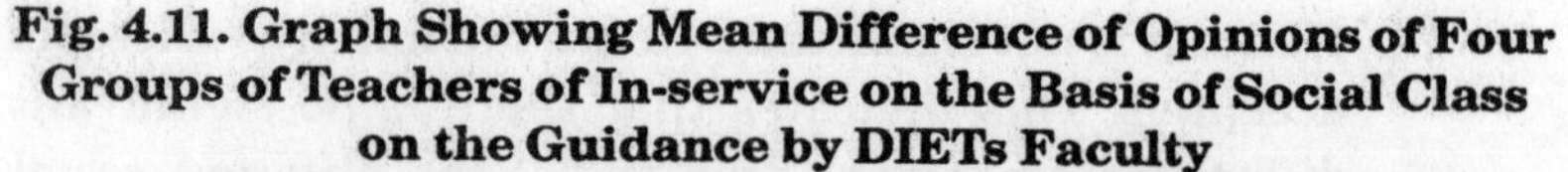

Fig. 4.11. Graph Showing Mean Difference of Opinions of Four Groups of Teachers of In-service on the Basis of Social Class on the Guidance by DIETs Faculty

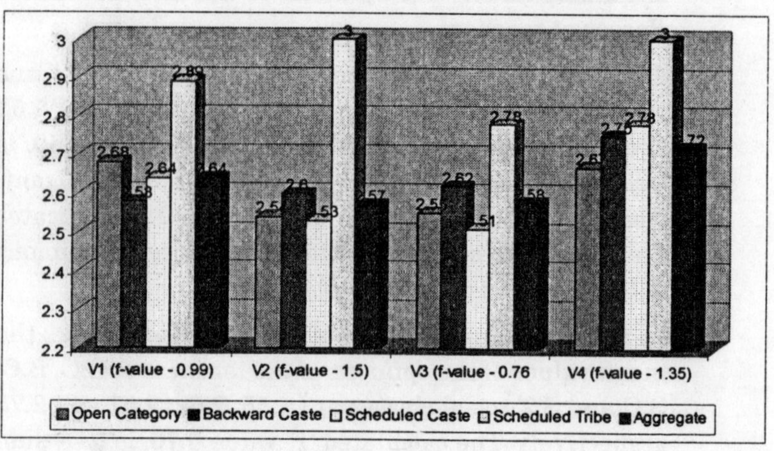

1. Regarding preparation of question banks the means of opinions of the three nativity groups of teachers are 2.61, 2.68 and 2.78 respectively. The generated 'F' value 0.70, is less than the table value. Hence it is not significant. Hence the null hypothesis is accepted. This indicates that there is no significant difference among the opinions of these teachers of three nativities. It can be inferred that the nativity of the teachers has no significant impact on their opinions on the preparation of question banks.

2. With regard to the preparation of students Hand-books the means of opinions of teachers belonging to three nativities are 2.53, 2.64, 2.56 and 2.57 respectively. The generated 'F' value 1.16, is less than the table value. Hence it is not significant. Hence the null hypothesis is accepted. This indicates that there is no significant difference in the opinions of the teachers belonging to different nativities.

3. With regard to the preparation of teachers' Hand-books the means of the opinions of the teachers are 2.59, 2.55 and2.78 respectively. The calculated 'F' value 0.62, is less than the table value. Hence it is not significant. Hence the null hypothesis is accepted. This indicates that there is no significant difference in the opinions of the teachers of three nativities.

Table 4.19. Table Showing Mean Difference Values of Opinions of Three Different Nativity In-service Teachers

Nativity / *Activities*	*Rural N=203*		*Urban N=133*		*Tribal N=9*		*Aggregate N=345*	
	Mean	*SD*	*Mean*	*SD*	*Mean*	*SD*	*Mean*	*SD*
The guidance given by lecturers in the preparation of question banks is satisfactory	2.61	0.70	2.68	0.58	2.78	0.44	2.64	0.65
The guidance given by lecturers in the preparation of student Hand-books is satisfactory	2.53	0.70	2.64	0.61	2.56	0.53	2.57	0.66
The guidance given by lecturers for the preparation of teachers Hand-books is satisfactory	2.59	0.63	2.55	0.62	2.78	0.44	2.58	0.62
The use of teaching learning material during classroom transaction by lecturers is satisfactory.	2.69	0.59	2.77	0.52	2.67	0.71	2.72	0.57
Total	10.42	1.77	10.64	1.62	10.78	1.48	10.51	1.71

Table 4.19a. Table Showing ANOVA Values of Opinions of Three Groups of Different Nativity In-service Teachers on the Guidance by DIETs Faculty

Activities	*Sum of squares*		*Mean square*		*F*
	Between	*Within*	*Between*	*Within*	
The guidance given by lecturers in the preparation of question banks is satisfactory	0.60	146.55	0.30	0.43	0.70
The guidance given by lecturers in the preparation of student Hand-books is satisfactory	1.01	149.50	0.51	0.44	1.16
The guidance given by lecturers for the preparation of teachers Hand-books is satisfactory	0.49	133.73	0.24	0.39	0.62
The use of teaching learning material during classroom transaction by lecturers is satisfactory.	0.45	110.84	0.22	0.32	0.69
Total	4.55	997.64	2.28	2.92	0.78

4. Regarding the use of TLM during classroom transaction, the means of the opinions of the three nativity groups of teachers are 2.69, 2.77 and 2.67 respectively. The generated 'F' value 0.69, is less than the table value. Hence it is not significant. Hence the null hypothesis is accepted. This indicates that there is no significant difference among the opinions of teachers of different nativities.

CONCLUSION

The opinions of teachers of the urban rural and tribal nativities are not significantly different regarding the above four activities. This indicates that the nativity of the teachers has no significant impact on their opinions regarding the four activities. All the teachers have responded positively and more or less similarly towards the guidance by DIET faculty towards the four activities.

Fig. 4.12. Graph Showing Mean Difference Values of Opinions of Three Different Nativity In-service Teachers

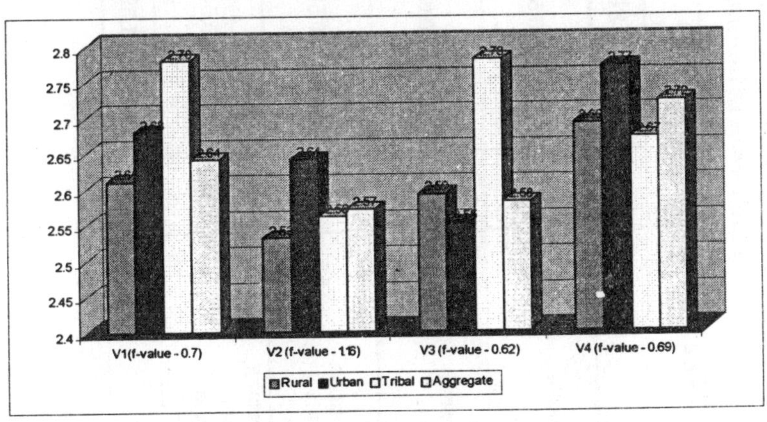

The above table shows the opinions of the teachers belonging to four localities of rural, urban, sub-urban and tribal.

1. Regarding preparation of question banks the means of opinions of the four localities of the teachers namely rural, urban, sub-urban and tribal are 2.61, 2.74, 2.30 and 2.47 respectively. The generated 'F' value 2.33 is more than the table value. Hence it is significant at 0.05 level. Hence the null hypothesis is

Table 4.20. Table Showing Mean Difference of Opinions of Groups of In-service Teachers of Different School Locations

School / *Activities*	*Rural N=197*		*Urban N=123*		*Sub-Urban N=10*		*Tribal N=15*		*Aggregate N=345*	
	Mean	*SD*	*Mean*	*SD*	*Mean*	*SD*	*Mean*	*SD*	*Mean*	*SD*
The guidance given by lecturers in the preparation of question banks is satisfactory	2.61	0.69	2.74	0.54	2.30	0.82	2.47	0.83	2.64	0.65
The guidance given by lecturers in the preparation of student Hand-books is satisfactory	2.58	0.67	2.59	0.63	2.3	0.82	2.47	0.74	2.57	0.66
The guidance given by lecturers for the preparation of teachers Hand-books is satisfactory	2.59	0.63	2.63	0.58	2	0.67	2.33	0.72	2.58	0.62
The use of teaching learning material during classroom transaction by lecturers is satisfactory.	2.72	0.57	2.73	0.54	2.9	0.32	2.53	0.83	2.72	0.57
Total	10.5	1.68	10.7	1.59	9.5	1.65	9.8	2.6	10.51	1.71

Table 4.20a. Table Showing ANOVA Values of Opinions of In-service Teachers of Different School Locations

Activities	*Sum of squares*		*Mean square*		*F*
	Between	*Within*	*Between*	*Within*	
The guidance given by lecturers in the preparation of question banks is satisfactory	2.96	144.19	0.99	0.42	2.33*
The guidance given by lecturers in the preparation of student Hand-books is satisfactory	0.97	149.54	0.32	0.44	0.74
The guidance given by lecturers for the preparation of teachers Hand-books is satisfactory	4.65	129.57	1.55	0.38	4.08**
The use of teaching learning material during classroom transaction by lecturers is satisfactory.	0.86	110.42	0.29	0.32	0.89
Total	22.17	980.02	7.39	2.87	2.57*

*Significant at 0.05 level.
**Significant at 0.01 level.

rejected. This indicates that there is significant difference among the opinions of the teachers of four localities. Hence it can be inferred that the locality of the school of the teachers has significant impact on their opinions on the preparation of question banks.

2. With regards to the guidance given by DIET lecturers in the preparation of students Hand-books, the means of opinions of the four locality of the teachers are 2.58, 2.59, 2.30 and 2.47 respectively. The calculated 'F' value 0.74 is less than the table value. This shows that there is no significant difference among the opinions of the teachers of the four localities. Hence the null hypothesis is accepted. Hence, it can be inferred that the locality of the school of the teachers has no significant impact in their opinions on the guidance given by DIET lecturers on the preparation of student Hand-books.

3. As far as the guidance given by DIET faculty for the preparation of teachers Hand-books is concerned, the means of opinions of the four locality teachers are 2.59, 2.63, 2.0 and 2.33 respectively. The obtained 'F' value 4.08 is more than the table value. Hence, it is significant at 0.01 level. Hence the null hypothesis is rejected. This indicates that there is significant difference among the opinions of the teachers of the four localities. Hence, it can be inferred that the locality of the schools of the teachers has significant impact on the opinions on the preparation of teachers' Hand-books.

4. With respect to the use of teaching learning material during classroom transaction by lecturers, the means of opinions of the four locality teachers are 2.72, 2.73, 2.90 and 2.55 respectively. The arrived 'F' value 0.89 is less than the table value. Hence it is not significant at both levels. Hence the null hypothesis is accepted. This indicates that there is no significant difference among the opinions of the teachers of the four localities. Hence, it can be inferred that the locality of the schools of the teachers has no significant impact on the opinions on the use of teaching learning material during classroom transaction by lecturers.

CONCLUSION

The locality of the schools of the teachers has significant impact on the opinions of teachers regarding the guidance given by the DIET faculty and in the preparation of question banks and in the use of teaching learning material by DIET faculty during class room transaction.

Fig. 4.13. Graph Showing Mean Difference of Opinions of Groups of In-service Teachers of Different School Locations

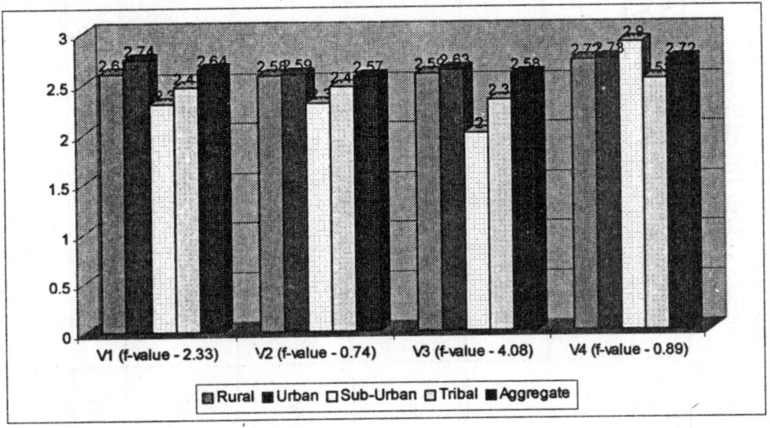

The above table shows the opinions of teachers possessing different general qualifications, regarding the four activities guided by DIET faculty.

1. Regarding the preparation of question banks, the means of opinions of teachers possessing different general qualifications like intermediate, degree and post-graduation are 2.70, 2.64 and 2.62 respectively. The calculated 'F' value 0.26, is less than the table value. Hence it is not significant. Hence the null hypothesis is accepted. This indicates that there is no significant difference in the opinions of the teachers possessing different levels of general qualifications.

2. With regards to the preparation of students Hand-books the means of the opinions of the three groups of teachers are 2.57, 2.56 and 2.59 respectively. The calculated 'F' value 0.05, is less than the table value. Hence it is not significant. Hence the

Table 4.21. Table Showing Mean Difference of the Opinions of the Groups of In-service Teachers Possessing Different General Qualifications

General qualifications / *Activities*	*Intermediate N=44*		*Graduation N=185*		*Post graduation N=116*		*Aggregate N=345*	
	Mean	*SD*	*Mean*	*SD*	*Mean*	*SD*	*Mean*	*SD*
The guidance given by lecturers in the preparation of question banks is satisfactory	2.70	0.59	2.64	0.68	2.62	0.64	2.64	0.65
The guidance given by lecturers in the preparation of student Hand-books is satisfactory	2.57	0.55	2.56	0.68	2.59	0.67	2.57	0.66
The guidance given by lecturers for the preparation of teachers Hand-books is satisfactory	2.55	0.59	2.56	0.64	2.61	0.62	2.58	0.62
The use of teaching learning material during classroom transaction by lecturers is satisfactory.	2.80	0.46	2.75	0.55	2.66	0.63	2.72	0.57
Total	10.61	1.47	10.51	1.79	10.47	1.67	10.51	1.71

Table 4.21a. Table Showing ANOVA Values of Opinions of Groups of In-service Teachers Possessing Different General Qualifications

Activities	*Sum of squares*		*Mean square*		*F*
	Between	*Within*	*Between*	*Within*	
The guidance given by lecturers in the preparation of question banks is satisfactory	0.22	146.92	0.11	0.43	0.26
The guidance given by lecturers in the preparation of student Hand-books is satisfactory	0.04	150.47	0.02	0.44	0.05
The guidance given by lecturers for the preparation of teachers Hand-books is satisfactory	0.23	133.99	0.11	0.39	0.29
The use of teaching learning material during classroom transaction by lecturers is satisfactory.	0.86	110.43	0.43	0.32	1.33
Total	0.62	1001.57	0.31	2.93	0.11

null hypothesis is accepted. This indicates that there is no significant difference in the opinions of the three groups of teachers possessing different general qualifications, which infers that there is no impact of general qualifications on the preparation of student Hand-books.

3. As to the preparation of the teachers' Hand-books the means of the opinions of the three groups of teachers are 2.55, 2.56 and 2.61 respectively. The calculated 'F' value 0.29, is less than the table value. Hence it is not significant. Hence the null hypothesis is accepted. This indicates that there is no significant difference among the opinions of the differently qualified teachers on the preparation of teachers' Hand-books.

4. In the case of use of TLM during classroom transaction, the means of the opinions of the teachers possessing different general qualifications are 2.80, 2.75 and 2.66 respectively. The calculated 'F' value 1.33, is less than the table value. Hence it is not significant. Hence the null hypothesis is accepted. It can be inferred that there is no significant difference in the opinions of teachers possessing three levels of general qualifications.

CONCLUSION

The possession of higher general qualifications i.e. graduation and post graduation caused no significant difference in their opinions regarding the four activities guided by DIET faculty. All the teachers opined more or less similar on the guidance by DIET.

Fig. 4.14. Graph Showing Mean Difference of the Opinions of the Groups of In-service Teachers Possessing Different General Qualifications

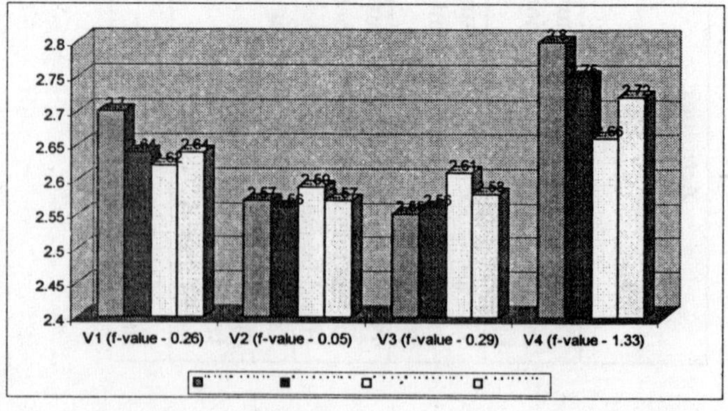

Table 4.22. Table Showing Mean Difference of Opinions of the Group of In-service Teachers Possessing Different-Professional Qualifications

Professional qualification / *Activities*	*TTC N=44*		*D.Ed. N=185*		*B.Ed. N=116*		*Aggregate N=345*	
	Mean	*SD*	*Mean*	*SD*	*Mean*	*SD*	*Mean*	*SD*
The guidance given by lecturers in the preparation of question banks is satisfactory	2.67	0.64	2.62	0.67	2.70	0.60	2.64	0.65
The guidance given by lecturers in the preparation of student Hand-books is satisfactory	2.65	0.63	2.50	0.69	2.77	0.50	2.57	0.66
The guidance given by lecturers for the preparation of teachers Hand-books is satisfactory	2.57	0.60	2.57	0.66	2.63	0.49	2.58	0.62
The use of teaching learning material during classroom transaction by lecturers is satisfactory.	2.81	0.48	2.69	0.60	2.63	0.61	2.72	0.57
Total	10.69	1.49	10.39	1.86	10.73	1.26	10.51	1.71

Table 4.22 a. Table Showing ANOVA Values of Opinions of Groups of In-service Teachers Possessing Different Professional Qualifications

Activities	*Sum of squares*		*Mean square*		*F*
	Between	*Within*	*Between*	*Within*	
The guidance given by lecturers in the preparation of question banks is satisfactory	0.24	146.91	0.12	0.43	0.28
The guidance given by lecturers in the preparation of student Hand-books is satisfactory	2.77	147.75	1.38	0.43	3.20*
The guidance given by lecturers for the preparation of teachers Hand-books is satisfactory	0.11	134.11	0.05	0.39	0.14
The use of teaching learning material during classroom transaction by lecturers is satisfactory.	1.19	110.10	0.60	0.32	1.85
Total	8.33	993.87	4.16	2.91	1.43

The above table shows the opinions of teachers possessing different professional qualifications regarding the four activities guided by DIET faculty.

1. Regarding the preparation of question banks the means of opinions of teachers possessing different levels of professional qualifications are 2.67, 2.62 and 2.70 respectively. The generated 'F' value 0.28, is less than the table value. Hence it is not significant. Hence the null hypothesis is accepted. It can be inferred that there is no significant difference among the opinions of the three groups of teachers possessing different professional qualifications.
2. With regard to the preparation of students Hand-books, the means of opinions of the three differently professional qualified groups of teachers are 2.65, 2.50 and 2.77 respectively. The generated 'F' value 3.20, is more than the table value. Hence it is significant at 0.01 level. Hence the null hypothesis is rejected. This indicates that the opinions of the three differently professional qualified teachers are significantly different. This infers that the B.Ed qualified teachers opined more better than the TTC/D.Ed teachers. It can also be inferred that higher the professional qualification, the more positive the professional opinion.
3. Regarding preparation of teachers Hand-books the means of opinions of the three different professionally qualified teachers are 2.57, 2.57 and 2.63 respectively. The calculated 'F' value 0.14, is less than the table value. Hence it is not significant. Hence the null hypothesis is accepted. This indicates that there is no significant difference in their opinions.
4. Regarding the use of TLM, the means of opinions of teachers with different professional qualifications are 2.81, 2.69 and 2.63 respectively. The generated 'F' value 1.85, is less than the table value. Hence it is not significant. Hence the null hypothesis is accepted. This indicates that there is no significant difference in the opinions of the differently professionally qualified teachers.

CONCLUSIONS

The opinions of teachers possessing different professional qualifications is not significant regarding the three activities of preparation of question banks, preparation of teachers' Hand-books, and use of TLM during class room transaction. But regarding preparation of students' Hand-books the higher professional qualified teachers opined significantly better than the TTC/D.Ed qualified teachers.

Fig. 4.15. Graph Showing Mean Difference of Opinions of the Group of In-service Teachers Possessing Different-Professional Qualifications

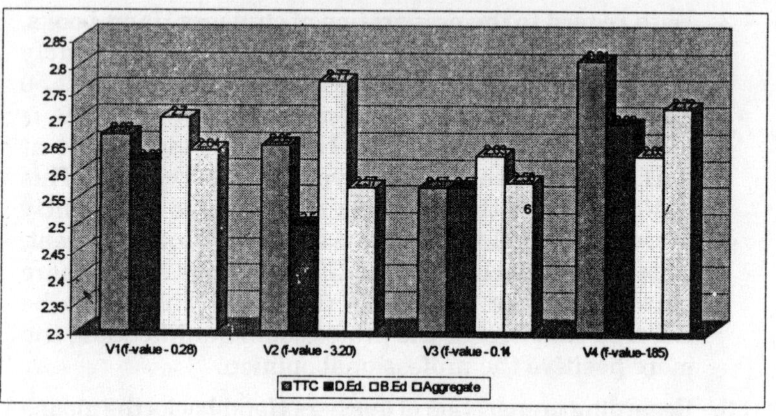

The above table shows the opinions of the teachers with different lengths of teaching experience – namely up to 10 years, eleven to twenty years and above twenty years regarding the four activities guided by DIET faculty.

1. Regarding the preparation of question banks the means of the three groups having different teaching experience are 2.60, 2.70 and 2.66 respectively. The calculated 'F' value 0.79, is less than the table value. Hence it is not significant. Hence the null hypothesis is accepted. It indicates that there is no significant difference in the opinions of the teachers having different lengths of teaching experience.

Table 4.23. Table Showing Mean Difference of Opinions of Three Groups of In-service Teachers Possessing Different Teaching Experience

Teaching experience / *Activities*	*Up to 10 years N=158*		*10 to 20 years N=115*		*Above 20 years N=72*		*Aggregate N= 345*	
	Mean	*SD*	*Mean*	*SD*	*Mean*	*SD*	*Mean*	*SD*
The guidance given by lecturers in the preparation of question banks is satisfactory	2.60	0.70	2.70	0.61	2.66	0.61	2.64	0.65
The guidance given by lecturers in the preparation of student Hand-books is satisfactory	2.52	0.67	2.63	0.67	2.59	0.62	2.57	0.66
The guidance given by lecturers for the preparation of teachers Hand-books is satisfactory	2.57	0.64	2.63	0.61	2.51	0.61	2.58	0.62
The use of teaching learning material during classroom transaction by lecturers is satisfactory.	2.67	0.61	2.78	0.53	2.73	0.53	2.72	0.57
Total	10.36	1.72	10.73	1.69	10.49	1.71	10.51	1.71

Table 4.23 a. Table Showing ANOVA Values of Opinions of Three Groups of In-service Teachers Possessing Different Teaching Experience

Activities	*Sum of squares*		*Mean square*		*F*
	Between	*Within*	*Between*	*Within*	
The guidance given by lecturers in the preparation of question banks is satisfactory	0.67	146.47	0.34	0.43	0.79
The guidance given by lecturers in the preparation of student Hand-books is satisfactory	0.76	149.75	0.38	0.44	0.87
The guidance given by lecturers for the preparation of teachers Hand-books is satisfactory	0.63	133.59	0.31	0.39	0.80
The use of teaching learning material during classroom transaction by lecturers is satisfactory.	0.81	110.47	0.41	0.32	1.26
Total	8.96	993.23	4.48	2.90	1.54

2. In case of preparation of students Hand-books, the means of opinions of the three groups of teachers are 2.52, 2.63 and 2.59. The generated 'F' value 0.87, is less than the table value. Hence it is not significant. Hence the null hypothesis is accepted. This indicates that there is no significant difference among the opinions of the three groups.
3. With regard to the preparation of teachers Hand-books the means of opinions of the three groups of teachers with different teaching experience are 2.57, 2.63 and 2.51 respectively. The generated 'F' value 0.80, is less than the table value. Hence it is not significant. Hence the null hypothesis is accepted. This indicates that there is no significant difference in the opinions of these three groups.
4. Regarding the use of TLM the means of the opinions of the three groups of differently experienced teachers are 2.67, 2.78 and 2.73 respectively. The generated 'F' value 1.26, is less than the table value. Hence it is not significant. Hence the null hypothesis is accepted. This indicates that there is no significant difference in the opinions of these three groups.

Fig. 4.16. Table Showing Mean Difference of Opinions of Three Groups of In-service Teachers Possessing Different Teaching Experience

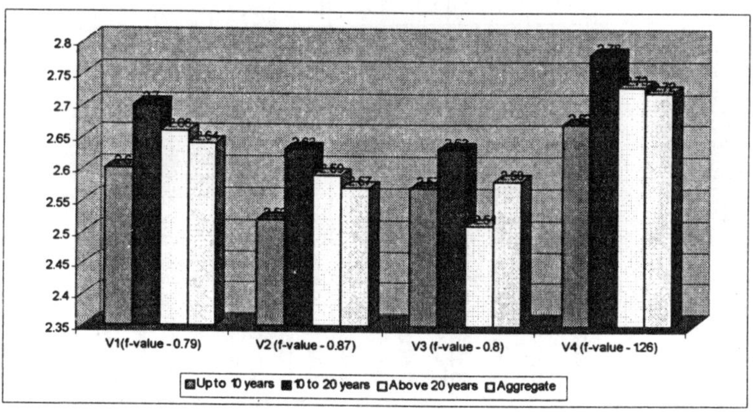

Table 4.24. Table Showing Mean Difference of Opinions of Groups of In-service Teachers Teaching Different Classes in School Regarding the Four Activities of Guidance by DIETs

Teaching classes / *Activities*	*1 & 2 Classes N=80*		*3 to 5 Classes N=183*		*6 & 7 Classes N=82*		*Aggregate N=345*	
	Mean	*SD*	*Mean*	*SD*	*Mean*	*SD*	*Mean*	*SD*
The guidance given by lecturers in the preparation of question banks is satisfactory	2.55	0.73	2.64	0.64	2.73	0.61	2.64	0.65
The guidance given by lecturers in the preparation of student Hand-books is satisfactory	2.58	0.67	2.59	0.66	2.52	0.67	2.57	0.66
The guidance given by lecturers for the preparation of teachers Hand-books is satisfactory	2.59	0.59	2.56	0.65	2.61	0.6	2.58	0.62
The use of teaching learning material during classroom transaction by lecturers is satisfactory.	2.79	0.5	2.72	0.57	2.66	0.63	2.72	0.57
Total	10.5	1.56	10.51	1.76	10.52	1.74	10.51	1.71

Table 4.24 a. Table Showing ANOVA Values of Opinions of Groups of In-service Teachers Teaching Different Classes Regarding the Four Activities

Activities	*Sum of squares*		*Mean square*		***F***
	Between	*Within*	*Between*	*Within*	
The guidance given by lecturers in the preparation of question banks is satisfactory	1.34	145.81	0.67	0.43	1.57
The guidance given by lecturers in the preparation of student Hand-books is satisfactory	0.25	150.26	0.12	0.44	0.28
The guidance given by lecturers for the preparation of teachers Hand-books is satisfactory	0.17	134.05	0.08	0.39	0.21
The use of teaching learning material during classroom transaction by lecturers is satisfactory.	0.67	110.61	0.34	0.32	1.04
Total	0.02	1002.17	0.01	2.93	0.00

CONCLUSIONS

The opinions of the teachers having different teaching experience has no significant effect in the preparation of question banks, Hand-books and use of TLM in the class room. This may be due to some negative attitude of more experienced teachers towards change and new intervention, like question banks, Hand-books and use of TLM in the class room during transacting through new approaches.

The above table shows that the difference in the opinions of the teachers teaching different classes namely 1-2 classes, 3-5 classes and 6-7 classes, regarding the four activities of preparation of question banks, Hand-books and use of TLM guided by the DIET faculty.

1. Regarding the preparation of question banks the means of the opinions of the three groups of teachers are 2.55, 2.64 and 2.73 respectively. The generated 'F' value 1.57, is less than the table value. Hence it is not significant. Hence the null hypothesis is accepted. This indicates that there is no significant difference in the opinions of these three groups.

2. In case of preparation of student Hand-books the means of opinion of three groups of teachers are 2.58, 2.59 and 2.52 respectively. The calculated 'F' value 0.28, is less than the table value. Hence it is not significant. Hence the null hypothesis is accepted. This shows that there is no significant difference in the opinions of these three groups of teachers teaching various classes in these four activities.

3. With regards to the preparation of teachers Hand-books the means of opinions of these three groups are 2.59, 2.56 and 2.61 respectively. The generated 'F' value 0.21, is less than the table value. Hence it is not significant. Hence the null hypothesis is accepted. This indicates that there is no significant difference between the opinions of teachers teaching different classes.

4. With regards to the use of TLM during class room transaction, the means of opinions of the teachers teaching different classes are 2.79, 2.72 and 2.66 respectively. The generated 'F' value 1.04, is less than the table value. Hence it is not significant. Hence the null hypothesis is accepted. This

indicates that there is no significant difference between the opinions of the teachers regarding TLM use.

CONCLUSION

There is no significant difference in the opinions of the teachers teaching different levels of classes regarding the four activities of preparation of question banks, Hand-books and in the use of TLM during class room transaction. This indicates that the level of classes teaching has not much impact on the opinions of the teachers towards the four activities.

Fig. 4.17. Graph Showing Mean Difference of Opinions of Groups of In-service Teachers Teaching Different Classes in School Regarding the Four Activities of Guidance by DIETs

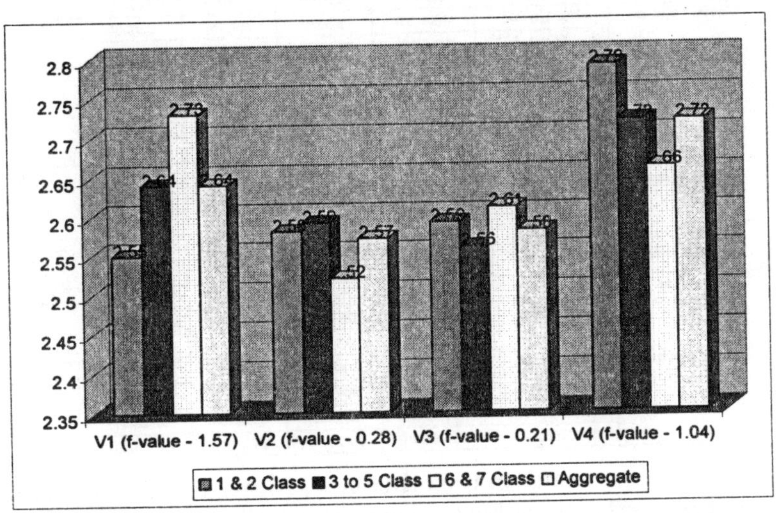

Age – Variable

It is to find out the difference of opinion in terms of the age of the teachers on MLL programme. The chi-square value is used.

The calculated chi-square value 55.09, is more than the table value. Hence it is highly significant at 0.01 level. Hence the null hypothesis is rejected. This indicates that there is significant difference among the opinions of teachers of the three age groups. More over 31-45 years aged teachers are more positive

Table 4.25. Table Showing Chi-square Values of Significance of Opinions of In-service Teachers Variable-wise on Minimum Levels of Learning Training Programme

Variable	*Group*	*Most useful*	*Useful*	*Less useful*	*Total*	*Chi-square*
Age (in years)	Below 30	40 (11.59)	10(2.90)	8 (2.32)	58 (16.81)	55.09**
	31 – 45	150(43.48)	40(11.59)	23(6.67)	213(61.74)	
	Above 45	21(6.09)	19(5.51)	34(9.86)	74(21.45)	
Sex	Male	100(28.99)	30(8.70)	44(12.75)	174(50.43)	9.86**
	Female	111(32.17)	39(11.30)	21(6.09)	171(49.57)	
Social class	OC	120(34.78)	22(6.38)	23(6.67)	165(47.83)	32.12**
	BC	70(20.29)	30(8.70)	26(7.54)	126(36.52)	
	SC	20(5.80)	15(4.35)	10(2.90)	45(13.04)	
	ST	1(0.29)	2(0.58)	6(1.74)	9(2.61)	
Nativity	Rural	150(43.48)	33(9.57)	20(5.80)	203(58.84)	40.77**
	Urban	55(15.94)	34(9.86)	44(12.75)	133(38.55)	
	Tribal	6(1.74)	2(0.58)	1(0.29)	9(2.61)	
Marital status	Un-married	15(4.35)	2(0.58)	5(1.45)	22(6.35)	1.78
	Married	196(56.89)	67(19.42)	60(17.39)	323(93.62)	
School location	Rural	145(42.03)	35(10.14)	17(4.93)	197(57.10)	47.27**
	Urban	51(14.78)	27(7.83)	45(13.04)	123(35.65)	
	Sub-urban	5(1.45)	3(0.87)	2(0.58)	10(2.90)	
	Tribal	10(2.90)	4(1.16)	1(0.29)	15(4.35)	
General qualifications	Intermediate	26(7.54)	12(3.48)	6(1.74)	44(12.75)	19.40*
	Graduation	130(37.68)	30(8.70)	25(7.25)	185(53.62)	
	Post graduation	55(15.94	27(7.83)	34(9.86)	33.62)	
Professional qualifications	T.T.C/ D.Ed	199(57.68)	55(15.94)	61(17.68)	315(91.30)	6.80*
	B.Ed	12(3.48)	10(2.90)	8(2.32)	30(8.70)	
Teaching experience (in years)	Up to 10	105(30.43)	37(10.72)	16(4.64)	158(45.80)	35.01**
	11 to 20	70(20.29)	26(7.54)	19(5.51)	115(33.33)	
	Above 20	36(10.43)	6(1.74)	30(8.70)	72(20.87)	
Classes teaching	1,2 classes	61(17.68)	10(2.90)	9(2.61)	80(23.19)	120.25**
	3-5 classes	140(40.58)	30(8.70)	13(3.77)	183(53.04)	
	6,7 classes	10(2.90)	29(8.41)	43(12.46)	82(23.77)	
	Total	211(61.16)	69(20.00)	65(16.84)	345(100.0)	

to this programme than the other two groups. It can be inferred that this may be due to better awareness and adequately matured ness over the other groups.

Sex Variable

It is to find out the difference of opinion in terms of the sex of the teachers on MLL programme. The chi-square value is used.

The calculated chi-square value 9.86, is more than the table value. Hence it is highly significant at 0.01 level. Hence the null hypothesis is rejected. This indicates that there is significant difference in the opinions of the teachers in respect of their sex. The female teachers' opinions are more better than male teachers' opinions. This may be due to more number of female teachers working for lower classes which is more applicable to lower classes and hence pro to minimum levels of learning programme than those male teachers who are working more in number for higher classes.

Variable – Social Class

It is to find out the difference of opinion in terms of the social class of the teachers, on MLL programme. The chi-square value is used.

The calculated chi-square value 32.12, is more than the table value. Hence it is highly significant at 0.01 level. Hence the null hypothesis is rejected. This indicates that there is significant difference in the opinions of the teachers.

Variable – Nativity

It is to find out the difference of opinion in terms of the nativity of the teachers, on MLL programme. The chi-square value is used.

The calculated chi-square value 40.77, is more than the table value. Hence it is highly significant at 0.01 level. Hence the null hypothesis is rejected. This indicates that there is significant difference among the opinions of the teachers belonging to the three nativities. This may be due to their cultural and climatic differences.

Variable – Marital Status

It is to find out the difference of opinion in terms of the marital status of the teachers, on MLL programme. The chi-square value is used.

The generated chi-square value 1.78, is less than the table value. Hence it is not significant. Hence the null hypothesis is accepted. This indicates that there is no significant difference in the opinions of the married and un-married teachers. It is inferred that the marital status of teachers has not incurring much influence on the opinions of the married or un-married teachers.

Variable – School Location

It is to find out the difference of opinion in terms of the school location of the teachers, on MLL programme. The chi-square value is used.

The calculated chi-square value 47.27, is more than the table value. Hence it is highly significant at 0.01 level. Hence the null hypothesis is rejected. This indicates that there is significant difference among the opinions of the four school localities teachers, which may be due to their environment of work and locality of school and the standards of the children.

Variable – General Qualifications

It is to find out the difference of opinion in terms of the general qualifications of the teachers, on MLL programme. The chi-square value is used.

The calculated chi-square value 19.40, is more than the table value. Hence it is significant at 0.05 level. Hence the null hypothesis is rejected. This indicates that the opinions of these three categories of teachers are significantly different. This may be due to their different academic backgrounds. (disciplines)

Variable-Professional Qualifications

It is to find out the difference of opinion in terms of the professional qualifications of the teachers, on MLL programme. The chi-square value is used.

The generated chi-square value 6.80, is more than the table value. Hence it is significant at 0.05 level. Hence the null hypothesis is rejected. This indicates that there is significant difference between the opinions of these two categories of D.Ed and B.Ed qualified teachers, which may be due to the difference in their level of professional qualifications.

Variable – Teaching Experience

It is to find out the difference of opinion in terms of the teaching experience of the teachers, on MLL programme. The chi-square value is used.

The generated chi-square value 35.01, is more than the table value. Hence it is highly significant at 0.01 level. Hence the null hypothesis is rejected. This indicates that there is significant difference in the opinions of teachers with varied teaching experience. This may be due to learning by teachers out of their varied experiences and varied exposures during their long service.

Variable – Classes Teaching

It is to find out the difference of opinion in terms of the classes teaching by the teachers, on MLL programme. The chi-square value is used.

The generated chi-square value 120.25, is more than the table value. Hence it is highly significant at 0.01 level. Hence the null hypothesis is rejected. This indicates that there is significant difference among the opinions of teachers teaching different classes. This may be due to the level of lookout, subject exposure, Methodology applying by the teachers and the level of children and the standard of children.

CONCLUSION

In total for the training programme on Minimum Levels of Learning (MLL) out of 345 total teachers 61.16% have opted most useful and 16.84 have opted less useful, whereas 20% have chosen useful which indicates that there is highly significant difference among the opinions of teachers in terms of all the ten variables discussed so far above.

B. TRAINING PROGRAMME ON ACTIVITY METHOD

The second sub item is training programme conducted on Activity Method. The usefulness of this programme is taken on the three point scale as most useful, useful and less useful. The significance of opinion is calculated by using all the ten variables as follows.

Age – Variable

It is to find out the difference of opinion in terms of the age of the teachers, on the Activity Method. The chi-square value is used.

Table 4.26. Table Showing Chi-square Values of Significance of the Opinions of In-service Teachers Variable-wise on Activity Method Training Programme

Variable	*Group*	*Most useful*	*Useful*	*Less useful*	*Total*	*Chi-square*
Age (in years)	Below 30	45(1304)	10(2.90)	3(0.87)	58(16.81)	60.42**
	31 – 40	180(52.17)	30(8.70)	3(0.87)	213(61.74)	
	Above 45	35(10.14)	20(5.80)	19(5.51)	74(21.45)	
Sex	Male	133(38.35)	32(9.28)	9(2.61)	174(50.43)	2.34
	Female	127(36.81)	28(8.12)	16(4.64)	171(49.57)	
Social class	OC	125(36.23)	31(8.99)	9(2.61)	165(47.83)	29.55**
	BC	105(30.43)	14(4.06)	7(2.03)	126(36.52)	
	SC	28(8.12)	9(2.61)	8(2.32)	45(13.04)	
	ST	2(0.58)	6(1.74)	1(0.29)	9(2.61)	
Nativity	Rural	151(43.77)	32(9.28)	20(5.80)	203(58.84)	27.75**
	Urban	108(31.30)	22(6.38)	3(0.87)	133(38.55)	
	Tribal	1(0.29)	6(1.74)	2(0.58)	9(2.61)	
Marital status	Un-married	17(4.93)	3(0.87)	2(0.58)	22(6.35)	0.31
	Married	243(70.43)	57(16.52)	23(6.67)	323(93.62)	
School location	Rural	150(43.18)	39(11.30)	8(2.32)	197(57.10)	104.92**
	Urban	100(28.99)	18(5.22)	5(1.45)	123(35.65)	
	Sub-urban	8(2.32)	1(0.29)	1(0.29)	10(2.90)	
	Tribal	2(0.58)	2(0.58)	11(3.19)	15(4.35)	

General qualifications	Intermediate	26(7.54)	10(2.90)	8(2.32)	44(12.75)	21.66**
	Graduation	133(38.55)	41(11.88)	11(3.19)	185(53.62)	
	Post graduation	101(29.28)	9(2.61)	6(1.74)	116(33.62)	
Professional qualifications	T.T.C/ D.Ed	255(73.91)	57(16.52)	3(0.87)	315(91.30)	214.09**
	B.Ed	5(1.45)	3(0.87)	22(6.38)	30(8.70)	
Teaching experience (in years)	Up to 10	130(37.68)	20(5.80)	8(2.32)	158(45.80)	56.52**
	11 to 20	100(28.99)	10(2.90)	5(1.45)	115(33.33)	
	Above 20	30(6.70)	30(6.70)	12(3.48)	72(20.87)	
Classes teaching	1,2 classes	70(20.29)	7(2.03)	3(0.87)	80(23.19)	100.02**
	3-5 classes	162(46.96)	17(4.93)	4(1.16)	183(53.04)	
	6,7 classes	28(8.12)	36(10.43)	18(5.22)	82(23.77)	
	Total	260(75.36)	60(17.39)	25(7.25)	345(100.0)	

*Significant at 0.05 level.
**Significant at 0.01 level.

The generated chi-square value 60.42, is more than the table value. Hence it is highly significant at 0.01 level. Hence the null hypothesis is rejected. This indicates that there is significant difference among the opinion of teachers of different age groups. This difference may be due to difference in their attitudes due to age gap and due to life experiences indirectly due to more professional experience.

Sex – Variable

It is to find out the difference of opinion in terms of the sex of the teachers, on the Activity Method. The chi-square value is used.

The calculated chi-square value 2.34, is less than the table value. Hence it is not significant. Hence the null hypothesis is accepted. This indicates that there is no significant difference between the opinions of male and female teachers.

Variable–Social Class

It is to find out the difference of opinion in terms of social class of the teachers, on the Activity Method. The chi-square value is used.

The generated chi-square value 29.55, is more than the table value. Hence it is highly significant at 0.01 level. Hence the null hypothesis is rejected. This indicates that there is highly significant difference among the opinions of the teachers belonging to the four social classes.

Nativity – Variable

It is to find out the difference of opinion in terms of the nativity of the teachers, on the Activity Method. The chi-square value is used.

The calculated chi-square value 27.75, is more than the table value. Hence it is highly significant at 0.01 level. Hence the null hypothesis is rejected. This indicates that there is significant difference in the opinions of the teachers belonging to the four nativities. This may be due to their cultural, climatic and environmental differences.

Variable – Marital Status

It is to find out the difference of opinion in terms of the marital status of the teachers, on the Activity Method. The chi-square value is used.

The calculated chi-square value 104.92, is more than the table value. Hence it is highly significant at 0.01 level. Hence the null hypothesis is rejected. This indicates that there is highly significant difference in the opinions of the married and unmarried teachers. This may be due to change in their life styles.

Variable – School Location

It is to find out the difference of opinion in terms of the school location where the teachers are working, on the Activity Method. The chi-square value is calculated.

The calculated chi-square value 104.92, is more than the table value. Hence it is highly significant at 0.01 level. Hence the null hypothesis is rejected. This indicates that there is high significant difference among the opinions of the teachers of the four school locations. This may be due to cultural and climatic differences in different school locations, the standard of the children which impacts on the opinions of the teachers.

Variable – General Qualifications

It is to find out the difference of opinions in terms of the general qualifications of the teachers, on the Activity Method. The chi-square value is calculated.

The calculated chi-square value 21.66, is more than the table value. Hence it is significant at 0.01 level. Hence the null hypothesis is rejected. This indicates that there is significant difference in the opinions of these three categories of teachers with varied general qualifications. This may be due to difference in their out-look due to more and more additional qualifications acquired by them. The more the qualified the more the positive attitude towards the Activity Method is observed.

Variable – Professional Qualifications

It is to find out the difference of opinions in terms of professional qualifications of the teachers on the Activity Method. The chi-square value is calculated. The calculated chi-square value 214.09 is more than the table value. Hence it is highly significant at 0.01 level. Hence the null hypothesis is rejected. This indicates that there is significant deference between the opinions of D.Ed. and B.Ed qualified teachers. This may be due to their professional training and level of teaching. The TTC / D.Ed. qualified are more positive than B.Ed qualified teachers.

Variable – Teaching Experience

It is to find out the difference of opinion in terms of teaching experience of the teachers on the Activity Method. The chi-square values is calculated. The calculated chi-square value 56.52 is more than the table value. Hence it is highly significant at 0.01 level. Hence the null hypothesis is rejected. This indicates that there is significant deference among the opinions of the teachers having varied experience. This difference may be due to their professional trainings and better understating of the educational concepts. The moderately experienced are more positive than the less or more experienced teachers.

Variable – Classes Teaching

It is to find out the difference of opinion of teachers in of classes teaching by the teachers, on the Activity Method. The chi-square value is calculated. The calculated chi-square value 100.02, is more than the table value. Hence it is highly significant at 0.01 level. Hence the null hypothesis is rejected. This indicates that there is significant deference among the opinions of the teachers teaching different levels of classes. This may be due to application of Activity Method to different levels of children and as the method is more applicable to lower classes than for higher classes.

Age – Variable

It is to find out the difference of opinion in terms of age of the teachers on Work-Experience Training Programme. The chi-square value is calculated.

The calculated chi-square value 15.18 is more than the table value. Hence it is significant at 0.01 level. Hence the null

Table 4.27. Table Showing Chi-square Values of Significance of the Opinions of In-service Teachers Variable-wise on Work Experience Training Programme

Variable	*Group*	*Most useful*	*Useful*	*Less useful*	*Total*	*Chi-square*
Age (in years)	Below 30	42(12.17)	11(3.19)	5(1.45)	58(16.81)	15.18**
	31 – 40	193(55.36)	11(3.19)	8(2.32)	213(61.74)	
	Above 45	60(17.39)	9(2.61)	5(1.45)	74(24.45)	
Sex	Male	149(43.19)	17(4.93)	8(2.32)	174(50.43)	0.35
	Female	146(42.33)	15(4.35)	10(2.90)	171(49.57)	
Social class	OC	151(43.77)	10(2.90)	4(1.16)	165(47.83)	41.17**
	BC	113(32.75)	10(2.90)	3(0.87)	126(36.52)	
	SC	26(7.54)	9(2.61)	10(2.90)	45(13.04)	
	ST	5(1.45)	3(0.87)	1(0.29)	9(2.61)	
Nativity	Rural	187(54.20)	12(3.48)	4(1.16)	203(58.84)	14.56**
	Urban	113(32.75)	17(4.93)	3(0.87)	133(38.55)	
	Tribal	5(1.45)	3(0.87)	1(0.29)	9(2.61)	
Marital status	Unmarried	20(5.80)	1(0.29)	1(0.29)	22(6.35)	0.67
	Married	275(79.71)	31(8.99)	17(4.93)	323(93.62)	
School location	Rural	185(53.62)	7(2.03)	5(1.45)	197(57.10)	57.03**
	Urban	100(28.99)	15(4.35)	8(2.32)	123(35.65)	
	Sub-urban	3(0.87)	5(1.45)	2(0.58)	10(2.90)	
	Tribal	7(2.03)	5(1.45)	3(0.87)	154.35)	

	Tribal	7(2.03)	5(1.45)	3(0.87)	154.35)	
General qualifications	Intermediate	40(11.59)	3(0.87)	1(0.29)	44(12.75)	21.47**
	Graduation	170(49.28)	10(2.90)	5(1.45)	185(53.62)	
	Post graduation	85(24.64)	19(5.51)	12(3.48)	116(33.62)	
Professional qualifications	T.T.C/ D.Ed	280(81.16)	22(6.38)	13(3.77)	315(91.30)	33.60**
	B.Ed	15(4.35)	10(2.90)	5(1.45)	30(8.70)	
Teaching experience (in years)	Up to 10	140(40.58)	13(3.77)	5(1.45)	158(45.80)	8.18
	11 to 20	100(28.99)	10(2.90)	5(1.45)	115(33.33)	
	Above 20	55(15.94)	9(2.61)	8(2.32)	72(20.87)	
Classes teaching	1,2 classes	75(21.74)	3(0.87)	2(0.58)	80(23.19)	27.50**
	3-5 classes	160(33.62)	10(2.90)	13(3.77)	183(53.04)	
	6,7 classes	60(17.39)	19(5.51)	3(0.87)	82(23.77)	
	Total	295(85.51)	32(9.28)	18(5.22)	345(100.0)	

*Significant at 0.05 level.
**Significant at 0.01 level.

hypothesis is rejected. This indicates that there is significant deference among the opinions of the three age groups of teachers regarding the Work-Experience Programme. Among the three groups, 31-45 aged group teachers opinion is more better than below 20 years and above 45 years age group teachers, which may be due to having moderate experience.

Sex – Variable

It is to find out the difference of opinion in terms of sex of the teachers, on Work Experience Training Programme. The chi-square value is used.

The generated chi-square value 0.35 is less than the table value. Hence it is not significant. Hence the null hypothesis is accepted. This indicates that there is no significant difference between the opinions of the male and female teachers regarding Work-Experience Programme.

Social Class – Variable

It is to find out the difference of opinion in terms of social class of the teachers, on Work-Experience Training Programme. The chi-square value is used.

The calculated chi-square value 41.17, is more than the table value. Hence it is highly significant at 0.01 level. Hence the null hypothesis is rejected. This indicates that there is significant difference in the opinions of teachers belonging to four different social classes.

Nativity – Variable

It is to find out the difference of opinion in terms of nativity of the teachers, on Work Experience Training Programme. The chi-square value is used.

The arrived chi-square value 14.56, is more than the table value. Hence it is significant at 0.01 level. Hence the null hypothesis is rejected. This indicates that there is significant difference in the opinions of the teachers belonging to rural, urban and tribal nativities, regarding Work-Experience Training Programme. This may be due to their regional and cultural exposure variations in their brought up.

Marital status – Variable

It is to find out the difference of opinion in terms of marital status of the teachers, on Work-Experience Training Programme. The chi-square value is used.

The calculated chi-square value 0.67, is less than the table value. Hence it is not significant. Hence the null hypothesis is accepted. This indicates that there is no significant difference in the opinions of married and un-married teachers.

Variable – School Location

It is to find out the difference of opinion in terms of school location, in which the teacher is working, on the Work Experience Training Programme. The chi-square value is used.

The generated chi-square value 57.03 is more than the table value. Hence it is significant at 0.01 level. Hence the null hypothesis is rejected. This indicates that there is significant difference in the opinions of the teachers working in the four different localities of schools, like rural, urban, sub-urban and tribal. It is inferred that this may be due to difference in the location which causes difference in their experiences. The rural teachers have more positive opinions than the teachers of other localities.

Variable – General Qualifications

It is to find out the difference of opinion in terms of general qualifications of the teachers, on the Work-Experience Training Programme. The chi-square value is used.

The generated chi-square value 21.47, is more than the table value. Hence it is significant, at 0.01 level. Hence the null hypothesis is rejected. This indicates that there is significant difference in the opinions of the teachers possessing different general qualifications. It can be inferred that this may be due to the difference in the level of their academic background. The intermediate qualified teachers are more positive than the graduation and post graduation qualified teachers.

Variable – Professional Qualifications

It is to find out the difference of opinion in terms of professional qualifications of teachers, on the Work-Experience Training Programme. The chi-square value is calculated.

The calculated chi-square value 33.60, is more than the table value. Hence it is significant at 0.01 level. Hence the null hypothesis is rejected. This indicates that there is significant difference in the opinions of the teachers possessing different professional qualifications. It can be inferred that it may be due to difference in the level of professional training received by the teachers. It is observed that TTC / D.Ed trained teachers have expressed more positive opinions than B.Ed trained teachers.

Variable – Teaching Experience

It is to find out the difference of opinion in terms of teaching experience of teachers on the Work Experience Training Programme. The chi-square value is calculated.

The calculated chi-square value 8.18, is less than the table value. Hence it is not significant. Hence the null hypothesis is accepted. This indicates that there is no significant difference in the opinions of teachers having three levels of teaching experience.

Variable – Classes Teaching

It is to find out the difference of opinion in terms of classes teaching on the Work Experience Training Programme. The chi-square value is calculated.

The calculated chi-square value 27.50, is more than the table value. Hence it is significant at 0.01 level. Hence the null hypothesis is rejected. This indicates that there is significant difference in the opinions of teachers teaching different levels of classes. It can be inferred that this may be due to difference in the classes they teach, which results in the level of teaching, way of teaching and other strategies. The teachers teaching 1,2 classes expressed more positive attitude than the teachers teaching next higher classes.

Variable – Age

It is to find out the difference of opinion in terms of age of the teachers, on the quality improvement training programme. The chi-square value is used.

Table 4.28. Table Showing Chi-square Values of Significance of the Opinions of In-service Teachers Variable-wise on Quality Improvement Training Programme

Variable	*Group*	*Most useful*	*Useful*	*Less useful*	*Total*	*Chi-square*
Age (in years)	Below 30	50(14.49)	4(1.16)	4(1.16)	58(16.81)	31.89**
	31 – 40	197(57.10)	11(3.19)	5(1.45)	213(61.74)	
	Above 45	50(14.49)	10(2.90)	14(4.06)	74(21.45)	
Sex	Male	155(44.43)	10(2.90)	9(2.61)	174(5043)	2.63
	Female	142(41.16)	15(4.35)	14(4.06)	171(49.57)	
Social class	OC	150(43.48)	10(2.90)	5(1.45)	165(47.83)	11.19
	BC	100(28.99)	11(3.19)	15(4.32)	126(36.52)	
	SC	40(11.54)	3(0.87)	2(0.58)	45(13.04)	
	ST	7(2.03)	1(0.29)	1(0.29)	9(2.61)	
Nativity	Rural	187(54.20)	13(3.70)	3(0.87)	203(58.84)	22.71**
	Urban	103(29.86)	11(3.19)	19(5.51)	133(38.55)	
	Tribal	7(2.03)	1(0.29)	1(0.29)	9(2.61)	
Marital status	Un-married	20(5.80)	1(0.29)	1(0.29)	22(6.35)	0.46
	Married	277(80.29)	24(6.96)	22(6.38)	323(93.62)	
School location	Rural	182(52.75)	12(3.48)	3(0.87)	197(57.10)	25.27**
	Urban	96(27.83)	9(2.61)	18(5.22)	123(35.65)	
	Sub-urban	7(2.03)	2(0.58)	1(0.29)	10(2.90)	

	Tribal	12(3.48)	2(0.58)	1(0.29)	15(4.35)	
General qualifications	Intermediate	40(11.59)	2(0.58)	2(0.58)	44(12.75)	**2.97**
	Degree	160(46.38)	15(4.35)	10(2.90)	185(53.62)	
	Post graduation	97(28.12)	8(2.32)	11(3.19)	116(33.62)	
Professional qualifications	T.T.C/ D.Ed	292(84.64)	16(4.64)	7(2.03)	315(91.30)	**149.20****
	B.Ed	5(1.45)	9(2.61)	16(4.64)	30(8.70)	
Teaching experience (in years)	Up to 10	147(42.61)	8(2.32)	3(0.87)	158(45.80)	**17.31****
	11 to 20	92(26.67)	13(3.77)	10(2.90)	115(33.33)	
	Above 20	58(16.81)	4(1.16)	10(2.90)	72(20.87)	
Classes teaching	1,2 classes	78(22.61)	1(0.29)	1(0.29)	80(23.19)	**133.42****
	3,5 classes	180(52.17)	2(0.58)	1(0.29)	183(53.04)	
	6,7 classes	39(11.30)	22(6.38)	21(6.09)	82(23.77)	
	Total	297(86.09)	25(7.25)	23(6.67)	345(100.0)	

**Significant at 0.01 level.

The calculated chi-square value 31.89, is more than the table value. Hence it is significant at 0.01 level. Hence the null hypothesis is rejected. This indicates that there is significant difference in the opinions of teachers with different age groups. It can be inferred that this may be due to difference in the age and the indirect effect due to more experience and exposure. The teachers with 31-40 years age group have expressed more positive opinions than the more or less aged groups of teachers.

Variable – Sex

It is to find out the difference of opinion in terms of sex of the teachers, on the quality improvement programme. The chi-square value is calculated.

The calculated chi-square value 2.63, is less than the table value. Hence it is not significant. Hence the null hypothesis is accepted. This indicates that there is no difference in the opinions of male and female teachers. However the male teachers showed a littlie more positive opinions than the female teachers.

Variable – Social Class

It is to find out the difference of opinion in terms of social class on the quality improvement training programme. The chi-square value is used.

The generated chi-square value 11.19, is less than the table value. Hence it is not significant. Hence the null hypothesis is accepted. This indicates that there is no significant difference in the opinions of the teachers of different groups of social class. However the B.C. community teachers have expressed less positive attitude towards the training programme than the teachers of other social classes.

Variable – Nativity

It is to find out the difference of opinion in terms of nativity of the teachers on the quality improvement training programme. The chi-square value is used.

The arrived chi-square value 22.71, is more than the table value. Hence it is significant at 0.01 level. Hence the null hypothesis is rejected. This indicates that there is significant difference in the opinions of the teachers of the three different nativities. It can be inferred that, this may be due to difference in the cultural and civilizational atmosphere of the teachers. However the rural teachers have more positive attitude than the urban and tribal teachers towards the quality improvement training programme.

Variable – Marital status

It is to find out the difference of opinion in terms of marital status of the teachers on quality improvement training programme. The chi-square value is used.

The generated chi-square value 0.46, is less than the table value. Hence it is not significant. Hence the null hypothesis is accepted. This indicates that there is no significant difference in the opinions of the married and un-married teachers.

Variable – School Location

It is to find out the difference of opinion in terms of school location of the teachers on quality improvement programme. The chi-square value is used.

The calculated chi-square value 25.27, is more than the table value. Hence it is significant at 0.01 level. Hence the null hypothesis is rejected. This indicates that there is significant difference in the opinions of the teachers of the four school localities. It can be inferred that this may be due to difference in their locality of work, aptitudes, interests and attitudes of their school children. How ever the rural teachers have expressed a littlie more positive opinions than the teachers of other localities.

Variable – General Qualifications

It is to find out the difference of opinion in terms of general qualifications of the teachers, on the quality improvement training programme. The chi-square value is used.

The calculated chi-square value 2.97, is less than the table value. Hence it is not significant. Hence the null hypothesis is accepted. This indicates that there is no significant difference in the opinions of teachers possessing the three levels of general qualifications.

Variable – Professional Qualifications

It is to find out the difference of opinion in terms of professional qualifications of the teachers, on the quality improvement training programme. The chi-square value is used.

The calculated chi-square value 149.20, is far more than the table value. Hence it is highly significant at 0.01 level. Hence the null hypothesis is rejected. This indicates that there is significant difference in the opinions of the teachers possessing different levels of professional qualifications. It can be inferred that, this may be due to the impact of professional qualifications on the opinions of the teachers on the quality improvement programme. However the TTC / D.Ed qualified teachers have expressed more positive attitudes than the B.Ed qualified teachers towards the quality improvement programme.

Variable – Teaching Experience

It is to find out the difference of opinion in terms of teaching experience of the teachers, on the quality improvement training programme. The chi-square value is used.

The calculated chi-square value 17.31, is more than the table value. Hence it is significant at 0.01 level. Hence the null hypothesis is rejected. This indicates that there is significant difference in the opinions of teachers with the three levels of teaching experience. It can be inferred that, this may be due to the impact of the length of teaching experience on the opinions of the quality improvement training programme. However the rural and urban teachers have more positive opinions than the tribal teachers regarding quality improvement programme.

Variable – Classes Teaching

It is to find out the difference of opinion in terms of classes teaching on the quality improvement training programme. The chi-square value is used.

The calculated chi-square value is 133.42, is far more than the table value. Hence it is highly significant at 0.01 level. Hence the null hypothesis is rejected. This indicates that there is significant difference in the opinions of teachers teaching different classes. It can be inferred that, this may be due to the impact of the level of classes teaching and the level of requirement of the quality improvement programme to those classes. However the lower the classes of teaching by the teachers is the higher the positiveness of opinions of the teachers is found. So the classes teaching has shown direct impact regarding the quality improvement training programme.

5

Summary and Conclusions

SUMMARY

The instrument of education is universally accepted as the main in bringing social change towards human development. It can bring economic growth, self sufficiency in food, employment and national integration. The development in the field of education should closely relate to the present needs and aspirations of the people and also in comparison to that of the external world. There certain factors that influence the quality of education like – the teacher's competence and character, the facilities, the mental health of the teacher are the most significant factors. A nation can not grow more than its teacher's attitudes aspirations and perceptions. The level of the education of a nation's citizens undoubtedly determines the pace and magnitude of the socio – economic development.

Education has been recognized as a fundamental right and a process of human resource development when the knowledge, skills and capabilities are sharpened to achieve a wide range of objectives. The education of the nation's masses can only bring success in the smooth running of democracy, development, community involvement, optimum utilization of physical and human resources, national integration , cultural emancipation universal brotherly hood and realization of oneness of humanity. A nation can only achieve any sort of development when due importance is given to its people's education. Inspite of glorious past history India could not maintain its glory simply due to improper attention towards its education. Since before independence several commissions and Comittees have been suggesting reforms. They were Macaulay's Minutes (1835), Woods Dispatch (1854), Hunter Commission (1884), Indian University Act (1904), Sadler Commission (1918), Radha Krishnan Commission (1948), Mudaliar Commission (1952), Kothari Commission (1964-66), and national policy on education (1986). Many philosophers and social reformers like Mahatma Gandhi (1988), Swamy Vivekanda (1985), Rama Krishna Paramahamsa (3rd edition, 1959), Rabindranadh Tagore (1992) and Raja Ram Mohan Roy (3rd edition 1959), have all stressed the need for educating all sections of the society.

In a country like India the level of the commitment and concern on the part of the teacher to contribute his effort for the emancipation of school education. A teacher requires a wide range of skills like good communicative skills, exploratory skill and the skills of reasoning reinforcement and questioning. The teacher is expected to perform, his functions to the maximum perfection and he must be able to tap and utilize all the resources for the cause of education.

The primary teacher has such a place in the system of education that his word deed and his every moment makes deep unalterable impression on the minds of children and it leads the child, lifelong. Hence the teacher especially a primary teacher must be a model and ideal teacher, a good scholar an ideal social worker and a committed one who can help to improve the lot of the poor and downtrodden by extending to them educational opportunities. The teacher has to aware them by sensitizing them to claim their basic fundamental rights. The role of the teacher is not limited to the syllabus and the four walls of the class room but to the good life of the citizen.

The DIETs are also aimed at revitalizing the in-service teachers at elementary level by incorporating the new trends and interventions that are thought to be intruded into the system of education from time to time and day to day. For this purpose effective design and plan of action for renovating, refreshing, rejuvenating , renewing, revising and replenishing the longback trained in-service teachers with newly invented, innovative methods and techniques of teaching with clarifications for the hard spots in the revised content areas for making the teachers confident and more effective with renewed enthusiasm and spirit to dedicate himself herself to the cause of education.

For this purpose six more branches such as IFIC branch, Planning and Management branch, Work-Experience branch, CMDE branch, Educational Technology branch and DRU branch are established to look into the in-service training programmes.

A sound programme of professional education of teachers is essential for the qualitative improvement of education. Investment in teacher education can yield very rich dividends because the financial resources required are small when measured against the resulting improvements in the education of millions of Indian masses. It is known that educational reform can not be successful unless the quality of the teacher is improved, but in turn the quality of the teacher depends to a large extent as the quality of the teacher education. In reality the teacher education is the sine qua non of all educational improvements. The status and quality of teacher education in our country especially at the elementary level is far from satisfaction. The elementary teacher education should train the prospective teachers to take decisions regarding the application of basic educational principles to the existing school situations without over looking the characteristics of the learners. Thus the professional education of the elementary teachers must relate to pedagogy and the way instructional materials can be put to a judicious use. The above contentions have many ramifications and implications for the teacher education curriculum. It is gratifying to note that some significant developments have already taken place in this field.

The national policy on education (1986) suggested an over – hauling of teacher education at all levels. A national curriculum framework for elementary /secondary school stages was developed by the NCERT keeping in view the major thrusts of national policy on education. Setting up of district institute of education and training (DIETs) at the elementary level and upgrading some colleges of education as institutes of advanced studies in education (IASEs) and strengthening of colleges of teacher education (CTEs), are other significant steps taken in this direction. These institutions are expected to contribute their mite in improving their quality of the teacher education. It is now felt that to make the training experiences of the in-service teachers as well as the student-teachers purposeful and effective, different components of teacher education curriculum, especially at the elementary level need to be reviewed and revised.

The teacher training institutes of the primary level now modified as district institute of education and training (DIETs) play an important role in producing the required teachers for the primary and upper-primary levels, more over refreshes and renovates the masses of the in-service teachers in the revised content and methodologies when-ever required, to keep abreast the elementary teacher always suitable and capable to meet the current challenges. Great is the task and dynamic is their role indeed! Are these institutes producing quality teachers? Is the pre-service training programme provided by the DIETs effective in respects? Are the in-service training programmes organized by DIETs serving the purpose fully? What are the deficiencies in the DIETs? In what aspects DIETs are to be rectified? A survey of such questions are to be answered with empirical evidence for the further improvement of the quality of teacher education at the primary level.

It is there fore pertinent to collect data about the attitudes of Principals and facilities that are available in all the 23 DIETs in of Andhra Pradesh the state and the attitudes of pre-service student trainees and in-service teachers about their training programmes so as to get a better picture of the situation and to identify the means to improve the teacher education which help, produce quality teachers. So, the present study is an ardent effort in this direction.

STATEMENT OF THE PROBLEM

The present study is a descriptive study of the DIETs in Andhra Pradesh. It is to know whether the role and performance of the DIETs are appropriate according to the Guidelines by MHRD, Government of India, as envisaged by NPE 1986. It is also to know whether the teacher education programmes conducted by the DIETs are according to the Guidelines.

The present study is taken up to know whether the independent and dependent variables have any influence on the role and performance of DIETs with respect to pre-service and in-service programmes, activities for improvement and quality of DIETs in the state.

VARIABLES OF THE STUDY

As the present study bring out the role and performance of DIETs in the sense the elementary school teacher education programme in Andhra Pradesh on the basis of the attitudes of the student teachers, In-service teachers and Principals.

The dependent variables Studied are:

1. Attitudes of student teachers in different aspects of DIET.
2. Attitudes of student teachers towards the teacher educators in DIET.
3. Attitudes of student teachers towards the different aspects of the D,Ed syllabus.
4. Attitude of the student teachers towards facilities in DIET.
5. Attitude of student teachers towards the training programmes conducted by DIETs.
6. Attitudes of in-service teachers towards the treatment of teacher educators.
7. Attitudes of in-service teachers towards the facilities provided in DIETs.
8. Attitudes of in-service teachers towards the utility of the training programmes.

The independent variables studied are:

The independent variables considered in the study are of two kinds namely a) The student teacher (D.Ed. trainees) related personal and demographic variables and b) in-service teacher related personal and demographic variables. The student teacher related independent variables are Age, Sex, Marital Status, locality of DIET, nativity, educational qualifications and community (social class). The in-service teacher related independent variables are age, sex, marital status, nativity, general qualifications, professional qualifications subjects teaching and experience as elementary school teacher, school location of classes teaching, and community (social class).

DESIGN OF THE STUDY

The present study is essentially an explorative and descriptive in nature. The design of the study may be called as a survey type of research.

OBJECTIVES OF THE STUDY

The main objectives of the study were:

1. To study the structural aspects and performance of DIETs in Andhra Pradesh.
2. To study the role and performance of DIETs on the different aspects of teacher training progrmmes.
3. To study the pre-service teachers programmes and professional development.
4. To study the in-service teacher training programmes and professional development.
5. To find out the specific deviations from the MHRD Guidelines while performing the functions by the DIETs of Andhra Pradesh state.
6. To suggest measures for improving the quality in primary teacher education.

HYPOTHESES

1. The DIETs of Andhra Pradesh do not differ significantly with respect to their role and performance on the different aspects of teacher training programmes.
2. a. The DIETs in Andhra Pradesh do not differ significantly with respect to the general facilities in DIETs.

   b. The DIETs in Andhra Pradesh do not differ significantly with respect to the student welfare.

   c. The DIETs in Andhra Pradesh do not differ significantly with respect to the practice teaching and evaluation.

d. The DIETs in Andhra Pradesh do not differ significantly with respect to in-service training programmes.

e. The DIETs in Andhra Pradesh do not differ significantly with respect to pre-service training programme.

f. The DIETs in Andhra Pradesh do not differ significantly with respect to research activities.

3. a. The D.Ed teacher trainees do not differ significantly in the training programmes irrespective of their personal variables.

b. The D.Ed teacher trainees do not differ significantly in the training programmes irrespective of their demographic variables.

c. The D.Ed teacher trainees do not differ significantly in their professional development irrespective of their personal variables.

d. The D.Ed teacher trainees do not differ significantly in their professional development irrespective of their demographic variables.

4. a. The in-service teachers do not differ significantly in the training programmes irrespective of their personal variables.

b. The in-service teachers do not differ significantly in the training programmes irrespective of their demographic variables.

c. The in-service teachers do not differ significantly in their professional development irrespective of their personal variables.

d. The in-service teachers do not differ significantly in their professional development irrespective of their demographic variables.

POPULATION AND SAMPLING

Keeping in view the suitability and advantages the investigator adopted the following sampling methods for different subjects involved in the study.

The sample selected for the present study is of 3 categories, namely:

1. The researcher has taken the whole population of DIETs in Andhra Pradesh state i.e. Twenty three DIETs from all the twenty three Districts of Andhra Pradesh state for collection of data, from the DIET Principals by using checklist.
2. For the purpose of measuring the opinions of D.Ed. teacher trainees from each DIET, systematic randomn sampling method is applied by selecting each nth trainee i.e. each 6th second year trainee in each DIET, (as there are 100 trainees in each DIET) constituting the total sample of 345 D.Ed. teacher trainees, who are selected from 23 DIETs in the Andhra Pradesh state.
3. In the selection of in-service teachers area randomn sampling method is applied. From the in-service teachers gathered in district level in-service training programmes represented from all the mandals, in the district fifteen teaches from 15 mandals (one from each mandal on randomn basis) were taken for measuring their opinions, by questionnaire. Like wise in service teachers were selected from each of the 23 districts in the Andhra Pradesh state. There fore from 23 districts @ 15 in-service teachers, totaling to the sample 345 teachers.

TOOLS USED IN THE STUDY

For the collection of reliable data from the different persons in the field three tools were designed to cater to the type of data to be collected. They were

1. Checklist for collecting data relating to the facilities and functional aspects of DIETs from the Principals of DIETs.
2. Opinionnaire for knowing the opinions of D.Ed. teacher trainees about their course and their opinions towards the facilities and performance of DIETs.
3. An opinionnaire for collecting the opinions from the in service teachers on the in-service training programmes offered to them.

PLAN AND PROCEDURE

After thorough review of various previous investigations and related studies from journals, periodicals and books the researcher has prepared three different tools for collecting the data from different respondents namely, the Principals of 23 DIETs, the pre-service (D.Ed.) trainees of DIETs and the in-service teachers from 23 Districts.

(*i*) **The checklist** was prepared with 108 items and were got filled by the Principals of all 23 DIETs in Andhra Pradesh state.

(*ii*) **Opinionnaire for Pre-service Trainees**; was carefully prepared (in four areas of DIETs functions) and administered on pre-service trainees of 23 DIETs. About 60 Likert type of items were prepared in 3 point scale of agree / undecided / disagree including personal data. A pilot study was conducted on 50 (pre-service) teacher trainees. The responses were checked for any ambiguity. The responses were tested by using chi square test. Out of 60 items 53 were found significant. Hence those 53 items were retained for the final form of questionnaire. Fifteen trainees from each of the 23 DIETs were selected by using systematic randomn sampling method, totaling to 345 trainees. An appeal was made to the respondents to respond to all of the 53 statements.

OPINIONNAIRE FOR IN-SERVICE TEACHERS

By taking all necessary precautions the questionnaire was prepared by the researcher for in-service teachers for all the 23 districts. Two areas were selected mainly for preparing the items of the questionnaire. They were

(a) Training needs of the teachers and

(b) Guidance given by DIET faculty.

There were about 23 items prepared including personal data. The items were of both closed and open ended. Some items were given for rank ordering by the teachers and some were likert type with 3 point scale of agree / undecided / disagree, covering both areas.

A pilot study was conducted on 50 in-service teachers. The responses were checked whether there was any ambiquity with the terms. The responses were calculated by using chi-square test. Out of 23 items 20 items were found significant. These 20 items were selected for final form and administered the questionnaire on 345 in-service teachers from 23 districts selected by area randomn sampling method. An appeal was made to the respondents to respond to all of the items.

STATISTICAL TOOLS USED

The independent variables selected for the study were sex, age, general qualifications, professional qualifications, length of service, nativity, locality of the school, locality of the DIET, classes teaching, subjects teaching and community. The responses for the items of the opinionnaire were quantified by assigning numerical values as 3,2,1 for most useful, useful and lessuseful, agree, undecided, and disagree, respectively. The qualitative responses of some items were quantified and the total responses for each of the two opinionnaires were noted and classified variable wise all the responses. The responses received against each item variable wise were noted in a separate table and put for statistical treatment for arriving at inferences.

ANALYSIS

As the data collected through different statements in the tools from different subjects on specific aspects, the item wise analyses were carried out to identify the role and performance of DIETs specifically in different aspects. Statistics such as chi-square, t-test and F-test were employed to make the description more precise.

The total scores obtained in each of the opinionnaires from all the subjects on all the variables were computed. The data were carefully analysed by employing the appropriate statistical techniques the theoretical, statistical techniques such as t-test, F-test and chi–square were employed to test the null hypothesis. The numerical results obtained were interpreted meaningfully.

FINDINGS

The researcher has listed out the following findings from the analysis and interpretation of the study.

It is found that all the 23 DIETs have own buildings but sixteen DIETs out of them possessed minimum carpet area of buildings with 1000 sft as suggested in the MHRD Guidelines. Nine DIETs do not posses adequate number of rooms for different purposes like administration, classrooms and other purposes. Eleven DIETs do not possess toilets for male trainees. Seven DIETs did not possess toilet facility for trainees.

All the 23 DIETs have separate Principals' chambers and furniture outof which. sixteen have Principal chambers with attached toilets. Except four, all the DIETs Principals chambers possess computers. All the Principals chambers possess one land telephone. But MHRD Guidelines suggested two land telephones. The intercom facility as suggested by Guidelines is not provided for teaching staff in any DIET.

All 23 DIETs' office rooms are adequately furnished. Thirteen DIETs possessed computers in their office rooms. All the 23 DIETs offices are adequately furnished with tables, chairs, almirahs, fans and tube lights but not adequate in five DIETs as per MHRD Guidelines. Only four DIETs possessed attached toilets for office room.

As per the MHRD Guidelines seven departments were established in each of the 23 DIETs. Nine DIETs possessed computers in department rooms. In all the 23 DIETs departments, furniture like chairs, tables, almirahs and fans were provided. But in some DIETs the furniture is not adequate. Two DIETs departments did not possess almirahs. Six DIETs departments possessed attached toilets. Four DIETs possessed separate waiting hall with furniture and attached toilets for women.

Out of 23 DIETs four DIETs possessed computers for library work. Seventeen DIETs possessed more than 1000 text books in the library. Nine DIETs possessed more than thousand general books. Twenty one DIETs possessed more than thousand general books. All DIETs are contributing for journals, more over 11 DIETs are contributing more than ten journals. Almost all DIETs libraries possessed inadequate book-shelves, and fans.

Nine DIETs possessed separate reading hall as suggested in MHRD Guidelines for the faculty and trainees for their academic and professional development. The reading halls in twelve DIETs are furnished with tables, chairs, fans and tube lights. As per the suggestion of the MHRD Guidelines a minimum of ten journals are to be contributed. Fourteen DIETs are contributing ten or more journals for reading hall and the other nine DIETs are contributing less than ten journals.

Seven DIETs did not possess separate meeting hall. There is provision for construction of a separate auditorium for each DIET as per MHRD Guidelines. Out of sixteen DIETs are possessing meeting halls adequate furniture is available in two halls. As suggested in MHRD Guidelines the public addressing system is possessed by eleven DIETs out of twenty three.

Fifteen out of twenty three DIETs possessed dish-antenna for getting educational channel. MHRD Guidelines suggested the possession of the following minimum equipment by each DIET – two color T.V.s , three audio cassette players. one VCP, cassettes, one slide – projector, one 16 mm film-strip projector, two OHPs and three computers. Eighteen DIETs possessed two or more color T.V.s. Two DIETs possessed a minimum of three audio-casette players (2-in-ones) Twenty one DIETs possessed 3 or more computers. Thirteen DIETs possessed two OHPs as suggested and five DIETs did not possess even one OHP. Seventeen DIETs possessed one or more 16 mm film strip projectors, but six DIETs did not possess them. Eighteen DIETs possessed one or more slide projects but they are not possessed by five DIETs. Eighteen DIETs possessed one or more radios but five DIETs did not possess them. Nineteen DIETs possessed one or more VCP / DVDs and four DIETs did not have them. All DIETs have video and audio cassettes adequately.

MHRD Guidelines suggest student managed hotel with 150 – 200 seats to be maintained probably for in-service teachers than for pre-service trainees on no loss, no gain basis by using the infrastructural facilities provided in the DIET hostels. Sixteen DIETs are running students managed hostels with 100 to 200 seats. Eleven DIET hostels possessed cots ranging from 20 – 120, whereas twelve DIETs hostels did not mountain cots.

Nineteen DIETs possessed a bore well for water in the hostel and four DIETs are using general tank water.

Most of the DIETs have been achieving 100% results in I and II year D.Ed. public examinations for the last 5 years. A few DIETs could not achieve 100% results in some years, but the least percentage of achievement by a few DIETs is 66% and above.

All DIETs are encouraging the pre-service trainees to participate in Extra curricular Activities like games and sports. Out of them DIET Bheemunipatnam stood first by participating maximum eight events. Majority DIETs are involving in seven sports and games. Games like chess, and volley ball are organized by 19 DIETs, kabaddi and kho-kho are organized by 18 DIETs.

As suggested in MHRD Guidelines all DIETs are organizing some Work Experience Programmes like gardening, clean and green, TLM preparation and phenol preparation. Very few DIETs are giving training in Red cross and Scouting. So much so very few DIETs are giving training in book binding, file pad preparation and food items preparation.

All the DIETs are encouraging the teacher trainees for participating in co-curriculum activities like quiz competions, essay writing, elocution, debates, Science fairs, and cultural activities. Very few DIETs are encouraging trainees to participate in seminars, field visits and exhibitions.

All the 23 DIETs faculty members preferred the Child-Centred and Activity Method for the first rank, and the Demonstration Methods, for the second rank, Lecture Method, for the third rank, Discussion Method as the fourth, Project Method, as the fifth and Seminar Method as the sixth rank (least) in the order of their preference.

Seventeen out of 23 DIETs are organizing academic activities like seminars. All 23 DIETs are conducting workshops, number ranging from one to 17. Ten DIETs out of 23 are oraganizing conferences in which academic staff are participating.

As suggested in MHRD Guidelines there are 7 Senior Lecturer Posts, 17 Lecturer posts and one Craft Teacher post for each DIET. But in most of the DIETs they are not filled due to non-filling service commission quota of 30% of the posts. In four DIETs the Craft Teacher post was filled. All the seven Senior Lecturer posts were filled in four DIETs. In majority of DIETs less than ten lecturer posts were filled.

As per MHRD Guidelines all the Principal, Senior Lecturer, Lecturer and Craft Teacher posts are yet to be filled. There are four Principals posts which are felt vacant . In 19 out of 23 DIETs, 1-7 Senior Lecturer posts are left vacant. In all 23 DIETs there are so many Lecturer posts vacant ranging from 2 to 13 in number. The Craft Teacher posts are vacant in 19 DIETs.

As per MHRD Guidelines each DIET office had to be filled with one Superintendent, one Senior Assistants, 9 Junior Assistants, one Steno-cum-Typist, one Steno, one Technician, one Librarian two Laboratory Assistants, and ten Attenders. Majority DIETs are not filled with the above personal in the sanctioned posts fully (like Junior Assistants Typists, and Attenders). More over no DIET in the state got filled with the Steno, Technician, Librarian and Laboratory Assistants except one or two. The Technician post is very essential for Educational Technology Branch in DIETs which was neglected to fill except in one DIET. The Librarian post is so essential for proper utilization of DIET library by faculty as well as trainees and in-service teachers.

The vacancy position of non-teaching posts of DIETs is alarming. There are three office Superintendents, two Senior Assistants felt- vacant in the state. All DIETs are suffering due to non-filling of Technician post, Librarian post, two Laboratory Assistants posts and Steno post in all the 23 DIETs.

All 23 DIETs in the state are organizing and conducting in-service training programmes more or less similarly. These programmes are either centrally sponsored or founded by DPEP / SSA. All in-service training programmes are commonly scheduled at state level with similar time table, duration, content and objectives.

The self ratings given by DIET Principals to the in-service training programmes are as follows.

The Principals have rated content enrichment programme as the most effective and the motivation and innovative practices as the least effective, whereas the TLM preparation, methodology development, developing of positive attitudes in teachers and action research as moderately effective.

Majority DIETs are encouraging their faculty to take up research towards M.Phil. and Ph.D. degrees A few DIETs faculty have yet to secure the research degrees. Some DIET faculty are still undergoing research. All DIETs are organizing research projects. All DIETs have already given research training to a number of interested teachers. Many DIET faculty have conducted action research and also are guiding teachers in action research.

All the 23 DIETs Principals have self rated the developmental activities in their DIETs as follows. The norms set forth by NCTE in the MHRD Guidelines were kept in minds by the Principals while ranking.

The Principals have ranked the qualifications of the DIETs staff as most satisfied and the Art Education as the least satisfied, whereas the strength of the teaching staff, administrative accommodation, Science laboratories accommodation, academic accommodation, Physical Education accommodation, Educational Technology equipment, Work-Experience Craft furniture and games and sports equipment as moderately satisfactory.

The female student trainees have expressed more satisfaction than male student trainees regarding the four areas of facilities and resources, instruction, curricular and extra curricular activities and field work and records.

The age factor of D.Ed. student trainees has no bearing in their satisfaction on the facilities and resources in DIETs. The age factor did not make much difference in the satisfaction of D.Ed. trainees towards the a) field work and records, and b) Instruction. Both are not much satisfied.

The married trainees were more satisfied than un-married trainees regarding Co-curricular and Extra curricular Activities. But regarding field work and records both married and unmarried have expressed more or less equal satisfaction than the other three areas. Both married and unmarried trainees have expressed less satisfaction regarding the Co-curricular and Extra-curricular Activities.

The rural and urban trainees have more satisfied than tribal trainees towards DIETs facilities and resources. The rural and urban trainees have less satisfied than tribal trainees towards instruction in DIETs. The rural and urban trainees have more satisfaction than tribal trainees towards Co-curricular and Extra-curricular Activities in DIETs. All the three nativity trainees have more or less equally satisfied with the field work and records in the DIETs.

The locality of the DIET has much bearing on the expression of satisfaction by DIET trainees towards instruction, Co-curricular and Extra–curricular Activities and field work and records. The locality of DIET do not have any bearing on their expression of satisfaction towards facilities and resources.

The social class of the trainees has bearing on the expression of their satisfaction towards facilities and resources, Co-curricular and Extra–curricular Activities and field work and records. But the social class has no bearing on the expression of the trainees satisfaction towards instruction.

The qualifications of trainees has no bearing at all on their expression of satisfaction towards any one of the four areas of DIET activities.

Among the 345 sample of in-service teachers 12.8% are intermediate qualified, 53.6% are graduates and 33.6% are post-graduation, which means that more than 80% of them have improved their qualifications and have been rendering quality education.

Among the sample 8.7% of the in-service teachers have improved their professional qualifications (i.e) B.Ed. and have been offering quality education.

There are 20.9% teachers above 20 years experienced, 45.8% teachers are less than 10 years experienced, and 33.3% teachers are 10 to 20 years experienced among the in-service teachers.

Among the in-service teachers 53% teachers teach 3 to 5 classes and 23.2% teach 1 to 2 classes.

As the class master system is in practice in the elementary schools of Andhra Pradesh state every teacher has been teaching all subjects.

The in-service teachers have expressed by ranks for different school subjects on the basis of their usefulness in the in-service training programmes. The teachers have ordered Telugu Training Programme as most useful and Hindi and Work Experience Programmes as least useful. They have also expressed that Mathematics, English and Science Training Programmes as moderately useful.

The in-service teachers have ranked the methodologies basing on their difficulty level from more difficult to less difficult. They agreed that Mathematics Methodology is the most difficult and the Hindi as less difficult. Whereas English, Science, Telugu and Social studies as moderate in terms of difficulty.

The in-service teachers have rank ordered the school subjects according to their difficulty level from more difficult to less difficult. They opined that Mathematics as the most difficult and social studies subject as least difficult whereas English, Sciences and Telugu subjects as moderately difficult.

The sex of the in-service teachers has not much bearing on their opinions towards the guidance given by DIET faculty in preparing question banks, teacher Hand-books and student Hand-books, and in the use of teaching learning material.

The marital status of in-service teachers has no bearing on their opinions on the guidance given by DIET faculty towards the preparation of question – banks, teachers Hand-books students Hand-books and in the use of TLM during class – room transaction.

The age of the in-service teachers has no bearing on their opinions on the guidance given by DIET faculty for the preparation of question banks, teacher Hand-books, student Hand-books and in the use of TLM during class-room transaction.

The community of the in-service teachers has caused not much difference in their opinions on the guidance given by DIET faculty towards the preparations of question–banks, teacher

Hand-books, student Hand-books and in the use of TLM during class-room transaction.

The nativity of the in-service teachers has not much bearing on their opinions on the guidance given by DIET faculty towards the preparation of question banks, teacher Hand-books, student Hand-books and in the use of TLM during class – room transaction.

The locality of the school where the in-service teachers have been working has effected their opinions on the guidance given by DIET faculty towards the preparation of question banks and teacher Hand-books. But it has no bearing on their opinions on the preparation of student Hand-books and in the use of TLM.

The level of general qualifications of the in-service teachers has no bearing on their opinions on the guidance given by DIET faculty towards the preparation of question banks, teacher Hand-books ; student Hand-books and in the use of TLM.

The difference in professional qualifications of in-service teachers has no bearing on their opinions on the guidance given by the DIET faculty regarding the preparation of question banks, teacher Hand-books and in the use of TLM , but the B.Ed. qualified teachers have expressed more satisfaction than the others regarding the preparation of students Hand-books.

The teaching experience of the in-service teachers has no bearing on their attitudes towards the guidance given by DIET faculty for the preparation of question banks, student Hand-books, teacher Hand-books and in the use of TLM.

The classes taught by the in-service teachers has not much bearing on their opinions towards the guidance given by the DIET faculty for the preparation of question banks, teacher' Hand-books , student Hand-books and in the use of TLM.

The findings from the attitudes of in-service teachers with regard to the usefulness of the MLL training programme are as follows.

The age of the teachers has clear ;impact on in-service teachers attitudes towards the usefulness of the MLL training programme. The sex (male / female / has clear bearing on in-service teachers opinions on the usefulness of the MLL training programme. The social class of the teachers is effective on the in-service teachers attitudes towards usefulness of the MLL programme. The nationality of the in-service teachers has clear impact on perceptions on the usefulness of the MLL training programme. The marital status of the teachers has no bearing on their attitudes on the usefulness of the MLL training programme.

The location of the school of the in-service teachers has shown great impact over their opinions about the usefulness of the MLL programme. The general qualifications of the in-service teachers have impacted on the perceptions of the teachers over the usefulness of MLL programme. The professional qualifications of the in-service teachers have little bearing on their attitudes over the usefulness of the MLL programme. The teaching experience of the in-service teachers has great impact on their perceptions about the usefulness of the MLL programme. The classes for which the in-service teachers teaching (level of classes) has great impact on the attitudes of the in-service teachers on the usefulness of the MLL programme.

The findings from the opinions of the in-service teachers on the usefulness of the Activity Method Training Programme are as follows.

The age of the in-service teachers has great impact on their attitudes on the ;usefulness of the Activity Method. The sex (male / female) of the in-service teachers has no bearing on their perceptions about the usefulness of the Activity Method. The social-class of the in-service teachers has great impact on their opinions on the usefulness of the Activity Method. The nativity of the in-service teachers has great impact on their perceptions over the usefulness of the Activity Method. The marital status of the in-service teachers has no impact on their attitudes over the usefulness of the Activity Method.

The location of the school of the in-service teachers has great impact on their attitudes on the usefulness of the Activity Method. The general qualifications of the in-service teachers has great bearing on their perceptions about the usefulness of the Activity Method. The professional qualifications of the in-service teachers has much impact on their perceptions about the usefulness of the Activity Method. The extent of teaching experience of the in-service teachers has great bearing on their perceptions about the usefulness of the Activity Method. The classes-teaching by the teachers has great impact on their attitudes towards the usefulness of the Activity Method.

The findings from attitudes of the in-service teachers towards the usefulness of the Work-Experience Training Programme are as follows.

The age of the in-service teachers has impacted on their attitudes about the usefulness of the Work-Experience Training Programme. The sex (male / female) of the in-service teachers has not impacted on their opinions over the usefulness of the Work-Experience Training Programme. The social class of the in-service teachers has strongly impacted up on their opinions about the usefulness of the Work-Experience Training Programme. The nativity of the in-service teachers has also strong bearing on their attitudes about the usefulness of the Work-Experience Training Programme. The marital status of the in-service teachers has no impact on their perceptions towards the usefulness of the Work-Experience Training Programme.

The location of the school of the in-service teachers has strongly impacted their opinions on the usefulness of Work-Experience Training Programme. The general qualifications of the in-service teachers have much impacted their perceptions on the usefulness of the Work-Experience Training Programme. The professional qualifications of the in-service teachers have much bearing on their attitudes on the usefulness of the Work-Experience Training Programme. The teaching experience of the in-service teachers has no impact on their opinion on the usefulness of the Work-Experience Training Programme. The classes being taught by the in-service teachers have much effected their attitudes on the usefulness of the Work-Experience Training Programme.

The findings from the opinions of the in-service teachers towards the usefulness pf quality improvement training programme are as follows.

The age of the in-service teachers has much impacted their perceptions on the usefulness of the quality improvement programme. The sex (male / female) of the in-service teachers has not shown any effect on their attitudes about the usefulness of the quality improvement programme. The social-class of the in-service teachers has no bearing on their opinions about the usefulness of the quality improvement programme. The nativity of the in-service teachers has its bearing on their attitudes about the usefulness of the quality improvement programme. The marital status of the in-service teachers has no bearing at all on their attitudes towards the usefulness of the quality improvement programme.

The location of the school of the in-service teachers has much impacted their opinions on the usefulness of the quality improvement programme. The general qualifications of the in-service teachers could not impact their attitudes on the usefulness of the quality improvement programme. The professional qualifications of the in-service teachers has shown great impact on their perceptions about the usefulness of the quality improvement programme. The teaching experience of in-service teachers has its impact on their attitudes towards the usefulness of the quality improvement programme. The classes being taught by in-service teachers has large bearing on their perceptions about the usefulness of the quality improvement programme.

The DIET Principals have been sending 80% of their student trainees to Government schools, 15% to private schools and 05% to residential schools for practice teaching. In very few DIETs the faculty have been participating in seminars workshops and conferences. In most of the DIETs very few faculty members are being encouraged to participate in conference. In about thirteen DIETs the faculty have been participating in workshops, seminars and conferences ranging from one to ten times.

Very few faculty from DIETs have published about 86 articles. A very few DIETs have alumni associations , but performing no activities. The faculty from 13 DIETs were being called for public functions organized by them in the practicing schools. But the faculty from 10 DIETs are not being invited by the practicing schools for functions organized by them.

The following activities are being organized by DIETs after the in-service training programmes. School monitoring activities are being conducted by 13 DIETs to see the actual implementation of the new pedagogy. Children language improvement programme monitoring by visiting the schools for actual implementation. Monitoring the school complex meetings, to see how effectively they are organized. TLM preparation workshops were organized to train them in TLM preparation.

Twelve DIETs out of 23 have been organizing innovative training programmes like radio-programmes, training on non-monitory basis, low-cost no-cost TLM preparation, training for tribal teachers , research and evaluation, puppetry , SLM cards, organizing melas etc. In about 12 DIETs staff have been pursuing research projects. Some have submitted and a few have yet to be submitted.

In fifteen DIETs developmental activities are being taken up like leveling of play-ground, development of garden, construction of toilets, over-head tank, bore-well, internal road-formation, compound-wall, fencing, repairs to existing buildings etc. A few DIETs have been enjoying say two donations to a maximum of 5,000/- per anum. No endowments are available for any DIET.

Developmental grants are being given very rarely by Central / State Government for constructing new buildings DPEP /SSA has been strengthening DIETs and their infrastructural facilities like furniture equipment and library.

CONCLUSIONS

On the basis of the Principals checklist it has been found that Principals have perceived that, the following aspects are worth mentioning.

Most of the DIETs in Andhra Pradesh do not possess adequate rooms for different purposes like administration and class-rooms. There are no toilets for male trainees in any DIETs. A few DIETs do not possess toilets for trainees. Some Principals chambers do not possess attached toilets. There is one land-line telephone in all DIETs MHRD Guidelines suggested two land line phones for all DIETs. No DIET in Andhra Pradesh has possessed inter-com facility. Many DIETs have not possessed computers for their office staff. A few DIETs do not possess adequate furniture in their DIET offices. All most all DIETs offices do not possess attached toilets.

Majority DIETs branches rooms do not possess computers and attached toilets. A few DIETs branches do not possess adequate furniture. Majority DIETs do not possess a separate ladies waiting hall furniture and attached toilets. Majority DIETs do not possess computer for library work. A few DIETs do not possess even 1000 reference books and 1000 general books. Majority DIETs do not possess even 1000 text books. All most all DIETs libraries do not possess adequate book rakhs, shelves, tube lights and fans. Majority DIETs do not possess a separate reading hall. Nine DIETs have not been still contributing at least for 10 journals.

Seven DIETs do not possess a separate meeting hall. Even then where the meeting halls are available there is no adequate furniture in them. Majority DIETs do not possess public addressing system. Seven DIETs do not possess dish-antenna. Majority DIETs do not poses Radio-cum-Tape recorders (Two-in-ones), and OHPs. A few DIETs do not poseess two colotr T.V.s , computers in E.T. branches, 16 mm projects, slide projectors, radios VCP / DVDs.

Seven DIETs do not possess cots in the hostels. Four DIETs' hostels do not possess a bore well. Majority DIETs have been achieving 100% results in I & II year D.Ed. public examinations for the last 5 years. Five DIETs have not been participating in majority games and sports. The cricket is not being played by majority DIET trainees which is a very popular game now-a-days. Very few DIETs have been giving training for their pre-service trainees in Red-cross and Scouting. Very few DIETs have been giving training in Work Experience Activities like book binding, file pad making and in preparation of food items. Very few DIETs in the state have been encouraging trainees to participate in seminars, field visits and exhibitions. In all the 23 DIETs the Child-Centered Method was preferred as number one and the Lecture Demonstration and Demonstration Methods were second preferred by the faculty members. Five DIETs have not been organizing seminars. A few DIETs only have been organizing workshops. Majority DIETs have not been organizing conferences where academic staff have to participate. In 19 DIETs the Craft Teacher post is not yet filled. In 19 DIETs the vacancy position of Senior Lecturers is ranging from 1-6. In majority DIETs vacancy of Lecturer posts vary from 2-13 in each DIET. A few Principal posts are felt vacant, for the last 3 years. In all the 23 DIETs the posts of Technician for E.T. branch, the Librarian and the Laboratory Assistant posts are not filled so far. The vacancy position of non-teaching staff is alarming. Three office Superintendents and three Senior Assistant posts are felt vacant in the state.

The self ratings by Principals about the in-service training programmes are as follows. The content enrichment topped in developing positive attitudes, action research motivation and innovative practices are ranked second. Some DIETs have not been yet taken up research activity. A few DIETs have not been guiding teachers in action research. The self rating by Principals about their DIETs are as follows. qualifications of DIET staff was ranked top (I). Strength of faculty and Art Education are ranked VIII. Games & sports equipment Physical Education accommodation VII rank. The furniture got VI rank and Work-Experience ranked IV.

The following deficiencies were noticed by going through the questionnaire on the attitudes of the D.Ed. trainees. The items were selected in four areas namely facilities and resources Instruction Co-curricular and Extra-curricular Activities and field work & records.

The questionnaire is statements on three point scale to express their degree of satisfaction, to see whether there is any significant difference in their attitudes, independent variable wise. The age factor has no significant difference in their attitudes on their satisfaction regarding the four areas. The married trainees were much satisfied than unmarried trainees regarding Co-curricular and Extra curricular activities. The tribal trainees are less satisfied than the other two nativity trainees regarding, DIETs facilities & resources, instruction and Co-curricular and Extra-curricular Activities. The social class of the trainees has much bearing on the expression of their satisfaction towards facilities and resources, Co-curricular and Extra curricular Activities and field work & records. The locality of the DIET has much bearing on their expression of satisfaction regarding Co-curricular and Extra curricular Activities, field work and records. The age and qualifications of the trainees has no bearing on their expression of their attitudes. The social class also has no bearing on their attitudes on instruction.

The in-service teachers are asked to assign six ranks to the subjects basing on their usefulness in the in-service training programmes from more useful to less useful. Hindi and Work-Experience are assigned VIII rank. Physical Sciences is given VI rank, Biological Sciences and Social Studies are assigned V rank. The in-service teachers rank the methodologies basing on their difficulty level from more difficult to less difficult. Mathematics Methodology is given rank – I indicating more difficult. English Methodology is given rank–II as next difficult. Sciences Methodology is given rank–III as next difficult. The in-service teachers have ranked the school subjects basing on their difficulty level from more difficult to less difficult. The teachers have ranked I, II, and III for Maths, English and Science respectively from more difficult to less difficult.

Regarding the guidance given by DIET faculty in preparing teacher and student Hand-books, question banks and in the use of teaching learning material. The sex, marital status, age, the social class, the nativity, the general qualifications, professional qualifications, the teaching experience, the classes teaching have not much bearing on their expression of significant difference of opinion. The locality of the school where the in-service teachers have been working has bearing in causing the significant difference of opinion on the guidance given by DIET faculty towards the preparation of question banks and teacher Hand-books.

The following are the opinions of in-service teachers towards the usefulness of the in-service training programmes.

1. The age sex, nativity, location of the school , general qualifications, professional qualifications teaching

experience and classes teaching of the in-service teachers have clear impact on the in-service teachers attitudes towards usefulness of MLL training programme.

But the marital status of the in-service teachers has no bearing on their attitudes towards the usefulness of the MLL training programme.

2. The age, the social class, the nativity, the location of the school, the general qualifications, the professional qualifications, the teaching experience and the classes teaching have much bearing on their opinions of in-service teachers over the usefulness of the Activity Method.

But the sex and the marital status have no impact on the attitudes of the in-service teachers on the usefulness of the Activity Method Training Programme.

3. The age, the social class, the nativity, the location of the school, the general qualifications the professional qualifications and the classes teaching have shown much impact on the attitudes of the in-service teachers over the usefulness of the Work-Experience Training Programme.

The sex, the marital status and the teaching experience have not shown any impact on the attitudes of the in-service teachers over the usefulness of the Work-Experience Training Programme.

4. The age, the nativity, the location of the school the professional qualifications, the teaching experience and the classes teaching have much impacted on the attitudes of the in-service teachers over the usefulness of the quality improvement training programme.

The sex, the social class, the marital status and the general qualifications, have shown no effect on the attitudes of the in-service teachers over the usefulness of the quality improvement training programme.

The following are the findings of quality aspects from data collected through Principals' check-list and by the personnel observation of the investigator.

All most all the DIETs have not been sending their student trainees to other than Government schools, for practice teaching lessons. Most of the DIETs have not been encouraging all the faculty members for participating in seminars, workshops and conferences. Majority faculty from DIETs have not been contributing articles for publication. Majority DIETs have not formed alumni association and where they have formed they have not been running any activities. The teaching practice schools have not been inviting 10 DIETs faculty for the functions being organized in their schools. Fifty percent of DIETs have not been monitoring the schools to see the implementation of the new pedagogy, CLIP implementation, school complex meetings and organizing TLM workshops to train the teachers in the TLM preparation.

Eleven DIETs out of 23 have not been organizing innovative training programmes like radio programmes, training programmes on non-monitory basis, low-cost no-cost TLM preparation, training for tribal teachers, action research training, puppetry, SLM cards preparation, good class-room and organizing melas etc. Eleven DIETs' faculty have not been pursuing research projects at all.

In eight DIETs developmental activities are not being done like leveling of play-ground , growing of garden, construction of toilets and over-head tank, laying of bore-wells formation of internal roads, compound-wall fencing and repair of existing buildings etc. All most all DIETs have not encouraged local public for donations for DIETs. Any endowments were not being enjoyed by any of the 23 DIETs. Very rarely the DIETs are in receipt of developmental grants from State / Central Government for construction of new buildings.

EDUCATIONAL IMPLICATIONS AND RECOMMENDATIONS OF THE STUDY

In the light of the major findings and conclusions of the study the following educational implications and recommendations are made by the investigator.

1. The Principals of all the 23 DIETs in the state have to prepare perspective plans of the respective DIETs with the vision of the institutional plans every year, so as to focus the deficiencies of the respective DIETs regarding the infrastructure facilities and structural aspects, as per MHRD Guidelines and local specific needs of the respective districts, geographical and demographical specialties.
2. The Principals have to encourage and motivate the faculty to effectively effort to implement the various developmental activities.
3. There must exist healthy atmosphere in the functioning of DIETs for implementing various programmes with the mutual co-operation of Principal, and faculty members.
4. The Principals have to request the Government for the allocation and release of necessary budgetary funds for the fulfillment of deficiencies which may hinder the proper and healthy implementation of the various activities in the DIETs.

   The following general deficiencies are identified in all the 23 DIETs in Andhra Pradesh state.
5. Lack of adequate accommodation (rooms), toilet facilities, two land-line phones, intercom facility, adequate computers adequate furniture, ladies waiting halls, computer facility in the library, necessary text books, reference books, journals and periodicals for library, separate furnished reading hall, a big meeting hall with addressing system, dish-antenna for getting educational channels, adequate educational technology equipment (electronic and electrical), hostel facility with necessary equipment for students, games and sports equipment, library furniture etc.
6. The Principals and faculty have to collectively take necessary steps to improve the performance of the DIETs recognizing its role realizing the importance of the following activities which are lagging behind in many

DIETs. They have encourage trainees regularly to participate in games and sports, to use the library for the effective teacher-hood, to read journals and periodicals on pedagogy to keep abreast innovative and latest developments, use Educational Technology equipment, to stay in hostels, to achieve 100% results, to train the teacher trainees in Red-cross Scouts and Guides, participate actively in Work-Experience activities, to participate in subject clubs workshops and field visits, exhibitions and Science fairs etc regularly.

7. All the DIETs' Principals and faculty members have to organize and conduct seminars, conferences workshops, field trips and exhibitions.
8. The Government has to take necessary steps to fill the vacant posts of Principals faculty positions and office staff and attenders especially those which are common and unfilled posts since the inception of DIETs, like Steno, Librarian, Technician, Craft Teacher Statistician, Art Education Lecturer, Laboratory Attenders in all the 23 DIETs.
9. All DIETs have to encourage teachers to take up action research so as to identify their professional problems and solve them selves, in a Scientific Method.
10. All DIEt faculty have to see that the activity approach to be properly implemented wherever applicable by all in-service teachers and the same message to be carried forward by pre-service trainees.
11. Games sports and Work-Experience Activities have to be encouraged in DIETs as well as in elementary schools.

The D.Ed. trainees have expressed their attitudes in the three point Likert type scale towards the four areas of DIETs role and performance, which makes the investigator to recommend as follows.

12. The facilities and resources of DIETs have to be improved to the satisfaction of the D.Ed. trainees by improving all infrastructural facilities like laboratories, library, sufficient faculty, demonstration lessons, Physical

Education Training, keeping the classrooms neat and tidy providing comfortable furniture in the class-rooms, providing toilet facilities, properly displaying institutional information on the notice board, by taking necessary medical care, and by maintaining good relationship between staff and student trainees.

13. The D.Ed. trainees need certain improved instructional facilities, which may be taken care of by the Principal and faculty members as to proper use of audio-visual equipment by the faculty, to use necessary TLM properly, to interact properly in the class room, to give proper awareness about action research to the trainees to make the computer lab for proper use, to provide useful tutorials to trainees by faculty and to conduct the examinations in a proper manner.

14. The Principal and faculty members have to take much care and interest in encouraging the D.Ed. trainees to participate and provide congenial conditions by providing activities such as conducting regularly the cultural activities in DIETs, organizing of symposia seminars, workshops, field trips, exhibitions and Science fairs, conducting quiz competitions, mock-parliaments, Work-Experience Activities, involving in project works, social service and welfare activities.

15. The Principal and all the faculty members of DIET have to organize the scheme of teaching practice lessons very effectively, to maintain proper co-ordination between Principal and staff, to maintain proper and effective supervision on teaching practice and give proper guidance and constructive suggestions for their further improvement, to co-operate all D.Ed. trainees to complete the schedule of practice lessons in time and properly, to guide trainees in preparing the lesson plans properly, to involve all trainees in surveys and investigations, to give good model demonstration lessons in all subjects not less than five per subject, to provide proper conditions for the development of good teaching skills in all trainees to guide trainees for the proper

preparation of annual plans, unit plans, lesson plans and appropriate teaching learning material.

The major objectives of establishment of DIETs is to bring quality in elementary education by refreshing, renovating the in-service teachers of elementary education by way of various in-service training programmes. In this context the attitudes of in-service teachers depict certain deficiencies in the conduction organization of these programmes at different levels, and the following recommendations are made to make the in-service training programmes more fruitful and yield expected level of quality in the field of elementary education.

16 Assessment of in-service teachers' training needs is the key to identify the areas on which in-service training programmes are to be planned and designed. Hence well planned need based assessment may be done in the end of the every academic year so as to enable the state level officials to plan for the resources like finance, human resources, designing of academic calendar, to get approved by the Government and to chalk out the three tier hierarchical stages of training programmes, for successful completion, so as to enable the teachers implement the training inputs immediately to get expected out comes in student achievement. In this connection hard spots and difficult areas are to be much more concentrated. Again feed back from in-service teachers after any training programme has to be taken and due attention to be focused to fill the gaps or weak areas.

17. The Teacher educators and state level district level mandal level and cluster level resource percons are to be well trained and their selection also play major role in the success of bringing quality education.

18. The in-service training programmes in introducing an innovative pedagogy like activity oriented child centred approach accrues great importance. More over the difficulty level of subjects and pedagogy are to be identified and due care to be taken to fill the gaps.

19. The area of monitoring and extension services of DIET faculty towards the quality elementary education in coordination with DPEP / SSA is to be properly linked and effective monitoring by DIET faculty yields best quality.

    The DIET faculty with the academic support of SCERT and State Project Ddirector DPEP / SSA have to well conduct the district level programmes and in turn monitor supervise mandal level / cluster level training programmes.

    Much care to be taken in giving proper guidance to the teachers in the preparation of text books, Hand-books, work books, question banks and achievement test papers for the necessary examinations to be conducted and in preparation of TLM and in the exhibition of the TLM.

20. i. The investigator has personally visited the DIETs and has observed the real situation of DIETs in various districts of Andhra Pradesh state.

    ii. Most of the DIETs do not run a model school, hence they have been facing hardships to give Demonstration Lessons by the faculty. Hence all DIETs may be accommodated with a model school which is very essential.

    iii. The in-service training programmes being conducted by DIETs have also been facing hardships in providing the participants lodging and boarding facilities in rural localities where the DIETs are situated. Hence all DIETs have to run a hostel more for in-service teachers than for student trainees.

    iv. Residential campus life, for both trainees as well as faculty members to be provided. Hence sufficient quarters are to be constructed in the DIET campus.

    v. It is observed that the hostels are in bad shape with lack of clean surroundings adequate furniture, water and low quality food, etc. To over come these deficiencies the responsibilities are to be entrusted to the in-mates as was the case in basic training courses, where the trainees completely manage the hostels, grow vegetables, purchase commodities, cook and cater food. The technical, non-teaching and menial staff are to be adequately posted to DIETs.

vi. It is felt that the State Education Department has to plan training programmes for Principal and faculty on human resource management, good administration, academic matters and financial aspects from time to time for more acceptable, dynamic amicable and smooth functioning of DIETs personnel.

Thus producing quality teachers has become a pre-requisite to achieve qualitative improvement in education at any level. Both central and state Governments have to come forward to enhance the budgetary allocations on teacher education and to recruit suitably qualified teachers and with ideal qualities as teacher educators.

It is suggested that a separate directorate in the state may be established for the teacher education and as being existed in some states. The linkages between pre-school teacher education institutions, DIETs, CTEs, IASEs and SCERT to be strengthened and on the other hand the linkage between teacher education and DPEP / SSA are also to be improved.

The privatization of teacher education is nothing but giving scope to deterioration of education because commercializing the teacher education is nothing but preparing a commercial teacher. Hence state as well as central Government should stop privatization of teacher education at once and the Government may establish sufficient teacher education institutions as per the need and demand from time to time.

SOME GENERAL RECOMMENDATIONS

- Those who have commitment to the profession are to be selected to the profession.
- The teachers are to be well equipped with the latest developments in the field of teaching profession.
- The DIETs are to be fully equipped with all required men and material for their effective role and performance.
- DIETs are expected to become role modals in terms of meticulous, efficient and effective planning and pioneer in performing their functions.

- All the training programmes given to the teachers are to be need oriented and objective oriented so as to improve ultimately student achievement.
- The teacher trainees are to be enabled to experiment, discover, practises and innovate to learn themselves for better teaching practices so as to make the learners learn easily effectively and happily.

SUGGESTIONS FOR FURTHER RESEARCH

1. Future researchers may undertake teacher educators, and parents of the student teachers to study with regard to their attitudes to make generalizations.
2. Similar studies also may be under taken on DIETs in other states.
3. A comparative assessment of DIETs of Andhra Pradesh with other states may be undertaken so as to adopt good practices implemented in other states for bringing better quality teacher education.
4. For identifying further deficiencies in the training programme other aspects, other than Principals, student teachers and in-service teachers may be taken up and can offer some more suggestions for the betterment of teacher education.
5. The present study is limited to certain personnel and demographic independent variables such as age, sex, experience, qualifications (general and professional) nativity, location of the school, location of the DIET, classes teaching by in-service teachers. Further the future researchers may also concentrate on other psycho-sociological variables of the subjects involved.
6. This study has not taken in to consideration the institutional variables such as year of establishment and perceptions / attitudes of teacher educators. Such variables may help to identify the variations between good and poor institutions, studies in this direction may help us to improve the status of teacher education further.

Bibliography

Aaron, (1996), "Teacher Effectiveness - Some Possible Correlates", the Journal of Karnataka University, Social Sciences, 2, 108-116.

Adaval, S.B., (1968), "The Third Indian Year Book of Education on Educational Research", NCERT, New Delhi,

Adval, S.B., (Ed.) (1978), "teacher education in the 3rd year Book of Educational Research" , NCERT, New Delhi.

Aggarwal, J.C., (1966), "Educational Research – An Introduction", Arya Book Depot, New Delhi,

Aggarwal, J.C., (1985) "Theory and Practices of Education" Philosophical and Sociological Basic of Education, 12th Edn. Vikas Publishing House Pvt. Ltd., New Delhi.

Aggarwal, J.C., (1985), "National Policy on Education 1986, A Frame work", Doaba House, New Delhi.

Arora, K., Dasagupta, H., Chopra, R. and Puri, P. etel, (1974), "National Survey of Teacher Education at Elementary Level". Department of Teacher Education, NCERT, New Delhi.

Banerjee, J.C., (1967), "Training of Primary Teachers in India": A Survey of Research in Education, (1974). M.B. Buch (ed.).

Barr, A.S., (1950), "Teaching Competencies, Encyclopedia of Educational Research", Revised Edition.

Bellack, A..A.R., (1960), & Huebner "Teaching Review of Educational Research", 30.

Betagiri, Suresh (1996), "Competencies and Training Needs of DIET Faculty Members in DPEP District of Karnataka" Dissertation Regional Institute of Education. Mysore.

Buch , M.B., (1991), "Fourth Survey of Research in Education" (1983-88) Vol.2, NCERT, pp.899-916.

Buch, M.B. (Ed), (1988), "Third Survey of Research in Education", NCERT, New Delhi.

Buch, M.B., (1974), "A Survey of Research in Education", Centre for Advanced Study in Education" (CASE), M.S. University, Baroda.

Buch, M.B., (1997), "Fifth Survey of Research in Education". New Delhi : National Council of Educational Research and Training.

Buch, M.B., (Ed), (1979), "Second Survey of Research in Education", Society for Educational Research and Development, Baroda.

Buch. M.B., and Singh, S. (1978), "Third All India Educational Survey of Teachers". NCERT New Delhi.

Chakravarthy, S.R. (1977), "Audio-Visual Aids in Education", New Delhi : Sagar Publications.

Chaurasia, G., (1967), "New Era in Teacher Education" Sterling Publisher, Delhi.

Desai, A.R. (1959), "Social Background of Indian Nationalism", 3rd Edn, Popular Book Depot., Lamington Road, Bombay.

Deve Gowda, A.C., (1973), "Teacher Education in India". Bangaloru: Printersall. (Pvt.) Ltd.

Edward, A.L., (1969), ."Techniques of Attitude Scale Construction", Bombay: Vakils, Feffer and Simons.

Edward, A.L., (1969), "Statistical Analysis", New York: Holt, Rinehard and Winston Inc.,

Gage N.Y., (1963), "Hand Book of Research Teaching", Rand Mc, Nally and Company, Chicago.

Gar., (1997), "Teacher Preparation", NCTE, New Delhi

Garrett, H.E & Wordsworth, R.S., (2001), "Statistics in Psychology and Education", Vakitsfelter and Simons Ltd., Bombay.

Gayatri, A.., (1996), "An Investigation into the Perceptions of Student -Teachers on Their Teacher Training", M.Ed. Dissertation. S.V. University. Hyderabad.

Good & Watt., (1959), "Methods of Social Research", Mc. Graw Hill Co., New York.

Good C.V. (Ed) (1959) : "Dictionary of Education", (2nd edition) Mc Grant Hall & Co. / New York.

Good, et al., (1941), "The Methodology of Educational Research", Appleton Century Crafts Crafts, New York.

Gopalan, Beena, (1993), "A Case Study of Few District Institutes of Education and Training in Kerala" , Kerala.

Guilford, J.P., & Fruchter, B., (1978), "Fundamental Statistics in Psychology and Education", McGraw - Hill Publishing Co., inc., Tokyo.

Gupta, S.P., (1971), "A Study of Admission Procedures in Elementary and Secondary Teacher Training Research in Education", M.B. Buch (ed), Centre of Advanced Study in Education, Baroda.

Harper, E., Dass Gupta, B., "Preparation and Use of Audio-visual Aids". Prentice Hall of India, New Delhi.

Harris, C.W., (1979) "Encyclopaedia of Educational Research", The McMillion Company, New York.

Hornby, A.S., Cowie, A.P. and Lewis, J.W., (1968), "Oxford Advanced Learner's Dictionary of Current English", The English Language Book society, Oxford University Press, London.

John W. Best & James V. Kahn (1995) "Research in Education" 7th Ed, Prentice Hall of India Pvt. Ltd., New Delhi.

John. W. Best & James, V. Kahn, (2005), "Research in Education", 9th Edition, Prentice Hall India Ltd., New Delhi,

Joshi, D.C., (1974), "A Study of Innovations in Teacher Training Institutions". V.B. Teachers College, Udaipur.

Khan, M.S., (1978), "Teacher Education in India and Abroad", Chugh Publications, Allahabad.

Khanna, S.D., (1989), et al "Education in the Emerging Indian Society", Doaba House, New Delhi.

Kohili, V.K., (1992), "Indian Education and Its Problems", Vivek Publishers, Ambala City.

Koshala, D.N.(Ed), (1998), "Curriculum Framework for Quality teacher education", NCTE, New Delhi.

Koshala, D.N.(Ed), (2003), "Competency Based and Commitment Oriented Teacher for Quality School Education", Education-in-service Education, NCTE, New Delhi.

Koshala, D.N.(Ed), (2003), "Envisioning Teacher Education" – In the 10th Plan and beyond", NCTE, New Delhi.

Kothari, C.R.,(2003), "Research Methodology-Methods and Techniques", Wishwa Prakasam Publications, New Delhi.

Kundu, C.L., (1997), "Presidential Address, President of Indian Association of Teacher Educators", Ponda, Goa.

Likert. R.A., (1932), "A technique for the Measurement of Attitudes", Achieves of psychology.

Lomac, D.E., (1972), "A Review of British Research in Teacher Education", Review of Educational Research, 42 (10, 331).

Madhavi, G., (1996), "Attitude of Student Teacher of DIETs Towards Teaching Profession ". Dissertation Abstract Kintr,.

Manoj Praveen, G., (1993), "Competencies and Training Needs of DIET Faculty Members in DPEP Districts of Kerela" Dissertation, RIJE, Mysore.

Mohammed Pasha, (1988), "A Study of the Problems Faced by the Primary Teacher Training Institutes in practice— Teaching in Practicing Schools"; Dissertation Abstr. Intr,.

Mooney, R.L., and Gorban, L.V., (1950), "The Mooney Problem Check-list Manual", New York: The Psychological Corporation.

Morgan, J.J.B, (1934), "Keeping a Sound Min", New York: Me Millan, Second Education.

Mukerjee, R.K., (1951), "Ancient Indian Education", London: Macmillan, and Co.,

N.C.T.E., (1988), "teacher education", NCTE publications New Delhi.

NCTE, (1998), "Policy Perspectives in Teacher Education", NCTE Publication, New Delhi.

NCTE, (1999), "Profile of Teacher Educators", NCTE Publication, New Delhi.

Prakash ,A., and Mehrotra, R.N.,(1974), "An Exploratory Study of the Use of Audio Cassette Recordings in the Supervision of Student-Teacher". Central Institµte of Education. New Delhi.

Rai, B.C., (1989), "Problems of Indian Education", Prakashan Kendra, Lucknow.

Ramachandra Rao, R., (1993), "Degree English", Tonic Writers Educational Publishers, Markapur, India.

Ramamurthy, (1994), " A Study of the Problems Faced by the Trainees in Schools during the Practice Teaching Progaramme": Dissertation Abstr. Intr.

Rao, M.R., (1980), (Ed) "Teacher Education at Cross Roads", Sourvenir, A.J. College of Education, Machilipatnam, (A.P.).

Ravindranadh Tagore, (1992), "On Education", Balasahiti Book Trust, Hyderabad.

Reddy, P.A., (1990), "Adult Education Programmes in India", Allahabad : Chugh Publications.

Sabharwal, N., (1981), "Studies and Investigations on Teacher Education in India", (1973-75), NCERT, New Delhi.

Safla Sultana, (1976), " A Study of Academic Difficulties of Student – Teachers" Department of Education, Aligarh Muslim University. (NCERT financed).

Sen Gupta, D., (1975), "Attitudes of Teachers" M.Ed. Dissertation, V.B.V. University, West Bengal.

Sharma R.A., (1993) 1st Ed, "Advanced Educational Technology" Eagle Books International, Meerut Cantt.

Sharma R.A., (1993), "Advanced Education Technology", Om Shivrani Computers, New Delhi.

Sharma, M.C., Teacher Education through Distance: An Indepth Study", Indian Journal of Open Learning, 10(2), 193-202.

Sharma, R.A., (1985), "Fundamentals of Educational Research", Loyal Book Depot, Meerut, U.P.

Shrivastava, R.C., "Teacher Education in India: Issues and Perspectives", Regency Publication, New Delhi.

Shukla, P.D., (1990), "The New Education policy in India", Sterling Publishers Pvt. Ltd.

Shukla, R.S., (1978), "Emerging Trends in Teacher Education", Chugh Publications, Allahabad, pp.89-93.

Singh Raghuram, M., (1998), "Research in Teacher Education" The Hindu Daily News, October, 13,1998.

Singh, L.C(Ed), (1990), "Teacher Education in India-A Research Book", NCERT, New Delhi.

Srivastava, R.C. (1970), "Evaluation of Practice Teaching in Teacher Training Institutions", Central Institute of Education. New Delhi.

State Institute of Education (Gujarat). (1966), "Case Studies of Primary Teacher Trainees of the Primary Teacher's Institutions of Gujarat, Ahmedabad.

Sujaya Krishnan, (1996), DPEP Calling (News Letter) a DPEP Bureau Publication, MHRD, New Delhi.

Swami Vivekananda, (1985), "On Education" Sri Ramakrishna Mission Vidyalaya, Coimbatore, Tamilnadu.

Vijai Naraian & Ajit Kumar, (1970), "Professional Development of Teachers", Rajasthan University and College Teachers Assn.

Wittich, Waltair Arno and Schuller, Charles Francis (1953), "Audio-visual Materials", New York : Harper and Brothers Publishers.

REPORTS ON EDUCATION

—"Discussion Document on Curriculum Framework for Teacher Education". National Council for teacher education, 16, Mahatma Gandhi Marg, I.P. Estate, New Delhi— 110 002.

"Report of the Calcutta University Commission" (1920), New Delhi: Government of India press.

Govt of India, Ministry of Education: "Report of the Teacher Education Commission" —1. New Delhi.

Govt. of India, (1985), "Challenges of Education – A Policy Perspective", MHRD, New Delhi.

Govt. of India, (1986), "National Policy on Education - 1986", MHRD, Dept of Education, New Delhi.

Govt. of India, (1986), "Programme of Action , National Policy on Education -1986", MHRD, Department of Education, New Delhi.

Govt. of India, (1989), "DIET Guidelines", MHRD Department of Education, New Delhi.

Indian Education Commission (1964-66), (1966), Ministry of Education, Government of India.

Mudaliar, A.L., (1954), "Report of Secondary Education Commission, Ministry of Education", Government of India, New Delhi.

Radha Krishnan, S., (1948), "Report of University Education Commission", Ministry of Education, Government of India, New Delhi.

Report, (1997), "On Manpower Planning for Teacher Education" Central Expert Group on Manpower Planning for Teacher Education, NCTE, New Delhi.

SIERT Rajasthan, (1966), "Teacher Education at Primary Level in Rajasthan",

U.G.C., (1966), "Report of Review on Education", New Delhi.

Agarwal J.C., (1983) (2nd Ed.) "Landmarks in the History of Modern Indian Education", Vikas Publishing House, Delhi-32, India.

Bisva Ranjan Purkait, (1992), "Milestones in Modern Indian Education", New Central Book agency, Calcutta, India.

National Council for Teacher Education, (1988), "Gandhi on Education", Member Secretary National Council for Teacher Education.

PH.D. THESES

Ghosh, R., (1974) "A Survey of the Present System of teacher education in the USA, the UK and the India", Ph.D. Thesis, A.C.T. College, West Bengal.

Mallaya, (1968), "Teacher's Training in Madhya Pradesh Ph.D. Thesis", Edu., Saugar University, Madhya Pradesh.

Rai, V.K., (1982), " A Survey of the Problems of Teachers Training Colleges with Regard to Practicing Schools", Ph.D. Thesis, Edu., Gujarat University.

Rama Mohan Babu, V., (1992), "Job Satisfaction, Attitude Towards Teaching, Job Involvement, Efficiency of Teaching and Perception of Organizational Climate of Teachcrs of Residential and Non-residential Schools", Ph.D. thesis,. Edu,. Sri Venkateswara University, Tirupati.

Reddy, C.R., (1991), "Quality Improvement of Pre-service Education of Primary School Teachers in Andhra Pradesh", Unpublished Ph.D thesis, Osmania University, Hyderabad.

Sharma, M., (1982), "Progress and Problems of teacher education in India", Ph.D. Thesis, Edu., Patna University.

Sharma, R.C., (1984), " Teaching Aptitude, Intellectual Level and Morality of Prospective Teachers", Ph.D. thesis, edu., Mohanlal Sukhadia University.

Sinha, P. (1982), "An Evaluative Study of teacher education in Bihar", Ph.D. Thesis, Edu., Patna University.

Sujatha, B.N., (1979), "An Enquiry into the Under – graduate Teacher Training Programme in the State of Karnataka" Ph.D. Thesis, Edu., Mysore University.

Tripathi, S.L., (1964), "The Training of Teachers of Basic Schools", Ph.D. Thesis, Edu, Vikram University.

Upasani, N.K., (1966), "An Evaluation of the Existing Teacher Training Programme for Primary Teachers in the State of Maharashtra with special reference to Rural Areas" , Ph.D. thesis , Edu., Poorna University.

Verma, D.R., (1979), "A Study of Teacher Training as a Catalyst of Change in Professional Attitudes of Student –Teachers", Ph.D. Thesis, Edu., Banaras Hindu University.

Viswananathappa, (1992), "An Evaluation Programme of DIETs in Andhra Pradesh", Ph.D. Thesis, Edu., Mysore University, Mysore.